An Archaeology
of Socialism

An Archaeology of Socialism

VICTOR BUCHLI

Oxford • New York

First published in 1999 by
Berg
Editorial offices:
150 Cowley Road, Oxford, OX4 1JJ, UK
838 Broadway, Third Floor, New York, NY 10003-4812, USA

Paperback edition printed in 2000

Berg is the imprint of Oxford International Publishers Ltd.

Library of Congress Cataloging-in-Publication Data

A catalogue record for this book is available from the Library of
Congress.

British Library Cataloguing-in-Publication Data

A catalogue record for this book is available from the British Library.

ISBN 1 85973 426 X (Cloth)

Typeset by JS Typesetting, Wellingborough, Northants.
Printed in the United Kingdom by Biddles Ltd, Guildford and
King's Lynn.

For the memory of my grandmother
Evdokia Feodorovna Zborowski

Contents

Acknowledgements

A number of institutions and individuals were crucial to the realisation of this work. First, I want to thank Sidney Sussex College at Cambridge University for having me as a Research Fellow and permitting me the time, support and good company which sustained me while writing this book. Second, the International Research and Exchanges Board (IREX) funded and supported me as an Exchange Scholar in 1992 when I did the bulk of the research for this project. At IREX, Moscow, I am particularly grateful for the support and friendship provided by the Director at that time, Elizabeth McKeon. Before going out in 1992, I was supported in my preliminary field research by a Stilgoe Fellowship from the Department of Anthropology, Columbia University, and a Harriman Institute Pepsico Fellowship, Columbia University. At the Harriman Institute I am particularly grateful to a group of inspiring teachers: Mark von Hagen, Natalia Sadomskaia and Vera Dunham. Similarly, I am thankful to Jean-Louis Cohen for his generosity towards an interloping ethnoarchaeologist.

Here at Cambridge, however, I am profoundly indebted to Ian Hodder, my PhD supervisor, for his indefatigable support and trust, which gave me the confidence to see my ideas through. Also, Caroline Humphrey has been an inspiring and critical voice that has seen me through the later stages of this work. Throughout, Catherine Cooke's infectious enthusiasm, extraordinary eye for scholarly detail, and warm support and generosity have sustained me through the various stages of this work. Lynn Meskell also provided inspiring conversation while directing me to the work of Judith Butler.

In Moscow, I am most profoundly grateful to the people who live and have lived at the Narkomfin Communal House. Over the course of the year following the breakup of the Soviet Union, they graciously endured a bearded foreigner in their midst, patiently tolerating his numerous and annoying questions, while generously providing him with their warmth, home-made cakes and tea and, when circumstances required, a bracing shot of vodka. In particular, I am extremely grateful for the friendship, warmth and gracious help of Aleksei Taits. Without his assistance and friendship, this work would have been something altogether different and considerably diminished. In addition, Vladimir Ginzburg, Ekaterina Miliutina, Viktoria Zaitseva and Nadezhda Afan-asieva – having patiently and graciously endured innumerable questions – very kindly allowed me access to their family archives. I am also indebted to Andrei Meerson, Rimma Krupnova, Alla Kazakova, Sergei Ingal and Liudmilla Belova for their insights and generous help. I also owe thanks to Anna Grekulova, editor of the *Entsiklopedia Domashnego Khoziaistva*.

A number of key institutions and their staff were extraordinarily helpful in the research for this project in Moscow: The Lenin Library; The State Shchusev Museum of Architecture, Moscow; The State Historical Library, Moscow; TsMADSN (Tsentral'nyi Moskovkii Arkhiv Na Spetsial'nikh Nositeliakh); RGAKFD (Rossiiskii Gosudarstvennyi Arkhiv Kinofotodokumentov); Muzei Istorii i Rekonstruktsii g. Moskvy; the MARKhI Library; and the collective at REU-9, Krasnopresnenskii Raion, Moscow. To all of them I am extremely grateful for their profess-ionalism and kind help.

I thank the editors of the *Journal of Design History* for permission to reprint sections appearing from 'Khrushchev, Modernism and the Fight against *Petit-Bourgeois* Consciousness in the Soviet Home', *Journal of Design History*, vol. 10, no. 2, 1997 in chapter 7. While at Berg, I am extremely grateful to Kathryn Earle and Nigel Hope for their kind and patient editorial help as well as the generous comments of two anonymous reviewers. Mitchell Bates's care and many acts of kindness sustained me while writing this. But in everything, as always, I owe my deepest gratitude to my parents Svetlana and Edward Buchli, who have seen me through every stage leading up to and through this work, who never once flinched, and always gave fully of their love, support and inspiration.

List of Figures

Introduction

Probably the most fundamental concern of students of material culture is how we understand and interpret societies through their artefacts. Of all the material cultures produced by societies, architecture is probably the most durable, long-lasting and easily retrievable. Architecture is also the material cultural matrix which most other artefacts of material culture are associated with or related to. Hence our understanding of societies is almost invariably concentrated through an architectural ocular.

That architecture should focus our attention in this manner is not entirely the result of its oft-remarked robustness. Architecture – and domestic architecture in particular – coincides (it would seem) in almost iconic fashion with the most basic units of social organisation, such as the household. Often the way to understand a given society is to understand the physical and, by metaphoric extension, the social architecture of its organisation. Consequently, the issue of domestic architecture in studies of material culture and other disciplines is fraught with many coincidences of meaning and form related to a wide range of vital questions central to an understanding of any given society – ranging from the household, gender and social organisation to cosmological ordering principles, to name just a few. In short, when we are confronted with the domestic architecture of a given society, far too much seems to be going on. The physical architectural artefact and its attendant metaphors are confusingly and painfully pregnant with a superfluity of meaning. In this introductory chapter I want to discuss how this relational problematic and the superfluity of meaning associated with it have been dealt with in the past by various theorists, and propose an alternative, and I hope, more manageable approach to the problem of how we understand material culture and the societies we study. This excursus will set the scene, establishing the interpretative sensibility with which I approach the subject of this book – the archaeology, in the broadest sense of the word, of the various households living at the Narkomfin Communal House built by the Constructivist architects Moisei Ginzburg with Ignatii Milinis between 1930 and 1991 in that period of Russian history we now refer to in the past tense as Soviet (see figure 1).

The reason for examining this particular building was that the Narkomfin Communal House in Moscow was specifically created by the Bolshevik elite to overcome the unsettling social, economic and political contradictions of early twentieth-century industrial capitalism in Russia. The building is the embodiment of a grandiose project to overcome these antagonisms and realise the terms of the good life for the greatest number of people (see figure 2). It was a demiurgic *tour de force* to overcome the contradictions of life in all its minutiae and grandeur – totally. This was the foundational project of the Soviet state and the most complete realisation of European modernity. Now that the century is drawing to a close and these grand modernist Soviet projects have apparently been abandoned, this study provides us the

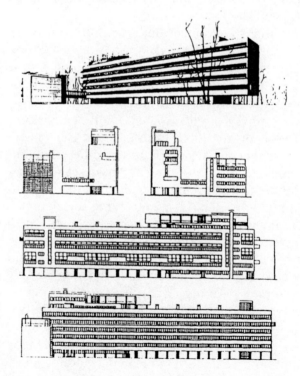

Figure 1 The Narkomfin Communal House, *Sovremennaia Arkhitektura*, 1929, no. 5, p. 158

Figure 2 Cover, *Krasivaia Zhizn'* (Beautiful Life), A. Kurella, 1930

opportunity for reflection by examining the micropowers at work in everyday life and the macropowers affecting changing state fortunes through the ocular of this building (see Boudon 1979 for a similar study of Le Corbusier's Pessac). I would like to understand how individuals coped with rapidly changing social contingencies by examining their negotiations of domestic architectural space; that space we most directly associate with the most fundamental structures of human society.

The pace of cultural change in the twentieth century requires an archaeological approach as we near the end of the century. The superfluity of information, the heightened pace of change, and the rapidly disappearing and changing nature of the material record of the twentieth century make an emphasis on the archaeological understanding of social change through its material cultural all the more pressing – in the twentieth century too many things disappear far too quickly before we are able to make any sense of them. At the same time, the materialist presumptions of archaeological work and the study of material culture in general are predicated on the same Marxian assumptions as the various projects of twentieth-century modernity, particularly the project that was the Soviet Union. Therefore the archaeological study of a twentieth century site, such as the Narkomfin Communal House, provides a unique opportunity critically to examine the assumptions upon which archaeologists and other students of material culture base their work.

This discussion will focus on the everyday and seemingly ordinary actions of individuals, such as those of Elena Andreevna who lived and died at the Narkomfin Communal House. In particular I want to understand the significance of the seemingly mundane aspects of quotidian life, such as the buffet cabinet she once regularly dusted in her apartment. This otherwise ordinary item of furniture contained the most extraordinary grouping of unlikely objects (see figure 3). An elaborate pre-Revolutionary (and otherwise 'counter-revolutionary' and 'petit-bourgeois') item of furniture contained – improbably – the collected works of Stalin juxtaposed with the works of Lenin, along with vials of holy water and the icons of saints. The buffet cabinet itself was situated in the apartment in the traditional Russian Orthodox red corner where icons are held and prayers uttered. How can such achingly antagonistic and contradictory objects be accommodated and literally contained by Elena Andreevna in her buffet cabinet which she regularly dusted, rearranged and cared for over her lifetime?

Why am I interested in looking at this? Namely because most of our interpretative tools leave us somewhat at a loss to understand something so seemingly 'perverse' as Elena Andreevna's buffet cabinet. But, as I shall discuss further on, social theorists such as Chantall Mouffe have stated that 'liberal' positions fail to cope adequately with fascism (in this case Soviet totalitarianism), relegating it to the margins of the 'evil' or 'perverse'. There is, however, a price to be paid for this marginalisation. We cannot afford to dismiss it as we have not quite come to terms with the collapse of the Soviet Union, and the

Figure 3 F-unit interior, 1992, Author's photograph

implications of this collapse for the nature of social change as well as the materialist assumptions upon which the intellectual projects of Soviet socialism and Western modernity are predicated. As we shall see in the course of this work, the role of architecture, space and material culture is central to an understanding of these issues. Thus the study of the Narkomfin Communal House becomes directly relevant both to our understandings of the relationship between social change and the realms of material culture that we study, and to our attempts to manage and come to terms with their infinite superfluity of meaning.

I hope to demonstrate, across a spectrum of concerns, the utility of shifting away from our preoccupation with presence (the material record and material culture in general) towards one of absence; that is, to move away from a desire to establish the 'structuration principles' of Anthony Giddens or the 'habitus' of Pierre Bourdieu and other such consensuses over a 'theory of material culture' towards – instead – a sensibility that embraces radical discontinuity, 'undecidability' and conflict. That is, those qualities which are very much characteristic of the Soviet and post-Soviet experience and which the 'consensus'-based approaches of much interpretative work in material culture studies fails to understand (see also Žižek 1992 for a discussion of these points in relation to the issue of post-Soviet nationalism). Such an approach, as I hope to demonstrate, will help students of material culture understand the dynamics of cultural change that belie the continuity of cosmologies and structures believed to be 'inscribed' within the material world waiting to be 'detected' or 'recovered'.

This approach I hope would discourage the prevailing preoccupation with the ethnographic and synchronic moment and be more concerned with the dynamics of culture change requiring a greater preoccupation with ethno-history and historical anthropology. I hope to show how the static conditions described within the ethnographic moment and the attendant preoccupation with 'systemness' create an overwhelming gravity in analysis that obscures the variability critical to understanding the dynamics of culture change. I hope to show how seemingly weighty, 'inscribed' and totalizing world-views (Blier 1987) or 'spatial logics' (Hillier and Hanson 1984) can be radically subverted – absolutely and discontinuously – by the most ephemeral manipulations of material culture. Thus, I hope to move away from Henrietta Moore's statement that 'any alternative interpretations, including the quotidian, practical interpretations of space, tend to be contained within the set of dominant interpretations' (Moore 1986:195). In turn we might be in a better position to suggest scales of analysis wherein variation, the manipulation of micropowers central to the dynamics of culture change, might be apparent along with their more ephemeral material cultural effects. Thus, variability might be better addressed and the role of the individual more clearly understood as well as the roles of the disempowered (those individuals who did not command the resources to build walls and other objects), whose only means to engage the material world was through the use of objects and spaces created by socially dominant others. It is these sorts of individuals who constituted the majority of people who lived under Soviet socialism and for the most part (though significantly for this study, not always) were the people who lived at the Narkomfin Communal House.

I want to suggest that the reason we have problems in trying to understand these issues is because there has been a rather stubborn tradition of positing a direct, iconic and at times homologous correspondence between an item of material culture and the society with which it is associated. Archaeologists in particular have been grappling with this correspondence for quite some time (see Parker-Pearson and

Richards 1994 for a good account of this engagement). This pre-occupation is part of an intellectual tradition that goes back a long way in Western thought. However, more recently it has been noted that the creation of these correspondences is a means of control; a discipline imposed on the apparent superfluity of meaning in an attempt to garner power for one individual, group or class (Foucault 1977; Smith 1988; Shanks and Tilley 1987, 1992). In a less sinister fashion, it is also a means of controlling something chaotic, destabilising and inherently uncontrollable. Thereby, it is an effective means of establishing order and tranquillity out of chaos.

For the purposes of this discussion and its Marxian context, it is relevant to go back to Lewis Henry Morgan, whose ethnographic work informed Marx and Engels, in order to pick up the 'axiological' imperative (Smith 1988) that evolved into this need to fix and constitute objects as linked to specific cultural, economic and social meanings and thereby limit superfluity. Morgan (1978), writing in the mid-nineteenth century, described a direct correspondence between the material base (or material culture) of a society, and its systems of kinship and degree of social complexity. Morgan's schema described a unilineal progression from 'savagery' to 'civilisation' with each stage along the way characterised by a particular complex of material culture, kinship system and social structure. Social change in this schema was mostly understood in terms of diffusion, that is, the diffusion of social and economic structures and their attendant forms of material culture.

Karl Marx and Friedrich Engels adopted this deterministic correspondence of Morgan and developed it further. Not only did the material base of a society determine the economic structure and social organisation of that society; it also predicated its consciousness (Marx 1983; 1986). These ideas in their turn had a profound impact on Soviet architects and other cultural workers attempting to realise the material terms of socialism. This Morganian/Marxian understanding was part of the Platonic foundationalist enterprise (Rorty 1980) of Western thought, which dominated much of social thought for most of the late nineteenth and early twentieth centuries. Works in semiology, literary theory and social theory began to challenge this Western 'axiological' and 'foundationalist' tradition which attempted to fix meaning and control its inherent superfluity. A new emphasis was placed on the context within which signifiers of meaning (such as material artefacts) were understood. That is, signifiers such as material artefacts were not denotative or inherently homologous within systems of meaning. Rather they were unfixed and 'free-floating', to use the language of post-structuralist theorists (Shanks and Tilley 1987, Babty and Yates 1990, Hodder 1986, Ricoeur 1991, Derrida 1976).

Within this emergent sensibility the works of two theorists in the social sciences, anthropologist Pierre Bourdieu and sociologist Anthony Giddens, had particular impact on the development of archaeological understandings of material culture (Moore 1986, Johnson 1993, Samson 1990). Both attempted to overcome the image of 'cultural dupes' enslaved to the fixed meanings and deterministic structures of a given society, where individuals were seen to respond in a mechanistic, and ultimately helpless, fashion to irresistible structural prerogatives as in the unilineal and deterministic tradition in Morgan, Marx and Engels and all the way through to structuralism (Levi-Strauss 1966, Chomsky 1968, Glassie 1975, Deetz 1977). The obvious criticism put forward by Giddens and Bourdieu was that the individual clearly had no active role. Cultural formations and structural prerogatives were 'out there' exerting an irresistible influence on an individual's actions. The obvious problem noted by these two theoreticians was that cultural change became very difficult to understand if the only obvious agents of such change – individual human beings themselves – seemed only to be responding mechanistically to some reified structuring prerogative outside the realm of the individual.

The solution to this dilemma was put forward in the form of two related concepts, namely a 'habitus' by Bourdieu (Bourdieu 1977) and a 'structuration principle' by Giddens (Giddens 1979). These concepts posited a higher-order generational structuring principle, open to the individual for creative and differentially competent manipulation through the course of that individual's negotiation of various social situations. This higher-order structuring principle involved the individual or agent as a creative manipulator, but it nonetheless resulted in the sorts of 'cultural dupes' Giddens and others were desperately trying to avoid (Bauman 1989, Smith 1988, Strathern 1991). Structuralism was merely replaced by higher-order structuration principles, just as deterministic and 'pre-wired' as any previous structuralist proposition. Ultimately, individuals were only creative and self-determining in terms of pre-existing structuration principles. However general they might have been, they were reified and beyond the scope of individual agency. People were again responding irresistibly to circumstances beyond their control. That this model should be static with little room for the description of cultural change, can in part be attributed to the nature of the ethnographic and ethnoarchaeological case studies used to develop these models which privileged the ethnographic moment over diachronic studies.

The idea of a habitus or structuration principle appears as a sort of higher-order structuralist generational grammar. Such higher-order generational grammars are attempts to make otherwise stiff and inflexible lower-order generational grammars more flexible (Chomsky 1968, Glassie 1975, Deetz 1977, Hillier and Hanson 1984, Rappaport 1982, Hodder 1986). That is, they make such generational models more sensitive to agency and the vicissitudes of culture change, such as the many post-structuralist attempts informed by Gadamer's hermeneutics (Hodder 1991, Shanks and Tilley 1987), the works of Paul Ricoeur (Moore 1986, 1990), and Bourdieu and Giddens (Johnson 1989 and Moore 1986). However these model grammars are not flexible enough to overcome determinism, and hence satisfactorily to evoke culture change. A considerable influence in archaeology have been hermeneuticists such as Ricoeur and Gadamer (Hodder, Moore) – as well as Phenomenologists like Merleau-Ponty and Heidegger (Tilley 1994, Gosden 1994). Both theoretical approaches are characterised by a certain preoccupation with a metaphysics of presence and are rather attractive to obsessively empirical archaeologists. Hermeneuticists place a great deal of emphasis on the text as the focus of analysis within a 'language tradition' (Gadamer) or interpretative 'community' (Ricoeur), constituting an ever-fixed, though admittedly shifting, axis about which consensuses are reached and the superfluity of meaning is contained. Similarly, phenomenological approaches (Heidegger, Merleau-Ponty, Husserl, Thomas and Tilley) privilege a similar axis of meaning, embodied within the physical artefact or the state of being-in-the-world (*Dasein*), which acts to contain superfluity as well. There is an irreconcilable tension produced by privileging some embodied 'objective' – however momentary or shifting an axis – created to contain superfluity. This tension arises as a result of trying to prevent the interpretative enterprise from exploding into chaos or some form of 'abject relativism', and alleviate its attendant anxieties. Additionally, the possibility of political action and social justice is predicated on the creation of such fixed axes of consensus or community – however shifting – that would contain superfluity. Hence Jürgen Habermas's proposal to create 'ideal speech communities' where such consensus can be reached equitably for all actors regardless of degree of empowerment (see Mark Leone (Leone and Potter 1992) for an archaeological implementation of Habermas's concepts in archaeological interpretation, as well as Shanks and Tilley (1992)).

Structures and generational schemes are, by their nature, generalising to the degree of being banal (Miller 1994). They are prevalent precisely because their banality enables them to function 'fuzzily', allowing greater flexibility and integration of diverse elements within their structuring boundaries (Bourdieu 1977). However, by insisting on these banal and rather 'fuzzy' structures, objects, traditions and variability are often conflated and equated because they participate within the same 'fuzzy' parameters. Ian Hodder (Hodder 1986:34–5) once made reference to the general 'systemness' that initially attracted some 'New Archaeologists' to structuralism. Nonetheless, this attraction to 'systemness' has prevailed in post-processual, structuralist and post-structuralist approaches as evidenced by the use of 'habitus' and 'structuration principles'. Such an attraction to 'systemness' within diachronic archaeological understandings favours the continuity of structures rather than adequately understanding nuances of variability – why structures change and why they might be discontinuous or rejected (or why in fact one should evince a structure at all and if so, to what end?).

Similarly, ethnoarchaeological and ethnographic understandings, despite the promises of 'structuration principles' and 'habitus', privilege the 'ethnographic moment' or synchronic 'snapshots' of structures that similarly skirt the issue of change and discontinuity (Moore 1986, Blier 1987, Carsten and Hugh-Jones 1995, Donley-Reid 1990). There is, nonetheless, despite an articulated desire to break away from the procrustean effects of such 'systemness', a strong desire to maintain it, to provide us with general models for cross-cultural comparison, to alleviate 'abject relativism', to provide us with a 'transparent language' or 'an adequate social theory', in short to prevent the entire interpretative endeavour from apparently splintering off into unintelligible chaos.

I shall discuss how those anxieties can be alleviated by taking, in a sense, a small step back, and embracing an assumption of radical discontinuity of action. The purpose of such an assumption is to alleviate the problem identified by the sociologist Zygmunt Bauman (1989), of hypostatisation. Thus I hope a more fluid and robust evocation of the dynamics of culture change will result and thereby be more amenable to satisfactory intervention within current political practices as a 'mediation on modernity', as suggested by archaeologists such as Mathew Johnson (Johnson 1993:183) and other students of material culture. Such an emphasis on radical disconstinuity will also permit expressions of the open-endedness and multi-vocality that our political and disciplinary conditions require, to cope more effectively with the contingencies of twentieth-century experience and the superfluity of meaning in which we are enveloped.

In short the problem with this superfluity is the problem of pluralism and multi-vocality and the anxiety caused by the fear of 'abject relativism'. This fear is not unlike the agoraphobia described by the feminist art historian Rosalyn Deutsche with its 'panicked reactions to the openness and indeterminacy of the democratic public as a phantom – a kind of agoraphobic behaviour adopted in the face of a public space that has a loss at its beginning' (Deutsche 1996:325). Thus, Deutsche argues, such fears take on a regulative function (Deutsche 1996:324, referring to Joan Copjec and Michael Sorkin). Lurking about as some great bogey man, it ensured the necessity to posit some ground or some foundationalist enterprise, which 'has a decisive voice in the real overcoming, but in no way coincides with it, and predicts the future only abstractly and inexactly' (Horkheimer 1978:438), thereby ensuring the necessity of an ultimately fixed and 'adequate social theory". In short, to turn the tables around, the fear of 'abject relativism' *must* necessarily be invoked in order to maintain otherwise 'foundationalist' enterprises with their decidedly regulatory functions.

Current developments in philosophy (particularly among the so-called Neo-Pragmatists) and social theory have attempted to address this anxiety concerning the fixity of meaning, in light of its disconcertingly evident superfluity and 'free-floating' nature, in a number of parallel and resonant ways. The examination of pluralism and superfluity requires a similarly pluralistic approach. With apologies in advance for these rather mercenary misappropriations and concatenations, I will address particular works of a group of rather heterogeneous theorists who, despite their specific disciplinary concerns, are related by a similar problem relevant to the issues of this discussion. They suggest in varying ways understandings towards its resolution and its application towards a more satisfactory understanding of material culture and particularly for the highly complex and conflicted experiences of Russia in the twentieth century. These theorists are Jacques Derrida, Michel Foucault, Richard Rorty, Barbara Herrnstein Smith, Marilyn Strathern, Judith Butler and Chantal Mouffe, all of whom in their various ways are deeply concerned with the superfluity of meaning and – in their respective ways – unafraid of it, and thereby establish a very useful sensibility for understanding the vicissitudes of the highly conflicted terms of cultural change that characterised the experience of Soviet socialism.

The exposition of the superfluity of meaning and the lack of fixity of signification that emerged in social and literary theory in the 1970s are heavily indebted to the school of deconstructionist theory most intimately associated with the works of Jacques Derrida. Central to Derrida's concerns was the desire to steer clear of the importance placed on empirical data or events such as the perception of the material world, its reflection and representation in language and its constituent signifiers. Derrida rejected the dominant metaphysics of presence of phenomenologists like Edmund Husserl, who privileged meaning in terms of the empirically perceived world. Rather, Derrida posited a sort of metaphysics of absence that focused not on fixed texts or signifiers, which he demonstrated not to exist, but on the dynamics of that signification, that is, *différance* or 'play'. Instead of controlling this superfluity, Derrida proposed simply to let it go and 'play'. As a result, notions of continuity, consistent transformation and progressive logical change are entirely absent from Derrida's conceptualisation of action. Rather, change and action are hardly happy, orderly and rational events but inherently violent. Since meaning is constituted precisely by the arrangement and spacing of signifiers, any change of a specific arrange-ment or 'trace' would dismantle that very 'thing' which imbues meaning and cause it to collapse.

In light of Derrida's rather microscopic insights into the minutiae of the generation of meaning through *différance* and the utter violence done by an individual semiotic act to constitutive structures or 'traces' it is apt to draw attention to Michel Foucault. His concept of power complements Derrida's concept of 'play' in the generation of meaning within those traverses of space that articulate meaning. Like 'play', Foucault's conception of power is essentially positive rather than negative (Foucault 1977:194). In addition, 'power is ubiquitous, not because it is able to assemble everything under its invincible unity, but because it is produced at every moment, at every point, or rather in every relation of one point with another' (Sheridan 1980: 184). The ubiquity of power places it in the domain of everyday activities and every individual (Sheridan 1980:218). Power therefore exists as a series of 'micropowers' which permeate every aspect of life; therefore power cannot be manipulated or overthrown institutionally, but locally in everyday, small situations (Sheridan 1980:139). Consequently, social change as we shall see in Russia in the course of this discussion, is the result of 'a plurality of instances, each a special case, distributed in an irregular way in time and space. Sometimes a broad series of resistances converge to bring about a major upheaval, a "revolution" but like power, and inextricably linked with it, resistance usually takes the form of innumerable, mobile, transitory points' (Sheridan 1980:185).

Both Derrida and Foucault attempt to expose the means, the 'play' and the 'power', by which meaning/knowledge/signification is generated; emphasising at once the passivity and frailty of human action, under the dominating and coercive influences of autonomous systems of signification appropriating and directing individual actions. At the same time, however, these mechanisms are revealed as being entirely within the scope of an individual to exploit, appropriate and act upon towards self-determination. Unfortunately, both ventures leave us with the problem of understanding how the two function together; how the individual manages or does not manage to create inalienable meaning under constantly alienating circumstances.

The Neo-Pragmatist Richard Rorty takes on the issues raised by *différance* and the manipulation of micropowers, and posits a sensibility directed towards action that links these issues raised by Derrida and Foucault. Rorty does this with his assertion of an anti-philosophical urge, which attempts to alleviate in one dramatic sweep the 'urge to philosophy' dominant in Western discourse from the days of Plato up to the 1970s. Rorty attempts to operationalise the notion of 'play' in Derrida's work within a Foucauldian political framework. If Foucault represents an aversion to speaking for others, rendering his politics mute and eliciting accusations of amorality, then Rorty picks up where Foucault was incapable of action and rather than being mute, encourages us to 'keep on talking', arguing for unlimited semiosis in the process of 'keeping the conversation going'.

As with Foucault, attempts at fixity, anchored in an adequate social theory, are attempts at closure, which often have highly pernicious effects. Certain empirical phenomena, such as counting and the observations of celestial motions, can be usefully enclosed and 'fixed' without necessarily inhibiting meaning. Observing four legs on a dog and accepting this observation will have little value in the elaboration of meaning concerning the problem of counting the number of legs on a dog. To assert otherwise would be nonsensical or surrealistic, but these other challenges do not undermine the practical project of counting the number of legs. However, such closure, inhibition of semiosis or Foucauldian 'discipline' cannot be adequate for something like the 'self', 'action', 'social justice' or 'structural change'. Closure in this realm is literally deadly and highly undesirable, as many thinkers in the tradition of critical theory have been saying for a very long time. Any foundationalist enterprise (e.g. Christian, logical positivist,

Marxian, National Socialist, structuralist) ultimately aims at inhibiting semiosis to one degree or another; in the sense of establishing closure, putting an end to an issue or conversation, or performing the indignity, repulsive to Foucault, of speaking for others (Sheridan 1980:114).

This is not to say that our hands are tied and our mouths are gagged, since to engage in any enterprise will result in some object, some totalising rhetoric or narrative which ultimately leads to repression and physical or symbolic violence. Rorty does not exhibit the pessimism of Foucault's muted position. On the contrary, he fully endorses the creation of precisely such objects, narratives and discourses for the very reason that by virtue of their articulation they generate further meanings, which other people then articulate *ad infinitum*.

The generation of all kinds of texts (e.g. open, closed, opaque) is crucial for the continuation of the process of semiosis. There must be a field against which a figure can be seen; there must be a text deconstructed in order to generate a further text. It is precisely the oscillation of that movement (Derridean *différance* or 'play') wherein meaning is generated. Consequently, Rorty argues that the generation of such narratives as conscious tropes – without pretensions to transcendentalism, objectivity, rigour or essences – is necessary to establish the creative tension propelling that movement towards further narratives generated to cope with changing contingencies. Such tropes become effective enabling devices or *Denkmittel* (means of thinking), to use the Pragmatist William James's apt term (James 1995). Thus the goal of intellectuals, according to Rorty, is to sustain semiosis and 're-weave' the community's web of belief 'by gradually literalizing, the new metaphors which the thinker has provided. The proper honour to pay to new, vibrantly alive metaphors, is to help them become dead metaphors as quickly as possible, to rapidly reduce them to the tools of social progress' (Rorty 1991:17).

Barbara Herrnstein Smith's work builds on Rorty's and elaborates a more nuanced understanding. Smith's main concern is literary theory. However, in discussing the objects of her analysis (e.g. literary texts and their interpretation), she assumes a sensibility directly relevant to the problem of the superfluity of meaning of text generally and material culture specifically. Like Rorty, Foucault and Derrida, Smith argues for a radical contingency of interpretation and echoes in unsentimental terms the violence inherent in semiosis. Like Rorty, she is compelled to argue for unfettered semiosis noting that such 'fixity would be unprofitable, in other words, to the extent that it prevents an organism from responding appropriately – that is, in a way that sustains the organism itself – to novel and emergent conditions' (Smith 1988:123).

Smith goes further than Derrida and Foucault and understands 'play' as a question of power and the means with which to realise these movements towards signification. Smith finds that these gaps, within which human motives are enacted and signification occurs in indeterminate fashion, are subject to radical and eternally shifting contingencies (Smith 1988:144). The resultant movements she calls 'scraps', which suggest the underlying violent aspect of Derridean 'play'. Her precise term for this condition is 'scrappiness', which characterises the instantiation of human motives and signification. The instantiation of motivations and significations is partial, contingent, inconclusive, open-ended, ultimately unfixable and – more significantly – inherently subject to contestation. Thus she alludes to another attendant meaning of 'scraps': 'our motives and behaviour are incomplete and hetero-geneous, like scraps of things, but also ("scrap" being a slang term for fight) that they are mutually conflicting or at least always potentially at odds' (Smith 1988:148).

In light of Rorty's problems with providing a satisfying politics of action (see criticisms of Rorty's position in (Bernstein 1987)), Smith provides a more suitable model. The constant foregrounding and dissolution of partialities, expressing the continuously contingent nature of the generation of meaning, offers a possibility for social justice that eludes Foucault, the Frankfurt School and Rorty, and offers a away to disperse the fears and anxieties over 'abject relativism'. Smith states that:

> Though not usually given in such terms, it is the fear that someone's acknowledging the fact and partiality of her perspective would make her authority –- that is, precisely the privilege of her perspective – vulnerable . . . But the securing of authority from interrogation and risk could hardly be thought an unqualified intrinsic good. On the contrary, it might be thought there was some communal value to ensuring that all authority was always subject to interrogation and always at risk. All authority: which must mean that of parent, teacher and missionary as well as tyrant, pope and state flunky. (Smith 1988:161)

Smith's process of interpretative authority resembles the 'ideal speech' situations of Jürgen Habermas, whereby in order to approximate the desired equity Habermas's moral imperative requires, differentially empowered agents relate to each other 'as if' the terms of commun-ication 'were' equitable. According to Smith, Habermas in effect denies the operation of any strategic contingency in his 'ideal speech' situation. He wants to factor out the 'scrappiness' inherent in the negotiation of contingencies, the very motivating force generating meaning, creating *différance*. In short, he proposes to neutralise the violent yet empowering vitality of semiosis. In the end, an 'ideal speech' situation would resemble the discussion over the four legs of a dog mentioned earlier; no one would have any strategic interest to take the matter any further, leaving us with an 'ideal speech' situation that by Habermas's definition can only be banal.

This emphasis on the play of 'gaps' and their resultant 'scraps' characterised by a violent 'scrappiness' echoes the concerns of social anthropologist Marilyn Strathern. Commenting on the conditions of interpretation in the anthropology of Melanesia, she speaks of an 'endless kaleidoscope of permutations' (Strathern 1991:xvii) that result in Smith-like 'scrappiness'. Strathern's discussion rests on the use of a metaphor derived from mathematical chaos theory, notably the nineteenth-century mathematical conundrum of Cantor's dust: 'begin with a line; remove the middle third; then remove the middle third of the remaining segments; and so on. The Cantor set is the dust of points that remain. They are infinitely many, but their total length is 0' (James Gleick in Strathern 1991:5).

Applying this metaphor to an anthropological inquiry, Strathern notes that every question or act of signification creates superfluity, a space – a 'remainder' in the Derridean sense of *différance* – so that 'each question in conjunction with its answer, or each position from which a new position is created, in turn becomes a position that one leaves behind' (ibid. xxii). Hence,

> at each juncture something more is generated than the answer requires, that something more acts as a kind of 'remainder', material that is left over, for it goes beyond the original answer to the question to encapsulate or subdivide that position (the question-and-answer) by further questions requiring further answers. Or, we might say, it opens up fresh gaps in our understanding. (ibid.)

Citing Frederik Barth's study of the Mountain Ok people of New Guinea (Barth 1987), Strathern notes that the very impetus for the generation of new meaning is in the creation of gaps/loss/absence/*différance*, as in the generation of further divisions of Cantor's dust. Rather than mournfully suffer from the violence of presumed information loss in Barth's account of the oral recreation of Ok mythology,

Strathern posits a contrary understanding: '. . . I have suggested the knowledge that they are lost [the knowledge of earlier myth] is not, so to speak, lost knowledge, it is knowledge about absence, about forgetting and about an unrecoverable background. That sense of loss stimulates the Baktaman initiators, it would seem, to making present images work' (Strathern 1991:97–8). Having to make do with what is at hand because of these 'absences'/gaps, the Baktaman elders' reworkings yield new information. Therefore, as with the void created by the play of *différance*, the gaps revealed in Cantor's dust are what create meaning. They are essential and predicative to the process of semiosis. "The important thing is that the gaps are preserved. They do not see themselves as recreating what they think is missing, but only what they know. It is as if they knew that by insisting on that absence they create their own identity.' (ibid. 98). Here Strathern relinquishes control of semiosis; something that other theorists despite their better intentions are too anxious not to do in their recourses to 'consensuses' and 'communities'; an anxiety resulting from the intellectual's absolute loss of transcendent authority (Smith 1988:74–7).

The process of semiosis involves extreme violence, 'scraps', fights and 'theft'. Referring to Marcel Griaule, Strathern reiterates his observation that 'ethnographic field work itself can be seen as intrinsically violent and intrusive extraction" (Stratern 1990:110); likewise the violence perpetrated in the constitution of the archaeological record through innately destructive excavation practices (Tilley 1989, and Parker-Pearson in Buchli 1995), and any other constitution of text or signification that inherently involves the Derridean concept of the 'theft' of speech (Derrida 1978:178). Nevertheless Strathern states unsentimentally: 'creativity in this view is thus what one makes do with, the recombining of parts unkindly cut from their original loci, even though one knows that those loci must have been cut from others' (Strathern 1991:110).

Strathern asserts that 'partiality' and the gaps of Cantor's dust 'makes people aware of their perceptual faculties in creating images" (ibid. 113). Thus she follows Foucault's calls for the revelation of micropowers to enable people to act and change their circumstances; Rorty's for the intellectual continuously to enable the process of semiosis 'by keeping the conversation going'; and Smith's for the necessity of 'scrappiness' for the most equitable conditions for our negotiation of our contingent circumstances. Strathern observes in addition, however, that 'Baktaman elders can only work with what is present. In so doing they create new information, new repositories of the differences they wish to impress on others, and thereby see in the background the presumed skills of past experts whose absent artefacts cannot be recovered' (ibid. 114).

Thus, these are powerful and enabling 'gaps', drawing our attention to our ability to negotiate these distances in the same way that the Baktaman elders know that they can create new meaning, engage in 'scraps' over the constitution of new significations. 'Gaps seem to give us somewhere to extend: space for our prosthetic devices' (ibid. 115). Our intellectual traverses over these absences or gaps allow us to make connections and create new meanings. Strathern likens these connections to prosthetics, a tool (or *'Denkmittel' pace* James) at once foreign to its immediate context/body but which enables it to engage other contexts: 'there is no subject–object relation between a person and a tool, only an expanded or realised capability' (Strathern 1991:38). Filling in gaps, these 'prosthetics' function in almost Rortian fashion towards '[making] a conversation work for me as a tool works, as I can make myself work in sustaining the conversation' (Strathern 1991:39).

Strathern is able to avoid containing superfluity about some axis or consensus, by acknowledging her ultimate powerlessness to contain meaning and reject any attempts to do so. Like Foucault, Strathern is 'indignant'; however, like Smith, Rorty and Derrida, she is optimistic, for by consciously relinquishing her power to contain superfluity, she facilitates the most equitable conditions for the generation of meaning and holds out the best hope for social justice.

Such radical discontinuity and lack of closure is what Judith Butler in her Queer/Feminist work strives to demonstrate as the necessary conditions for meaningful Queer and Feminist politics. Rather than being something we have to learn to live with, be 'weaned' off (Rorty) or endure as a 'communal value' (Smith), Butler sees the impossibility of closure as something that is positive, liberating and ultimately our only hope. In terms of feminist struggle she argues that the category of women can never be known and ought not to be known: 'That the category can never be descriptive is the very condition of its political efficacy. In this sense, what is lamented as disunity and factionalization from the perspective informed by the descriptivist ideal is *affirmed* by the anti-descriptivist perspective as the open and democratising principle of the category' (Butler 1993:221).

Butler comes to this affirmation of radical discontinuity through her argument, *pace* Derrida, Ernesto Laclau and Chantal Mouffe, that every 'closure' creates an 'outside' – that which is not contained and for democratic reasons never should be (Butler 1993:220). Thus, rather than being stoic like Smith about the impossibility of ever keeping the 'jackals at bay', Butler sees the lack of 'guarantees' as an absolute virtue, which would not only 'keep the conversation going' *pace* Rorty but provide its own assurance for the necessary terms of democracy. This process of perpetual dislocation and antagonisms, Butler argues, is the very guarantee of democracy that would keep Smith's 'jackals at bay'. Derridean *différance* is not something to be overcome or endured; his observation constitutes a necessary 'fact' that actually secures the field against the possibility of any one ever getting the axiological upper hand.

Butler's discussion of the constitution of genders and their bodies has direct implications for material culture if one takes the 'body' as an artefact and a peculiar instance of material culture (see Thomas 1998). Generally, the physicality or the 'materiality' of material culture is often taken for granted. The presupposition is that there is a material artefact with attributes that, once stripped away of its capabilities to signify socially and symbolically, can be understood in an unproblematised and straightforward manner such as 'reading the archaeological record' or 'letting the artefacts speak'. In terms of the scientific understanding of the physical qualities of the material object at hand this assumes an indisputable base-line and given; something about which few meaningful objections concerning their consensus could be expressed. Butler, however, posits an understanding of the body that rejects the unproblematised aspects of sexing and gender; an understanding that, stripped of social and symbolic meaning, there is a male and female body that can be known and exists in a particular relationship to each other. Butler rejects the sexed 'male' and 'female' body as neutrally and unconditionally sexed (invoking Thomas Laqueur's argument (Laqueur 1990); see also Moore (1994) and Broch-Due et al. (1993)). Thus Butler warns us in relation to the political work of feminist thinkers, with the question echoing an earlier one by James:

> To what extent in invoking received notions of materiality, indeed, in insisting that those notions function as 'irreducibles', do we secure and perpetuate a constitutive violation of the feminine? When we consider that the very concept of matter preserves and recirculates a violation, and then invoke that very concept in the service of compensation for violation, we run the risk of reproducing the very injury for which we seek redress. (Butler 1993:53–4).

The result of such an uncritical feminism is that inequalities become naturalised and those that do not fit the binaries established by the 'heterosexual matrix' fall outside where they do not 'matter' in both the physical and social sense. The old problem is reiterated that such axiality produces inevitable exclusions. However, *pace* Derrida, Butler acknowledges that such 'outsides' are necessary to enforce the objects they contain and thereby describe each other (ibid. 38–9). However, as with others these 'outsides', 'spaces' or 'gaps' offer great liberating potential and explanatory power if we move away from thinking about 'presences' (what 'things' are) to 'absences' (how 'things' are not).

However, Butler assumes a similar lack of sentimentality to Smith's: 'it is important to resist that theoretical gesture of pathos in which exclusions are simply affirmed as sad necessities of signification' (Butler 1993:53). Rather Butler is supremely optimistic:

> The task is to refigure this necessary 'outside' as a future horizon, one in which the violence of exclusion is perpetually in the process of being overcome. But of equal importance is the preservation of the outside, the site where discourse meets its limits, where the opacity of what is not included in a given regime of truth acts as a disruptive site of linguistic impropriety and unrepresentability, illuminating the violent and contingent boundaries of that normative regime precisely through the inability of that regime to represent that which might pose a fundamental threat to its continuity. (ibid. 53)

Butler sees that the uncertainty of such a position of radical discontinuity or contingency purged of the phantom of 'abject relativism' actually initiates the possibility of more equitable social interaction, which works precisely to disperse such phantoms and their attendant anxieties.

The political theorist Chantal Mouffe expands on this particular point in greater detail. Mouffe like Butler, focuses on indeterminacy and the necessity of what she calls 'antagonisms' in the negotiation of 'undecidables' as the best hope for social justice without recourse to foundations. Like Smith she argues against Habermas's 'boot-strap action' (Smith) of 'ideal speech situations' (Mouffe 1996b:246).

Butler draws on Mouffe's valorisation of antagonism as the essence of political life. According to Mouffe, to factor out antagonism – in terms of the position characteristic of 'abject relativism' (where no such antagonisms could be justified because everything is equally virtuous) – would end in the result that 'although it tends to be very critical of liberalism, that type of extreme pluralism, because of its refusal of any attempt to construct a "we", a collective identity that would articulate the demands found in the different struggles against subordination, partakes of the liberal evasion of the political' (Mouffe 1996b:247).

Mouffe argues further quoting her collaborator Ernesto Laclau:

> But by the simple fact of the presence of negativity and given the primary and constitutive character of any antagonism, the hiding of the 'ultimate' undecidability of any decision will never be complete and social coherence will only be achieved at the cost of repressing something that negates it. It is in this sense that any consensus, that any objective and differential system of rules, implies, as its most essential possibility, a dimension of coercion. (Laclau in Mouffe 1993:141)

Mouffe's political project is to

> reveal the danger of postulating that there could be a rational definite solution to the question of justice in a democratic society. Such an idea leads to the closing of the gap between justice and the law that is a constitutive space of Modern democracy. To avoid such a closure, we should relinquish the very idea that there could be such a thing such as a 'rational' political consensus – that is, one that would not be based on any form of exclusion. (Mouffe 1996b:253–4, see also Mouffe 1993:145)

However, in keeping with Butler and Derrida with her notion of the 'constitutive outside', Mouffe insists that the violence of exclusion is inevitable and that it is significant to recognise it as such as an assurance for progressive politics (Mouffe 1993:145). Mouffe embraces that which other – what she would call 'liberal' – theorists (Mouffe 1996b:255) reject.

The key element of Mouffe's argument, like Smith's 'scrappiness', is her concept of 'undecidability' where

> Undecidability is not a moment to be traversed or overcome and conflicts of duty are interminable. I can never be completely satisfied that I have made a good choice since a decision in favour of one alternative is always to the detriment of another one . . . Politicisation never ceases because undecidability continues to inhabit the decision. Every consensus appears as a stabilisation of something essentially unstable and chaotic. Chaos and instability are irreducible, but as Derrida indicates, this is at once a risk and a chance, since continual stability would mean the end of politics and ethics. (Mouffe 1996b:9)

Thus Mouffe's understanding of totalitarianism will be of direct relevance to the materials we will look at later on in this book. As she argues: 'In the end, the rationalist defence of liberalism, by searching for an argument that is beyond argumentation and by wanting to define the meaning of the universal, makes the same mistake for which it criticises totalitarianism: it rejects democratic indeterminacy and identifies the universal with a given particular' (Mouffe 1993:146) hence, 'the incapacity of liberal theorists to come to terms with the phenomenon of fascism [or totalitarianism]' (ibid. 3). As I hope to unfold in the following chapters, this incapacity inhibits our ability to come to terms with the confusing and contradictory ways in which people had carved out lives for themselves within the totalitarian system that was the former Soviet Union and thereby enable us to understand the improbable accommodations resulting from this experience and how someone like Elena Andreevna could keep house in the extraordinary way that she did, lovingly and diligently dusting her icons, along with her collected works of Stalin. In the next chapter I will trace the beginnings of these processes and the radicalisation of the domestic sphere in which they were played out.

Revolution and the Restructuring of the Material World

We are now at war, and the war is for the new life, for that which mere words cannot describe. Here every person is obliged, like a soldier, to overcome everything. (Ilyina in Rabotnitsa 1930, #4,13)

The early Bolshevik state in its attempts to restructure every aspect of the Tsarist world found itself in an agonistic relationship with every aspect of pre-Revolutionary life. According to prevailing Marxian assumptions of the material world and its social effects, the conditions of material life would determine consciousness. The most immediate arena to be restructured was the realm of daily life or *byt*, constituting it and focusing on the quotidian micropowers structuring the social fabric almost in anticipation of Foucault's own analysis. Loosely translated, *byt* encompasses all the following English terms: 'daily life', 'domesticity', 'lifestyle' or 'way of life'. Prior to the Revolution the term *byt* had largely ethnographic implications and was used to describe differences in daily life represented by traditional ethnographic subjects such as Siberian aboriginal groups, as well as traditional European peasant societies. With the Revolution and the problem of constructing a new socialist society the word *byt* assumed increasing political significance, moving to the forefront of discussions about the reconstruction of society in the aftermath of the Revolution and Civil War.

The socialist revolution in the eyes of Soviet theoreticians had two important fronts: external and internal. The battle on the external front was conventional, with men mobilised into armies intended physically to repulse and destroy the enemies of socialism. The period of 'war communism' during the Civil War saw most of the resources of early socialist society diverted towards the successful defeat of the enemy on this external front. Though of less immediate danger than an invading army, the internal or 'domestic' front was nonetheless essential to the long-term success of the socialist restructuring of society. In the eyes of Soviet Marxist theoreticians, the 'domestic' front was also the weakest. Viktor Shtein describes how the shift in the battle for socialism from the barricades of war communism to the domestic sphere 'carried over into our daily lives, and there the old world attempts to engage us in battle, attacking on all our weak as yet unfortified positions' (Shtein 1929:6). As the conventional Soviet Marxist wisdom went: *Bytie opredelaet soznanie* (Smidovich 1927:20; Rabotnitsa,1925,#9, pp.20–1) ["Daily life/being determines consciousness"]. *Byt* was central to the development of a worker's political and social consciousness. If workers' consciousness, predicated on the conditions of daily life, were not attuned to collectivist values they could not be developed elsewhere, particularly in economic and political life (Bordiugov 1987:151). The conventional external front of military conflict, fought by male foot soldiers, strove to purge the emergent socialist society of external dangers. The internal front in its turn, fought by female 'foot soldiers' at home, addressed dangers to the internal development and continuity of Soviet society. The battlefields for this conflict were less readily evident. Rather the threats were passive, underfoot and lurking everywhere in quiet resistance to the advances of socialism and the restructuring of society. This passive resistance, both real and imagined, was believed omnipresent. The new order had yet to be created that would replace and repulse it. The problem, however, was where the dangers lay and what exactly they were.

The Revolution had eradicated the old political and economic order, and accordingly the culture and social formations associated with the preceding economic base. A dilemma lay in the fact that a new base was in the process of being erected and an appropriate order was just being realised. Hence there was a very significant threat of cultural and social vestiges (*perezhitki*) from before the Revolution that were incompatible with the new economic base and passively inhibiting its development. The precise nature of these vestiges was a matter of great debate. Thoughts on this issue ranged from a radical repudiation of every aspect of pre-Revolutionary society to the conservative position that nothing further needed to be done. Amongst moderate and radical reformers the locus of these dangers was debated for a broad range of everyday behaviour: from manicures to industrial management. With rare exceptions, no one doubted the need to restructure society beyond the eradication of oppressive classes and foreign invaders; the issue was what needed to be refigured and how to go about doing it.

Before the Revolution, the writings of socialist theoreticians and utopianists held few concrete and programmatic understandings of what the new *byt* would be (Osipovich 1931:77). Such a new order was to be predicated on its economic base. All one could do was to speculate; yet few questions were raised about the fantastical nature of these musings without an appropriate infrastructure. In fact, some existing oppressive relationships were more amenable to reformist speculation. These included labour relations, ownership of capital, and relations between the sexes. These issues had long been worked through in nineteenth-century reformist thought. However, ancillary aspects of the new life had to be worked out through the unfolding reforms of socialist construction in the early 1920s. Hence, there was a great deal of speculation, experimentation and negotiation in these as well as other related areas.

The Battle for Socialist *Byt*

With the end of the Civil War, the following period of limited capitalist economic recovery known as the New Economic Policy (NEP), and the reconstruction of Soviet political and civil life, the issue of *byt* began to be directly addressed (Kostrov 1930:7). A key issue in the problem of *byt* was women's oppression. Most discussions from the beginning of the 1920s and throughout the Soviet period focus on *byt* as the concern for and of women. As the regulation of pre-Revolutionary daily life was associated most intimately with the domestic realm, women became the focus of concern regarding the petit-bourgeois 'hearth' (as the unreformed domestic realm was known) of post-Revolutionary Russia. Women were seen as oppressed by the patriarchal institutions of the petit-bourgeois 'hearth', as much as they were seen to exert control over it by deriving authority and social position from it. As such, women's 'deformed' consciousness was particularly problematic for the realisation of daily life according to socialist principles.

If, as Engels so famously observed, a wife was to her husband in the domestic sphere as the proletariat to the capitalist (Engels 1972:81–2), then the key to dismantling that oppressive structure was a change in the economic basis of that relationship. In terms of labour relations this required the socialisation of capital and the abolition of private ownership. Similarly regarding domestic relations, what was needed was the socialisation of the domestic sphere and the dismantling of the private realm of the family (Bordiugov 1987:151). The emancipation of women and the shattering of the institutions of the 'hearth' were thus intimately related.

Ideally the dismantling of the 'hearth' would involve the total emancipation of women from their exploited positions within the patriarchal petit-bourgeois family, just as the proletariat would be emancipated from the oppression of capitalism. Women could then join men as the equal citizens of a new socialist egalitarian society. Heterosexual men, however, were not victims of the patriarchal hearth in the private realm as they were the victims of capitalism in the public realm of the workplace; women, on the other hand, were victims twice over. Soviet Marxist theoreticians emphasised an industrialising economic base that predicated all other aspects of social and cultural life. This claim was underlined by the rather obvious fact that most Bolsheviks and Party members were male, conspiring for a hierarchy of concerns in the grand scheme of socialist construction. This state of affairs tended to place *byt*, the emancipation of women and the dismantling of the 'hearth' rather low on the list of priorities. Despite the fact that *byt* determined worker consciousness (Toporokov 1929:8; Nikiforov 1929:12), it was ultimately determined by economic structure (Kozhanyi and Pyzhova 1925:6); therefore large-scale economic matters such as industrialisation had priority.

Furthermore the dismantling of the 'hearth', while radically changing women's positions in society, threatened positions of male patriarchal authority within the private realm. It must be noted that in the works of Soviet domestic reformers and the makers of social policy at no time was *byt* and the problems of housework and child-rearing ever seen as a man's problem. It was not a matter of levelling men's and women's roles in the domestic sphere rather the dismantling of that sphere with the raising of women 'above' and 'out' into the public realm of men. There was little discussion of bringing men 'down' into the private domestic sphere by making them equal to women in the share of the housework and childcare. Men were already out of the domestic realm and had been placed in the public realm of labour and industry, thereby creating the industrial infrastructure that could eventually socialise all aspects of domestic work. Since the dismantling of the 'hearth' and the emancipation of women were envisioned as the eventual results of socialist industrialisation, the socialisation of the domestic sphere would have to wait until the economic base was suitably established.

Throughout the 1920s, discussions attempted to come to terms with how long one had to wait before the 'hearth' was dismantled, the degree to which this would happen and the extent to which the 'hearth's' functions would be socialised. More important, however, was the question as to who was to take the responsibility for its socialisation. That is, who was to pay for previously unpaid women's labour.

The period of war communism saw experiments with various sorts of living arrangements in an attempt to realise the socialist utopias envisioned by Fourier, Chernishevskii, Tolstoy and others. The experiments ranged from familiar religious communes to the more radical Marxist student ones (Stites 1989). In practice these experiments had little impact on a society in the throes of civil war. With the war's end in 1921 and the beginning of NEP, the process of building a socialist society could be undertaken in earnest. However, in the eyes of the Party and Marxist theoreticians, NEP was seen as a limited period of retreat from socialist goals. NEP capitalism was temporarily employed to invigorate the economy quickly after the devastation of civil war, after which one could begin socialist economic construction. Most of the attempts to define and address the problems relating to *byt* and women were influenced by this climate of retreat and accommodation.

Different Responses to *Byt*

During NEP a plurality of responses emerged that attempted to come to terms with NEP conditions and negotiate the new *byt* and women's roles (Khlevniuk 1983:147; Kozhanyi and Pyzhova 1925:9–10). Some engaged the pre-existing mode of domestic production that centred upon the segregated nuclear and extended family, using the unpaid work of women in the domestic realm and the waged labour of male household members in the public realm. For some families where the male labourer earned enough to maintain a wife devoted to domestic tasks this was an option. This, however, was officially discouraged by the Party and radical thinkers as a vestige of petit-bourgeois family life and consciousness.

A respectable alternative followed by many non-waged women of sufficient means was to engage in *obshchestvenaia rabota* or 'social work' in the *zhenotdel* or 'women's section' of the Party, or some other aspect of social work. Housework was perceived as a mark of women's shameful oppression under capitalism (Rabotnitsa 1924:#19p.30, Rabotnitsa 1925:#22 backcover, Rabotnitsa 1927:#22,pp.22–3). Women who did not perform wage labour were therefore encouraged to withdraw from the domestic realm and engage in useful 'social work'. Only then would they begin to realise the socialist ideal of the liberated woman in the public sphere. The 'social work' undertaken by these women was not remunerated for the most part, representing an unpaid labour force at the disposal of the Party (Sheftel' 1931:10). The potential of this free labour force did not go unnoticed: 'until now children's daycare was poorly staffed by worker's wives and housewives. The Five Year Plan remedies this deficit. Many wives of workers with families can, thanks to this, busy themselves with social work and will be drawn into the construction of socialism' (Rabotnitsa 1929:#40,14). These more fortunate liberated women could also have their former domestic responsibilities taken over by *domrabotnitsi* (live-in maids) who came to the city for food and employment in the wake of the 1930–1 collectivisation campaign. Women who were not able to find jobs in industry and managed to avoid prostitution could find employment as live-in maids in well-to-do urban households.

However, with industrialisation, women began to figure more in the workforce. Therein lay the foundation of what was to become the characteristic bane of women throughout the Soviet period: the double burden of unpaid household maintenance in addition to paid daytime work. During the 1920s household time-budget surveys pointed with increasing alarm to the double burden experienced by women having to work a regular shift as well as tend to children, find food, prepare meals and cope with housework. Typically men devoted considerably less time to household affairs, dismissing them as *bab'e delo* ('wench's affairs'). The effect of the double burden on women was less sleep, poorer diet, and increased exhaustion for waged women in comparison to their male counterparts.

The contradiction of the petit-bourgeois housewife with the labourer/ homemaker became rapidly intolerable in both ideological and practical terms. To remedy this situation a variety of strategies were proposed in the years before and during the First Five Year Plan. One such strategy was Taylorism (*NOT byta* [*Nauchnaia Organizatsia Truda byta*]), the rationalisation of housework according to Taylorist efficiency principles taken from industrial production and military management. Taylorist principles applied to housework were believed to make it more efficient, rational and less time-consuming in order to free women to pursue 'social work' and participate in the construction of socialism. If the 'hearth' (and its institutions) could not be immediately socialised or eliminated entirely then it could at least be rationalised to minimise its role in social life. Taylorism was a palliative measure: acknowledging the double burden and striving to relieve it by making it more efficient, and less burdensome.

Radical proposals existed that called for the complete obliteration of the domestic sphere. This was a full-frontal assault against the petit-bourgeois 'hearth'. Its most effective weapon was the institution of the *kommuna* or commune. *Kommuny* attempted to pool all the resources of a group of like-minded individuals. Inhabitants would perform domestic tasks such as cooking, cleaning, laundry and childcare by assigning individuals or teams on a rotating basis (Stites 1989, Larin and Belousov 1930, Cooke 1974). The more radical *kommuny*, usually composed of young, idealistic students, would go so far as to socialise everything. They practised the pooling of all wages earned, the sharing of a communal stock of underwear and perhaps the most extreme expression of communality: the sharing of sexual partners. Such *kommuny* were rare and represented an exceptional confluence of individuals, with similar backgrounds, earnings, experience and open-mindedness that seldom found sustained expression in practice (Stites 1989, Khlevniuk 1983:149).

Less radically socialised *kommuny* that might have only pooled individual wages or part thereof had an easier chance of acceptance. They represented an economic co-operative that responded effectively to the difficulties of low wages, high prices, incessant shortages and long queues for food during the NEP period. They also coincided with the prevailing notions of communalism (Stites 1989). One of the contradictory consequences of this type of *kommuna* was that, while the *kommuna* functioned in varying degrees of communality, it segregated itself from the rest of society forming a separate, independent and somewhat aloof entity (Bordiugov 1987:152; Rabotnitsa 1930:#8,18). Complaints of snobbery on the part of communards towards their less 'socialistically' inspired colleagues caused resentment from less radical Soviet citizens. Official assessments in the late 1920s began to reflect and report on this popular resentment. Comments concerning the extreme radicalism of such endeavours degenerated into accusations of petit-bourgeois self-absorption, anti-social-mindedness, vulgar egalitarianism, egotism and Trotskyism (Bordiugov 1987:152–3, Khlevniuk 1983:153–5).

Following the *kommuny* the next level of socialisation of the domestic sphere was the *zhilishchnye kooperativi* (housing co-operatives). These co-operatives attempted to socialise selected aspects of the domestic realm; notably, laundry, housing maintenance, the preparation of food, and to a limited degree, childcare. Instead of a full-frontal assault on the 'hearth', the co-operatives represented a sustained engagement with the 'enemy'. The female members of the housing co-operative would pool their labour and resources in order to provide domestic services to the co-operative as a whole rather than individually. Housework was not eradicated but engaged in communally. Aspects of co-operative maintenance that could not be performed by members of the community (e.g. plumbing, laundry, cooking) could be hired out at the co-operative's expense (Bakhterev and Razumovskii 1930:11). This solution had appeal as it socialised feminine domestic labour, inculcating with socialist values women who were otherwise individual 'petit-bourgeois' housewives. Its proponents also claimed that it increased personal liberty by pooling resources and streamlining redundant household labour as well as hiring outside help, leaving women more free to engage in useful 'social work'.

The housing co-operative movement was rather long-lived compared to other approaches (it was abolished as late as 1937). One of its prime advantages was its relative conservatism, both socially and fiscally. It did not involve a radical transformation of pre-existing domestic forms within the 'hearth' such as the eradication of the nuclear family or traditional women's roles. Nor did it require any financial input on the part of unions, the Party and the state. The nuclear family was left intact; only its most oppressive features were factored out (laundry, childcare facilities and the procurement of food) and socialised amongst the female members of the housing co-operative.

Usually the housing co-operatives leased or bought properties from local councils. Funds were collected from special co-operative housing loan schemes and on occasion from union, Party and factory sources. For the most part these co-operatives were self-funded and self-managed. Facilities for socialised functions were often ingeniously carved out from existing housing stock by appropriating apartments, or by using cellars or attics or at times pre-existing outbuildings (Kozhanyi and Pyzhova 1925:74–7). Labour was supplied by members themselves or hired specialists when local talents were lacking. Added to this, building materials were solicited from factory surpluses by the co-operative or acquired by various means by members independently (Kozhanyi 1924:58–61).

The day-to-day maintenance of the communal facilities fell to the women (Rabotnitsa 1934, #32–4, 10–12, Rabotnitsa 1931, #13, 10; Rabotnitsa 1930, #11, 14–15; Rabotnitsa 1930, #15, 16–17, Rabotnitsa 1929, #41, 12; Rabotnitsa 1929, #40, 15–16; Rabotnitsa, 1929, #46, 15; Rabotnitsa 1929, #18, 14; Smidovich 1927:31; Bakhterev and Razumovskii 1930:13). The co-operatives did little to eliminate the 'hearth' entirely; they merely socialised it, easing the double burden by pooling women's labour and finances. These housing co-operatives seemed to work most effectively where there existed free sources of female labour: domestic work being performed mainly by non-waged women or full-time housewives. Working women who would have profited the most from such co-operatives did not benefit (Central Committee of the Communist Party (Bolsheviks) of Ukraine 1929:26). One could easily speculate that such wage-earning women simply did not have the time away from their jobs in the course of the day to participate with the non-waged women in the maintenance of the housing co-operative. Nadezhda Krupskaia, a prominent feminist and Lenin's widow, observed this situation and objected that socialised child-rearing was the work of charitable ladies and not the work of labouring masses (Krupskaia 1930:22).

Though communalized, the services of the housing co-operative did not come free. These co-operatives were funded by member's dues and fees for services. Many waged women found that they simply could not afford to send themselves and their families to the communal dining rooms. Economies of scale kept the prices of the few functioning communal dining rooms high and out of reach of the single female worker, especially one supporting a family (Central Committee of the Communist Party (Bolsheviks) of Ukraine 1929:26–7). This left poorer women with the burden of having to procure and prepare foodstuffs for their families themselves (ibid. p. 26). Only educated non-labouring urban women who shared household incomes with their waged husbands had the means sufficient to pay for advance construction costs, co-operative fees and maintenance (Hazard 1939:12). Thus, the movement could only serve a narrow social stratum, specifically the professional urban population.

Advocates of the communal housing movement saw their policy less as a retreat dictated by the requirements of economic recovery but more as an end in and of itself, expressing the very spirit of communal and socialist life in its spontaneous, grass roots and independent nature (Larin in Larin and Belousov 1930:5–20). Through the 1920s, this local spontaneity gradually fell into disfavour with the increasingly statist, centralised and authoritarian regime born of Civil War-era 'war communism' (Fitzpatrick 1985:57–76).

In fact, aside from mere lipservice, the communal housing movement was divorced financially and administratively from the Party and trade unions (Central Committee of the Communist Party (Bolsheviks) of Ukraine 1929:38–9). By the late 1920s and early 1930s cultural workers and *byt* activists made increasing demands on Party, union, and

industrial authorities for resources for the communal housing movement, insisting on their importance for the realisation of socialist goals
(ibid., 38–9; Kulturnaia Revolutsia 1931, #6, 5–7; Rabotnitsa 1930, #22,
16–17; Rabotnitsa 1930, #4, 3; Artiukhina in Rabotnitsa 1929, #4, 3–4;
Rabotnitsa 1929, #21, 14–15; Rabotnitsa 1929, #10, 7–8; Rabotnitsa
1929, #7, 17; Kul'turnaia Revoliutsiia 1929, #24, 41–2; Kul'turnaia Revoliutsiia 1929, #15,17). Amid the cacophony of socialist programmes,
goals and projects struggling for acceptance during the years of the
Cultural Revolution, these demands fell on deaf ears; the party gave
little money to support these endeavours. Eventually the *zhenotdel,*
which undertook much of the *byt* agitational work, was disbanded by
the Party in 1931 (see Goldman 1993). Similarly, unions and factory
management provided very little in terms of support and finance despite
official rhetoric.

The reason most frequently cited for non-compliance was lack of
funds. Factory managers (desperately attempting to meet the rapid-
fire pace of industrialisation) found themselves hard pressed to devote
resources towards *byt* reform. Though *byt* reform was essential to the
well-being of the workforce in the long run, it did nothing to maximise
line items or production goals during the First Five Year Plan (Rabotnitsa
1929, #7, 17; Rabotnitsa 1929,#10, 7–8; Artiukhina in Rabotnitsa 1929,
#4, 3–4).

The structure of government directives concerning the funding of
byt programmes aimed at helping women only served to work against
them. Women were more expensive to employ because of additional
infrastructural expenditures such as childcare, and other facilities
required by the *byt* funds where significant numbers of women were
employed. This only exacerbated the situation women found themselves in: earning lower wages than their male counterparts while
tending to be employed in less prestigious lower-skilled sectors like
the textile and paper industries which men avoided. Also, women found
it harder to be promoted as *vydvyzhentsy* (workers advanced to more
responsible positions and higher education) (Sheftel' 1931:17). More
concerned with production goals, the Party gave little incentive to
factory managers to conform to the demands of *byt* activists. With the
Party having eliminated the largest base of *byt* activity – the *zhenotdel*
– there was little organised incentive to realise *byt* reforms.

Clements has argued that the *zhenotdel* and the Party's dedication to
women's issues were superficial, the Party having succumbed to
ingrained misogynistic tendencies in Russian and Soviet society
(Clements 1992). This without doubt was an element contributing to

the failure of *byt* reform. One cannot underestimate the degree of resentment amongst upwardly mobile male managers and labourers whose notions of propriety and status were based on high wages and a housewife at home. Anecdotes culled from the popular women's journal *Rabotnitsa* from the years 1928 to 1932 refer to women's growing concern and fear of male resentment. This resentment was directed towards women with daytime jobs engaging in social work within *byt* collectives after-hours, rejecting the duties of the 'hearth'. One piece of women's fiction from the era describes the resentment of a worker's husband who is so angered by her social work in the evening away from home that he eventually stabs her to death (Rabotnitsa, 1929, #46, 7). Women's journals like *Rabotnitsa* would warn of the resentment of husbands, their beatings, and the blind eye of unions, factories and Party cells towards such abuse (Rabotnitsa 1929:#11,12). Often the class enemy was the man to whom a woman was married. In many respects he was far more imposing a foe than any outside aggressor, considering the reluctance of the many so-called 'unenlightened' women who remained within the confines of the 'hearth' (Central Committee of the Communist Party (Bolsheviks) of Ukraine 1929:6–12).

Along with institutionalised misogyny, the expediencies of industrialisation ultimately conspired against the dedication of resources towards *byt* reform. Other factors were complicit: a population experiencing inordinate flux; social instability; shortages; and squalid housing. It would not seem unimaginable that the patriarchal 'hearth', in spite of its institutionalised inequality, was one small oasis of relative 'stability' not yet touched by the whirlwind of instability that characterised life in the 1920s. Reports of the dangers and horrors from the domestic front lines could only have stirred the more self-willed and determined segments of the female population into action. Those less capable of the Nietzschean heroism of *byt* activists – probably the majority of women – accepted the pre-existing stability of the old *byt* (see Rosenthal 1994 on the significance of the Nietzschean figure in Soviet culture).

Changing Party Support of *Byt* Activism

Although prevalent in Party rhetoric, official government and Party support for the *byt* communes and the reform of *byt* issues did not become fully articulated and operationalized until late 1929 and early 1930. VTsIK authorised on 20 February 1930 a directive for the Sovnarkom RSFSR (Soviet of Peoples' Commissariats of the RSFSR) to liaise and co-operate more directly with various *byt*-reforming collectives.

On 15 March 1930, additional instructions were given to register all *byt* collectives, to establish wholesale discounts for their inputs, and to put forward a recommendation of credit schemes. Additionally, government sectors such as the Presidium of the VTsIK, the Sovnarkom RSFSR, and Narkomtrud (People's Commissariat of Labour) established their own *byt* commissions between 1929 and 1930 (Khlevniuk 1983:150).

As government support was consolidated in the early months of 1930, criticism of the entire undertaking was beginning to be articulated in official circles. The Sixth Congress of VKP(b) assessed the various communal and collective housing schemes as 'having much that is very interesting, but without question much that is quite negative - with dependent and levelling tendencies' (Khlevniuk 1983:153). Likewise, the March 1930 First All Union Congress of *Byt* Communes noted the dangers that some highly structured and regimented *byt* communes could pose. They cited their disregard for volunteerism along with their vulgarisation of the process of collectivism by claiming their methods to be the sole legitimate ones (Bordiugov 1987:152).

Articulation of outright opposition to the very spirit of *byt* reforms came with the 16 May resolution of the Central Committee of VKP(b) entitled 'O Rabote o Perestroike Byta' ('On the work concerning the restructuring of daily life'). While generally supporting the idea for the creation of a new socialist *byt* and its relevance to the whole socialist enterprise, the resolution gave stern warnings against 'the unfounded half-fantastical, and therefore dangerous attempts by individual comrades who "with one leap" propose to skip over those obstructions to the socialist restructuring of daily life, whose roots are in the economic and cultural backwardness of the country'. Yet it emphasised that 'the unavoidable at this given moment, maximal dedication of all resources towards the speediest industrialisation of the country . . . establishes the real material preconditions for the deep-rooted reform of daily life' (Khlevniuk 1983:154, Bordiugov 1987:152–3).

By 5 October 1930, *byt* sections of city and village Party Soviets were ordered by government directives to facilitate 'the voluntary collectivism of worker's *byt*' (Khlevniuk 1983:154), thereby shifting the burden for organising and financing *byt* reform from the Party, government and industry onto the people themselves. By the June 1931 plenum of the Central Committee VKP(b), the increasingly frosty attitude towards *byt* reform became more pronounced. The issue of the abolition of individual kitchens – long considered by reformists as the key to women's emancipation and the realisation of socialism – was rejected amidst claims that a public infrastructure did not yet exist to replace the functions of the individual domestic kitchen.

In addition, the plenum called for militant vigilance in the realm of *byt* issues against 'right opportunism, which is against the Bolshevik tempo of socialist development of industry, and against the reform of the culture and *byt* of industrial and *kolkhoz* workers, as well against the leaps of "left" opportunist propagandists, coming out with every imaginable projected proposals [such as the abolition of the individual kitchen and the artificial imposition of *byt* communes]' (Khlevniuk 1983:155). In the pages of a 1929 issue of *Komsomol'skaia Pravda*, N. Krupskaia rejected radical projects with fully communalised child-care. She argued the ill-effects such communalisation would have on children, justifying individual upbringing as having no ill-effects in socialist terms since petit-bourgeois values were based on private property, which had long since been eradicated (Krupskaia 1930:22).

With regard to *byt* reform the Party and government policy's shift to spontaneous volunteerism (*samodeiatel'nost'*) made an official virtue out of the independent, self-funded strategies of earlier *byt* reformers. The previous experience of *byt* activists – struggling to manage, organise and fund *byt* programmes on their own – was invoked as the new model according to which *byt* reform was to proceed (Zheleznov in Rabotnitsa 1931, #32, 3–4; Ishkova in Rabotnitsa 1931, #?,17). In keeping with the plenum's support of spontaneous voluntarism in *byt* affairs, the issue of funding equally became 'voluntary' and 'spontaneous'. The means to reform *byt* were to be mobilised from within the population; 'work must be developed to mobilise the means of the population itself towards the restructuring of daily life' (Rabotnsitsa 1931, #?,17). The person to do so was 'the worker woman herself [who] must tend to these affairs' (Rabotnitsa 1931, #?,17). During the Civil War the heroic efforts of communist women were invoked when women alone provided the conditions for domestic life without any funding or support under the most trying of circumstances. Organised *byt* reform was further dismantled with the dissolution in 1931 of the *Zhenotdel* of the Communist Party. The unambiguous shift of the burden of *byt* reform from enterprises to individuals probably caused a collective sigh of relief amongst union officials and industrial management as well the vast majority of worker families unimpressed by the 'school-marmish' and judgmental attitudes of *byt* reformers regulating their daily lives.

In this new scheme of things, *byt* reform became less of an absolute right under state guarantee than a perk awarded to successful, enterprising workers – an incentive towards better work and productivity. Admission to communalised *byt* institutions, such as dining rooms and childcare centres, was increasingly reserved for the so-called worker aristocracy developing in the wake of the *vydvyzhentsy* and subsequent Stakhanovite movements. Elite workers received these former 'rights' as benefits, not simply because they could afford them, but because they deserved them as representatives of the more advanced and enlightened segments of socialist society (Sorokin and Markovich 1931:22). Offering rewards and advancement to highly valued and upwardly mobile workers became normal practice with the rise of the Stakhanovite movement. An example of this was the use of placards at the workplace to announce children's crèches as a reward for the best suggestion for production improvement by a female worker, who would otherwise be saddled with responsibility for childcare while working (Kul'turnaia Revoliutsiia 1931:#15,8). These and other such announcements followed the All-Union Congress of Labour Unions directive of February 1931 expressly stating that all childcare facilities are 'for the exclusive use of children of workers working at [their respective] factories and *sovkhoz*. Priority was given to female shock-workers and members of labour unions' (Osipovich 1931:76). Childcare was no longer a right, but a privilege extended to elite workers.

According to reports in the late 1920s the project of communalised *byt* was floundering financially; the withdrawal of financial aid by the Party, government and industry proved to be the death knell to this grand social enterprise. Even with the minimal funding of organised groups earlier, the communalisation of *byt* could not be realised. The withdrawal of institutional support exploited the ideologically respectable notions of *samodeiatel'nost'* or volunteerism. Consequently the role of women in the five years following the June Plenum of the Central Committee in 1931 began to take on a fundamentally different aspect. The nuclear family and the institutions of the 'hearth' were once again validated in the interest of fiscal expediency. In the absence of a viable public sector organising, controlling and funding domestic services and the rearing of children, these services became more efficiently and cost-effectively organised by reverting to the use of unpaid women's labour in the domestic sphere, which resulted in a revival of the 'hearth' and the cult of domesticity.

These debates both for and against the reformation of *byt* follow closely the complex infighting between various interests within the Communist Party hierarchy and Soviet society in general which were struggling for dominance in the vacuum following Lenin's death in

1923. Crudely put, this was the struggle between Trotsky, Bukharin and Stalin, and the group interests each respectively attracted, over the stewardship of the Party and the fate of the social reforms initiated by the Revolution (Fitzpatrick 1982; Trotsky 1972; Schapiro 1971; *History of the Communist Party of the Soviet Union (Bolsheviks)* 1939). The directions these competing positions took can be roughly characterised as follows. The Trotskyite 'left' represented the more extreme aspirations of the pre-Revolutionary radical intelligentsia. It called for 'perpetual revolution' and the 'withering away of the state' towards the creation of a society based on spontaneous organisation with minimal state interference temporarily overseen by a 'dictatorship of the proletariat'. The 'left' was vehement in its opposition to NEP: seeing it as a dangerous retreat from the construction of socialism. The most radical of *byt* reformers felt comfortable with the 'left' position as it called for a complete restructuring of society according to socialist principles in the shortest interval upon an industrialised base. Represented by Nikolai Bukharin, the 'right' found much that was positive about NEP: the limited forms of capitalist economics it entailed and the direction the capitalist economic sector received from the Communist Party. Despite their differences, the two positions together insisted on a limited role for the state, from the outright 'withering away' of state control in social and economic matters for the 'left', to the 'right's vision of Party-directed state stewardship of capitalist economic processes. Highly significant is the fact that both sides represented the dominant interests of the pre-Revolutionary intelligentsia. The 'left' appealed to the more radically minded, while the 'right' appealed to members of the former pre-Revolutionary intelligentsia ambivalent towards the Party and revolutionary struggle.

The 'centrist' position cultivated by Stalin positioned itself over the interests of the pre-Revolutionary intelligentsia, appealing directly to men and women typically of working class or peasant origin in the vast and numerically more populated provinces outside Moscow and Leningrad. It was in their name that the October Revolution was fought and the dictatorship of the proletariat maintained. It was a principle of Party policy that these individuals should be rapidly recruited into the ranks of the Party, as they were under the first 'Lenin Levy'. While encouraging their advancement in the creation of a truly proletarian intelligentsia designed to serve the Party and government bureaucracy, Stalin cultivated their sense of being the chosen inheritors of the Revolution, and appealed to their resentment against the established personages and interests of the pre-Revolutionary intelligentsia represented by the 'left' and 'right'.

The gradual consolidation of Stalin's power through his identification with these new upwardly mobile men within the Party and government apparatus gained considerable momentum with the defeat of the 'left' opposition, following the expulsion of Leon Trotsky and his supporters from the Party at the Fifteenth Party Congress in 1927. The Stalin faction was further strengthened by the infamous Shakhty trial of 1928 (Fitzpatrick 1982:132). Before the Shakhty trial there had been a 'gentleman's agreement' to avoid cultivating working-class antagonisms (Fitzpatrick 1982:132). The Shakhty trial broke this unspoken agreement and let those antagonisms loose into the contentious arena of the Cultural Revolution begun by the Stalin faction in 1928 on the eve of the Shakhty trial. Within the cacophony of the Cultural Revolution, various groups strove to achieve authority in the establishment of revolutionary orthodoxy in all spheres of public and social life. The environment of the Cultural Revolution favoured and idealised the proletariat. Stalin's consolidation of power within that climate harnessed the ambitions and desires of men and women who claimed highly favoured proletarian backgrounds propelling themselves and Stalin into power. In 1928 membership of the Party was approximately 1.3 million; by the end of the Cultural Revolution in 1933 its figure was 3.6 million (Fitzpatrick 1982:138). The majority of members came from working-class and peasant backgrounds and were given preferential access to education and rapid promotion.

These new men had very different ideas from their pre-Revolutionary Bolshevik seniors as to what the Revolution meant. Stalin recognised this friction and exploited differences in order to establish control over the Party apparatus by expanding it with men and women of his creation. The brand of socialism of these first sons and daughters of the proletariat emphasised education, social advancement and material security. For them, the new socialist *byt* differed greatly from the radical, ascetic and idealistic visions of the highly articulate pre-Revolutionary intelligentsia. *Byt* reformers, while attempting to establish orthodoxy in all matters of cultural and political life, mocked the aspirations and values of these *arrivistes*. Unfortunately the conditions of the Cultural Revolution did not favour the interests of *byt* reformers. They were overwhelmed by the torrent unleashed in the wake of the rapidly rising authority Stalin's new elite cadres were gaining in cultural and political matters and the drastic shifts in *byt* policy after the June 1931 Plenum.

As for *byt* reformers and their rhetoric, they changed gradually and inconsistently. Reformers desperately tried to accommodate the shifts in Party orthodoxies to their vision of socialist reform. *Byt* rhetoric would superficially fluctuate during these contentious years to suit ascendant orthodoxies, while fundamentally contradicting as yet unassailed points of belief. This almost irrational and contradictory accommodation has been attributed, by some observers, to the fervent belief of the intelligentsia (both pre-Revolutionary and Stalinist) in the supreme good of the Party and the socialist enterprise, despite 'temporary' setbacks, diversions or 'mistakes' perpetrated by individuals or factions (Fitzpatrick 1982, Thurston 1986). Nevertheless, their faith in the socialist enterprise was unshaken, and no matter how contradictory, every accommodation evinced Party orthodoxy. Eventually Stalinist orthodoxy in political and social matters was established and the discourse of *byt* reform was barely recognisable by the mid-1930s, in fact becoming no longer tenable. A uniform and fixed consensus was believed to be paramount to the successful realisation of socialism. This of course meant that there were to be many unruly and 'scrappy' things that needed to be left out, particularly former class enemies, the consciousness of the petit-bourgeois, and other vestiges and deviations inhibiting socialism. In short, it meant consolidation and a cleaning-out of superfluous elements. As we shall see, social hygiene and hygiene in general began to assume unprecedented significance for the creation of a sound axis about which Soviet socialism could be consolidated and achieved.

three

Soviet Hygiene and the Battle against Dirt and Petit-Bourgeois Consciousness

The Petit-Bourgeois has become a dwarf . . . but despite the fact that he is insignificant, he is nonetheless unhealthy, as unhealthy as dust, unhealthy as the fumes from a swamp and decaying organic gases. In the air we breathe it is not enough that there are none too few poisonous admixtures. This is all very unhealthy, with this we need to fight, claw and fist. (Gorkii [1931] in Bordiugov 1987:153)

You won't sweep out petit-bourgeois consciousness with a broom, neither with a steel one nor with a fiery one. It is corrosive. You have to get at it in print with books, and clubs and theatres and tractors. Bring up anew, a whole generation . . . (A.N. Tolstoi in Kisel'nikova 1985:74–5)

As the domestic sphere was the locus of the battle against petit-bourgeois values inhibiting the establishment of socialism, the issues of homemaking, domestic hygiene and taste became of paramount importance. As for other aspects of the domestic sphere, the organisation of domestic labour and space came under increasing scrutiny and rationalisation in the years following the Civil War, reaching its climax during the Cultural Revolution. In this respect socialist housework represented a form of guerrilla warfare; a prolonged engagement of sporadic but direct hostilities against the institutions of the petit-bourgeois 'hearth'. During the NEP period, guidebooks to housekeeping and domestic hygiene were very similar to their pre-Revolutionary and Western counterparts. However, they were distinguished by being the first exclusively to address workers and peasants (pre-Revolutionary guides addressed the issues of peasant and worker households rather from the point of view of bourgeois and aristocratic housekeepers (Agarov 1909, Andreev 1893, Avdeeva 1868)).

With the exception of the obligatory frontispieces proclaiming the new *byt* and successes of the Revolution, the content of much of these guides was remarkably unpolitical and pragmatic in the advice they provided. They had two goals: to help cope with the high cost of living and to instil distrust of NEP market economics. The objective was to promote self-sufficiency until the time when NEP market economics were no longer needed and the long-promised fully developed socialist economy could step in and provide desperately needed goods and services to support the domestic sphere (Sovety Proletarskoi Khoziaike 1924:91) By advocating self-sufficiency, household advice however simply strengthened the institutions of the 'hearth' and the role women played in them, reluctantly following the general 'retreat' from socialist goals under NEP.

Changing Perceptions of the Domestic Front

Within this body of household advice the domestic front began to be constituted, thereby setting the conditions for future changes. In the mid-nineteenth century, Ekaterina Alekseevna Avdeeva in her massive tome on household economy *Polnaia Khoziaistvennaia Kniga*, rather dismissively addressed the issue of *uiut* (comfort, cosiness or *Gemütlich-keit*) with regard to the lower orders of tsarist society: 'where poor people are concerned one cannot say much except to keep rooms clean and aired' (Avdeeva 1868:11). The sentiment had not altered significantly sixty years later when M.M. Zarina, the doyenne of socialist household advice, urged that 'cleanliness and order are the best decoration for any household' (Zarina 1928; Dubniak 1931:38). Because its achievement was predicated on a certain superfluity of material goods, *uiut* required a certain degree of prosperity, hinting dangerously at petit-bourgeois domestic values (see McCracken 1989 on 'homeyness'). In the course of the 1920s, *uiut* was to be increasingly problematic as it conflicted with developing notions of cleanliness and order. How could one be hygienic and therefore Soviet and proletarian, while living *uiutno* (comfortably)?

One of the first attempts to guide the housewife in the revolutionary reappropriated petit-bourgeois household was the 1924 guide *Sovety Proletarskoi Khoziaike* ('Advice for Proletarian Housewives'). This guide established the characteristic elements of the socialist household. It articulated the major themes and semantics of domestic space for the entire Soviet period. The guide defined *uiut* as a 'well-built and health-fully laid out table, a simple but beautiful dress; the little joys of the small household have become attainable for the proletariat' (ibid. 7). *Uiut* was not only desirable, but represented the achievement of the Revolution to improve the life of workers.

A worker's house could be easily and inexpensively decorated. To provide decorative effect plants such as philodendrons, ficuses and fuchsias were recommended (ibid.). Over the doors and windows, *shtori* or blinds were recommended as appropriate and *uiutno,* but heavy draperies were singled out as obscuring too much light and accumulating too much dust (ibid.). An illustration of acceptable proletarian drapes shows cut-away bordered drapery with appliquéd red communist stars (ibid.). Furniture could not be *krichashchego* (loud and blatant). However, one should have everything that is required. Furthermore, furnishings should not be veneered, as veneers eventually crack (ibid.). Instead they should be of simple lacquered wood, appealing to reformist notions of 'honesty' in Modernist design principles (ibid.). Though wood was advocated and used for most items of furniture, it was banned for the construction of beds, as wooden beds were believed to harbour bugs. Therefore one should have an iron frame bed instead (ibid.89).

The author advocates a small writing desk under a window, a place well-suited for *umstvenyi uiut* (intellectual cosiness), where a worker can think and further educate him- or herself in an attempt to realise the Marxian ideal of the multi-faceted worker/intellectual. Next to the writing desk should be a free-standing *etazherka* (etagère) for the storage and display of books (ibid.). In front of the table on the wall should hang a portrait of Lenin, alongside of which should be a portrait of whoever was the founding father of the profession in which the head of the household worked.

In the same room as the dining table should be a corner set aside for the children: an *Ugolok Diadi Lenina* (Uncle Lenin's Little Corner) where children can be instilled with love and respect for Lenin. Here also should hang a picture of Lenin, and images of the old pre-Revolutionary *byt* of children suffering under capitalism. Objects, from the home republic of the child's family, should be placed in the corner to instil love and knowledge of the republic – as well as a map of the entire USSR, images of the Soviet Union's flora and fauna and national cultural figures (ibid.).

Remaining areas of the room could be decorated with flowers in inexpensive vases, one or two allegorical figurines representing, for instance, 'Labour and Science', or 'Labour Fighting Capital'. All these decorative elements should not be displayed 'museum-like nor monastery-like but gaily, lively, dynamically and with variety' (ibid. 90–1). The author cautions that

> nonetheless, the proletarian housewife must maintain while decorating her household one thing in particular; not to stuff the apartment with unnecessary extra furniture, not to hang useless rags for decoration. These things not only significantly reduce the amount of light, but also harbour dust containing all manner of parasites, and poison the home with throngs of tiny bacteria which are extremely harmful to one's health. (ibid. 90–1)

In summation the author affirms, 'Let the proletarian house be light, spacious, decorated with flowers and only with those objects which preserve the health of the body and the health of the revolutionary spirit' (ibid.).

The *Sovety Proletarskoi Khoziaike* characteristically describes the standard elements of the socialist household and establishes the areas of conflict where anti-Revolutionary hazards may lie. The crucial elements are the sleeping area; the dining area; the study area; and the children's corner. Each area noticeably represents an arena of conflict between the proletarian housewife and vestigial petit-bourgeois values, whose containment and resolution was critical to the realisation of the Soviet socialist ideal.

The Bed

One point of contention was the bed. Wooden beds were rejected as unhygienic, despite other items of wooden furniture in the household and straw mattresses as more probable sources of vermin (Zarina 1928). Instead, industrially produced metal beds were favoured. Wood, the traditional material in East Slavic peasant architecture and material culture, signified the old *byt*. Wherever possible it was replaced with the products of Soviet industrialisation like metal and concrete: wooden peasant huts by concrete communal houses and wooden beds and dishes with metal ones (Rabotnitsa 1930:#8,18; Zarina 1928:80).

Other traditional elements of the pre-Revolutionary bed were rejected outright, especially the mound of down-filled pillows (*gorka*) that signified the prosperity of the family (Budina and Shmeleva 1989): 'Down, it pampers the body and besides which it does not allow the air to circulate.' (Zarina 1928:80). Ubiquitous and elaborate rugs hanging above the bed were problematic, too. These rugs protected against draughts and damp walls. Considering their usefulness despite their prestige value, some authors retained them yet warned that 'rugs require constant care, since they harbour various infectious diseases', causing an investment of household labour considered inappropriate by *byt* theoreticians (Zarina 1928:920). In general all that was 'soft' was considered hazardous to one's health: 'we must understand that every object takes away air, especially soft things – clothing, soft furniture, rugs or floor-coverings, table cloths and napkins' (Organovich 1928:70), for these spoil and take up air while collecting dust (Zarina 1928:78).

The Table

Another arena of contention was the table or dining area. Since communal dining rooms were not yet a feasible reality, dining areas within the house were retained but minimalised as much as possible. Tables were to be of simple lacquered wood without veneers (Sovety Proletarskoi Khoziaike 1924:90). Collapsible and extendible tables were preferred as they could be hidden from view and create space. (Rabotnitsa 1932:#29,6; Rabotnitsa 1931:,#?,16–17). The overall appearance of tables and chairs should be simple without any superfluous veneers and devoid of any ornamentation. Furniture should exhibit '*nichego lishnego*' (nothing superfluous) (Organovich 1928:77; Radchenko 1928: 13–14; Ivanova 1926:62). Pre-Revolutionary, non-modernist, and non-rationalist forms and ornamentation were believed to harbour all sorts of dangers to the body in the form of dust-born parasites and vermin, lurking within crevices of heavily ornamented furniture legs threatening everyone, in particular the vulnerable children of the new socialist society: 'smooth legs help to avoid the accumulation of dust and grime' (Ivanova 1926:62) ensuring that 'everything is such that it is simpler, so that there is more air in a room, so that there is less dust and dirt, and so that small children do not bruise themselves on carved sharp edges' (Radchenko 1928:13–14).

Beyond unavoidable items associated with the old *byt* and desirable ones of the new, all else was to be ruthlessly eliminated from the domestic realm. The motto '*nichego lishnego*' (nothing superfluous) prevailed in all matters of judgement. Trunks, chests, commodes and buffets 'took air away' from the household. Ideally all these objects should disappear into the walls in the form of built-in closets and collapsible furniture. (Radchenko 1928:13–14; Zarina 1928:77; Dubniak

1931:25, Kozhanyi in Rabotnitsa, 1930, #29,6; Rabotnitsa 1926:#3,10). However, since such collapsible and built-in furniture was not available, a commode for instance could be replaced with a *slavianskii shkaf:* a narrow cabinet where one could store clothing and other household goods (Zarina 1928:78) . The majority of furniture produced and used throughout the 1920s did not meet the specifications of reformists such as Kozhanyi who often lamented the production of 'unhygienic' furniture (Kozhanyi in Rabotnitsa, 1932, #29, 6) calling for workers to agitate in their notoriously recalcitrant labour unions for more 'rational' furniture to be produced.

Primuses and Other Household Appliances

The traditional *pech'* or oven was the embodiment of the 'hearth' itself and its symbolic connotations (see Baiburin 1983 for an excellent discussion of the semantics of the traditional East Slavic *izba* particularly in relation to the *pech'*). These ovens were categorically reviled by reformers but grudgingly tolerated as they were the prevailing means of heating and cooking (Zarina 1928:104). However, the *pech''s* urban analogues, the stove, primus and hotplate, were another matter. As the mainstay of the non-communal, individual petit-bourgeois kitchen, these objects represented the greatest threat. They were seen to shackle women to the hearth, preventing the collectivisation of social and daily life and keeping women from entering the industrial workforce. The ubiquitous pre-Second World War wood-burning iron stove, used for both cooking and heating was colloquially referred to as a *burzhuika* (the diminutive of the feminine for bourgeois); betraying its intimate association with feminine petit-bourgeois values. The agitational literature from the 1920s made persistent references to the '*ugneta primusov*' (the oppression of primuses), as well as other signifiers of domesticity such as pots and pans enslaving women (Okov in Rabotnitsa, 1925, #22, back cover).

This image of household objects as oppressive pervaded much of the rhetoric concerning domestic material culture. In a speech to the plenum of the MK VKP(b), the feminist agitator and editor of *Rabotnitsa* Artiukhina denounced attempts to introduce into industrial production efficient electronic household appliances based on Western models. She argued that it was better to suffer with the old-fashioned tools of domestic work until full socialism was realised, in anticipation of the elimination of housework, rather than use appliances reinforcing feminine domestic labour: 'why should we copy the bourgeoisie, who with these very same mops and pans oppress women workers even more tying them down to the very same kitchen?' (Artiukhina in Rabotnitsa, 1930, #4,3).

Icons

Nothing so cogently embodied the values of the pre-Revolutionary order than the rites and institutions of the Russian Orthodox Church. The socialist rejection of all forms of deism and its fierce affirmation of atheism needs no elaboration. The Party was firmly hostile towards all religious institutions, resulting in the wholesale destruction of sacred properties and artefacts (exceptions were works of art or artefacts too cumbersome to destroy). As the very embodiment of petit-bourgeois consciousness, any manifestation of religiosity was rejected and swiftly attacked. Thus, the fiercest foe in the arena of the domestic front was the icon that rested in its 'red corner' (krasnyi ugol) – the place of honour and semantic focal point of any traditional Russian Orthodox dwelling.

However, the removal of icons from the 'red corner' left it achingly bare. Portraits of Lenin and other Communist leaders provided appropriate substitutions. A. Agienko, reporting on the successes of recent campaigns to 'clean' dwellings of icons and crosses and replace them with photographs of Party leaders, stressed 'the necessity to fight further for the cleansing of houses of their religious paraphernalia and to work for more cultured furnished dwellings (with pictures, radios, bookshelves and the like)' (Agienko 1931:23). Period photographs illustrate this transformation wherein 'red corners' that once contained religious paraphernalia now appeared filled with portraits of communist leaders, shelves of Marxist literature, along with gramophones, radios and other industrial prestige goods. (Rabotnitsa 1931:#?,17 photograph of exhibition of new byt in the Moscow Park of Culture) (see figure 4).

The threat icons represented for the consolidation of Soviet socialism was obvious and did not need to be justified in the name of simple hygiene. Nevertheless, icons and their associated rituals were subject to strict standards of Soviet hygiene. Being profoundly 'contaminated' ideologically, icons were also believed to harbour all manner of bodily dangers. The Commissar of Health N.A. Semashko (who was to live at the Narkomfin Communal House) referred to the traditional Easter greeting of three kisses as bytovoi sifilis (domestic syphilis), thereby implicating the custom in all kinds of infections. Kissing an icon was believed to transmit contagious diseases such as syphilis, tuberculosis, diphtheria and scarlet fever (Semashko 1928:48, see also Bernstein 1998

Figure 4 (a) 'The family of a distinguished brigadier, 1938, RGAKFD: No. 039583, **(b)** 'Lenin corner in a worker's family organised by school children drinking tea', Krasnodarskii Krai, 1931, RGAKFD: No. 22649

for her discussion of Semashko and syphilis). The futurist writer Maia-kovskii expressed similar sentiments in his poetry (Maiakovskii 1923, quoted in Maiakovski 1930:170), as did various other *byt* agitators (Kul'turnaia Revoliutsiia 1929:#15,14).

'Red Corners' and Children's Corners

The removal of icons created an apparent void in the semantic per-ception of domestic space. Something had to be done with this highly charged symbolic area. One of the first responses, in addition to simply hanging portraits of Lenin, was the installation of the *Ugolok Diadi Lenina* (Uncle Lenin's Little Corner). The idea of Uncle Lenin's Little Corner transformed the pre-Revolutionary *krasnyi ugol* (red corner), representing patriarchy and Christianity, into the new opposing order of atheistic socialism. This transformation supplanted the place of honour reserved for the elder Orthodox patriarch with that of the socialist child.

Other responses to this semantic void were *detskye ugolki* (children's little corners), *Leninskii ugolok* (Lenin's little corner), *krasnyi ugolok* and the *ugolok razumnogo dosuga* (little corner of rational leisure) (Kozhanyi 1924:41). These different corners segregated various attributes conflated in the *ugolok Diadi Lenina* (later, the negotiation of this space would crystallise into separate *detskye ugolki* and *krasnye ugolki*). *Detskye ugolki* directly competed in degree of semantic intensity with the pre-Revolutionary *krasnye ugli* (see figure 5). One report from the Sverdlovka and Bol'shaia Kommuna factories relates how the children of the barracks created their own corner demanding that their parents remove their icons. When parents did not remove their icons, the children responded with 'let them stay up, it doesn't matter, our corner will defeat theirs'. Consequently, thirty-three families at the Proletarka barracks reportedly removed their icons and the *detskye ugolki* prevailed (Rabotnitsa 1935:#5-6,20). With the inclusion of a small desk and chairs for the child or children, such corners closely resembled more conventional *krasnye ugolki* with portraits of Revolutionary leaders and educational material about the Communist Party (see figure 5). Like their Christian predecessors, these corners occupied the best lit and aired corner of the room.

The pre-Revolutionary *krasnyi ugol*, lit by natural daylight from adjacent windows, served as the focus of the household, linking it to the patriarchal order and the world of Christianity beyond. It offered a vivid expression of that order, linking individuals through private and

Figure 5 (a) 'A child's corner', RGAKFD, no catalogue number; **(b)** 'A children's corner in a family', Moscow, 1929, RGAKFD, no. 238823

communal prayer, and ritual observances. The Soviet *krasnyi ugolok* (expressed in the diminutive to distinguish it from its Christian antecedent) served a similar function, describing the new secular order. The placement of Soviet Marxist agitational material, books, newspapers and pamphlets further amplified the expression of the new order. In most cases it was literally amplified in the form of *tarelki* (literally plates, or single channel radios) tuned into the Party-controlled state radio station (Kul'turnaia Revoliutsiia 1930:#6,23–5) (see figure 4). These new *krasnye ugolki* served as the new communal hearths of socialism. They supplanted the old individual petit-bourgeois 'hearth' and served as an important communal focus for agitational speeches, lessons and other group activities (Kul'turnaia Revoliutsiia 1930:#8–9,4–5)

The *krasnye ugolki* were as important as the icon corner in structuring pre-Revolutionary spatiality at the primary integrative level of the individual pre-Revolutionary household. Accorded singular importance for the restructuring of the new *byt*, they were the locus from which agitational material was disseminated by press and speech to local communities, bringing into people's lives the continuous process of *byt* reform. Initially they were not well received, and even resisted. At the time of the First Five Year Plan during the height of *byt* activism, only 12 per cent of housing co-operatives in Ukraine had *krasnye ugolki* (Central Committee of the Communist Party (Bolsheviks) of Ukraine 1929:29). Similarly, approximately 27 per cent of housing co-operatives (ZhAKT) in Leningrad (800 out of 3,000 co-operatives) had *krasnye ugolki*, the majority of which, the authors reported, functioned very poorly (Bakhterev and Razumovskii 1930:18).

How *krasnye ugolki* were resisted can be observed from various reports by *byt* activists. In Tver one *byt* activist, Comrade Kozorina, reported how in barracks number 122 of the Proletarka factory, the *krasnyi ugolok* was located in a damp basement accessible only through the courtyard and down a dark, narrow and grimy staircase. She noted that meetings held there were miserably unsuccessful as no one ever wanted to venture there under such conditions (Rabotnitsa 1929:#23,17;1929:#18,14). Tales of other *krasnye ugolki*, hidden away in uninhabitable places, were reported elsewhere (Surozhskii in Kul'turnaia Revoliutsiia, 1930, #11, 13, 15, 16). Like other aspects of *byt* reform, *krasnye ugolki* were not adequately funded by their communities. When they did come into being, *krasnye ugolki* were buried away unused, as reluctant attempts to appease the agitational work of *byt* activists (see Kotkin 1993:186).

Light

An overall, consolidating luminescence, facilitated by white- and pale-coloured walls, was deployed on the domestic front as a metaphorical weapon against all manner of darkness, ignorance and microbes associated with petit-bourgeois *byt*. As one worker was queried as to the name of the tool she was using to jet-spray whitewash on a newly constructed *Dom Kommuna* she responded that she did not quite know but that she and her colleagues were calling it a revolver. 'Why a revolver ?' the interlocutor asked. She responded with a big shining grin: 'It shoots the old *byt* dead!' (Rabotnitsa 1929:#41,12).

Luminosity was believed to destroy microbes, the source of disease (Dubniak 1931:7, 9, 23), while providing warmth and nurture for growing things such as plants and children (Zarina 1928:78). Traditional peasant houses were railed at for not bringing in enough light because of their dark wooden walls and small windows. As one could not build whole new buildings overnight to replace these old structures, one had to make do and try to improve them as much as possible. Whitewashing walls and painting furniture white (Dubniak 1931:7–9) were inexpensive and simple ways of employing reformist modernist elements in old structures. Naturally, one of the best sources of light in the mythic socialist project of dispelling darkness was the *lampa Ilyicha* (Lenin's lamp) (ibid.9) or the electrical lightbulb. This was the spearhead of the great electrification campaign of the 1920s which brought electricity and artificial light to thousands of rural villages. Along with Modernity and socialism, these lamps dispelled darkness, vermin and the spectre of petit-bourgeois consciousness by the purifying and illuminating effects of its rays.

Dirt and Petit-Bourgeois Consciousness

Early Soviet concepts of hygiene in the domestic realm associated cleanliness and good health with socialism and the new *byt* and dirt and ill health with pre-Revolutionary petit-bourgeois consciousness (see Bernstein 1998 for an excellent discussion of hygiene, women's health and gender inequality in the pursuit of socialist construction in the 1920s). Dirt itself as well as objects believed to harbour it become metonyms of the enemy lurking within: the ubiquitous consciousness of the petit-bourgeois. This metonymic substitution lay deep within Soviet Marxist thought and rhetoric. Lenin cogently summed up this association to explain failing worker-consciousness: 'Workers are building a new society without having become new people, cleansed from the dirt of the old world, and who still stand up to their knees in this filth' (Lenin, quoted in Nikiforov 1929:86). N. Nikiforov takes the association further.

> The dirt of the old world, the characteristics of the 'traditional psychology' not only appear in relations of production, in the inability to labour, the lack of labouring culture, but also in private life, in *byt*, where in particularly splendid colours burst forth the vestiges and traditions of the past, revealing the great tenacity of the spirit of petit-bourgeois individualism. (Nikiforov 1929:86)

Soviet theoreticians, concerning the innately 'filthy' and petit-bourgeois state of the vast majority of the Soviet population had to consider seriously whether or not reformist efforts could ever be successful. What can one do if one takes the worker out of the petit-bourgeoisie but cannot take the petit-bourgeois out of the worker? The tempo of reforms picked up, industrialisation under the First Five Year Plan permitted some housing construction. However, even new housing reflected pre-Revolutionary spatial arrangements with its individual kitchens and dining rooms. The building industry and labour unions proved to be intransigently conservative with regard to *byt* reform, much to the chagrin of reformers (Kul'turnaia Revoliutsiia 1929:#15, 14; Kul'turnaia Revoliutsiia 1930:#2,17–18; Rabotnitsa 1930:#8,20; Rabotnitsa 1925:#3,13–14;Kul'turnaia Revoliutsiia 1929:#11,21).

Despite new building construction that managed to accommodate various attempts at *byt* reform despite the conservatism of labour unions and local party cells, there arose the much-bemoaned condition of the two *byt*s – old and new – existing side by side. Vladimirskii and Sheftel' discussed the problem of

> inhabitants arriving in the new hearth of the new *byt*, with Primuses, icons, washboards and sundry trash, which has no place in socialist homes. People bring into new homes not only icons and Primuses, but old bulky, uncomfortable furniture. Can one blame them for this, when no one is concerned with the furnishing of new buildings appropriate to contemporary conditions, which is comfortable and occupies little space? (Vladimirskii and Sheftel' 1931:14)

Byt critics identified two realms of *byt* that arose out of the 1920s: one that was rationalised and industrial in the public realm of factories, and the other that was domestic and private (Toporokov 1929:132). People who brought the values of the petit-bourgeois 'hearth' with them into the factory were thought responsible for declining labour productivity (Toporokov 1929:134); frustrating *byt* reform at the factory as well as in the home. The activist Surozhskii echoed this frustration, commenting on the construction of new houses in Leningrad without facilities for the new *byt*. He complained that despite what was said in theory 'in practice we are continuing to fortify the old individualistic petit-bourgeois *byt* whilst fighting against it so energetically in words. We are building fortresses of the old *byt* with our very own hands' (Kul'turnaia Revoliutsiia 1930:#2,17). In addition, Surozhskii prophesised: 'We are creating a housing stock that the next generation will tear down. That generation will break through load-bearing walls, destroy the rodent hole-kitchens, move the walls of the family hearth into the common corridor, and on every storey create a common dining room mechanically distributing food from the local factory-kitchen' (ibid.18).

Conventional Marxist wisdom dictated that material conditions determined consciousness. Thus one could do as much as one possibly could to change people's attitudes (which *byt* reformers did with desperate energy), but if the material conditions were not there, nothing much could change conditions effectively (Kurella 1930). With regard to the furnishings of interiors, nothing could be done to reform them if the material culture of the worker's interior embodied petit-bourgeois, pre-Revolutionary values.

D. Arkin describes at length the frustration of *byt* agitators with the conservatism of the furniture and decorative arts industries and their reluctance to address issues of the new *byt* (Kul'turnaia Revoliutsiia 1929:#2(5),26; see also Markovnikov, in Larin and Belousov 1930). Arkin noted how in urban and rural markets there appeared to be an increasing demand for various decorative effects – plaster casts of roses, figurines depicting Mephistopheles, bathing girls and Revolutionary themes. 'These articles, born of the most reactionary petit-bourgeois tastes, come to the market, enter into use, thanks to the fact that our industry and cultural organisations don't give any attention to these matters' (D. Arkin, in *Kul'turnaia Revoliutsiia* 1929, #2(5), 27). Arkin blames this situation on the industry's reliance on trade agents 'who decide whether this design or another is appropriate for the market. This judgement arises further because of the influence of old tastes and traditions; attempts to instruct the consumer in new tastes is done very seldom' (ibid. 27). Arkin notes that new industrial designs are silenced by the same routine and thus remain on paper.

Uiut

Pervading these discussions of housekeeping, hygiene and petit-bourgeois taste was the nagging question of *uiut*. *Uiut*, its apparent superfluity and the desire for it, were all considered an attribute of petit-bourgeois consciousness. At the same time *uiut* was an indicator of material prosperity attainable for the first time because of the Revolution. However, most reform efforts were literally to contain, whitewash away and sweep out all the trappings and furnishings of the domestic 'hearth' leaving only the barest necessities of life.

The factors governing which items of material culture could be deemed socialist or petit-bourgeois were not always based on hygiene. Often these attitudes were formed by literary social satire emerging before and after the Revolution. The most notable of these satirists were Maksim Gorkii and Vladimir Maiakovskii. The great theoreticians such as Lenin, Engels, Marx and Lunacharskii did not provide their readers with specific material indicators of petit-bourgeois conscious-ness. (Lazar Kaganovich eventually made this case at the 1931 June Plenum of the Central Committee, with serious consequences for *byt* reform). Rather, literary satirists, while creating vivid images of the reviled petit-bourgeoisie, delineated its material world and the physical attributes of that consciousness through the creative use of metonymy, particularly Gorkii and Maiakovskii (Brown 1978:191; Kisel'nikova 1985; Starostenko 1990).

Maiakovskii, in his work for *Komsomol'skaia Pravda*, his poetry, and plays such as *The Bedbug* and *The Bathhouse*, battled at length with the vestiges of petit-bourgeois consciousness and its attributes. One of the most important pieces of literary satire was Maiakovksii's *O Driane* ('Concerning Trash') (Brown 1978:191; Kisel'nikova 1985:72), which identified the material components of petit-bourgeois consciousness. It formed the stock of popularly understood material attributes of petit-bourgeois consciousness, such as the images of cosy studies and bedrooms, samovars, scarlet framed portraits of Marx, cats sleeping on casually strewn copies of *Izvestia*, dresses decorated with hammers and sickles, and the ubiquitous singing canary (see Semashko's use of these images in Semashko 1929:89).

Uiut: Getting Comfortable and the Shift from Denotative to Contextual Understandings of Material Culture

Throughout these discussions in the 1920s material culture is assumed to represent unambiguously a particular set of values, one that is socialist and another that is petit-bourgeois. However, a variety of responses emerge attempting to sort out which artefacts signify petit-bourgeois consciousness and which not. As deliberations gained tempo during the course of the First Five Year Plan, a profound change emerged in attitudes towards material culture and the role it played in Soviet social negotiations. Perception of material culture shifted away from a denotative Marxian understanding which saw material culture as the physical signifier of a particular economic base. As the First Five Year Plan progressed, a worrisome contradiction emerged – that the emerging universe of material culture had not changed from its pre-Revolutionary and petit-bourgeois antecedents – and caused considerable concern amongst *byt* reformers. If the universe of material culture continued to signify petit-bourgeois values, then the future of socialist construction would be severely handicapped if not entirely compromised. However, the demands of rapid-fire industrialisation claimed all existing energies and resources that might otherwise have been used to create a new distinctly socialist universe of material goods. This was exacerbated further by industry conservatism and consumer demand resistant to 'rationalist' reforms.

This resistance served to reformulate prevailing denotative understandings of material culture in favour of an approach that was more contextual. Objects, in and of themselves, were not considered to possess any single meaning; rather it was the relationship between objects that was crucial. Put in another way, an object of material culture could no longer represent unambiguously petit-bourgeois values: a stuffed sofa could no longer simply represent *meshchanstvo* thereby identifying its owner as a petit-bourgeois. Rather, it was the relationship one had with the stuffed sofa which determined consciousness. In short, it was the context of use which defined whether or not a stuffed sofa could be categorised as petit-bourgeois or socialist. Therefore the pre-existing universe of material culture inherited from the pre-Revolutionary period could be tolerated and maintained under the emergent socialist conditions of the First Five Year Plan and be socialist by virtue of the context of its use and not in and of itself. Consequently, the attribution of petit-bourgeois consciousness became less fixed and far more ambiguous and predicated on the rules of its use and the vagaries of who decided what those rules were. Shifting to a contextual understanding empowered those who could determine the appropriate context of use, denying a universal standard claimed by modernist *byt* reformers. The shift from a fixed Bolshevist (and what was to become known later as a 'left') and denotative understanding of material culture to a Stalinist and contextual understanding developed gradually from the start of the First Five Year Plan in 1928, culminating through various accommodations by agitators in the Central Committee directives of 1930 and the June Plenum of 1931.

This shift coincided with the ascendancy of the Stalinist faction in the Party and its stand on matters of political and cultural orthodoxy. The reaction to denotative conceptions of material culture was triggered by the frequent discussions in the Soviet press as to what were or were not the material expressions of petit-bourgeois consciousness. As one *byt* theorist had noted, the use of specific denotative attributes and objects to determine petit-bourgeois consciousness was too easily manipulated; one could simply present a facade of socialist piety by superficially manipulating these attributes, while masking one's inner petit-bourgeois nature. By focusing on denotative attributes such as styles of furniture, dress, personal appearance, polite and profane speech to distinguish a petit-bourgeois sensibility from a proletarian one, judgements were passed too quickly and superficially.

This gradual modification of rhetoric on the part of some *byt* reformers, from a denotative to a contextual understanding of the role of material culture in Soviet social relations, instigated a re-evaluation of the thorny problem of *uiut*. As previously mentioned, *uiut* as a value and a goal was highly suspect. While it celebrated the new-found dignity and prosperity of Soviet workers, when taken to an extreme it betrayed a 'petit-bourgeois' consciousness : 'The petit bourgeois turns his back on all manner of social life (what use is it to him?); he lives only for the interest of his own *uiut*, his clothing; the miserable happiness of his family is the goal of his life' (Semashko 1929:89–90).

Given these new contextual understandings, *uiut* could be readily accommodated. In keeping with these changes, the Commissar of Health, Semashko, noted discussions where some individuals claimed that people who were clean and well-dressed, and lived in comfortable apartments were in actual fact petit-bourgeois. Semashko claimed that these attributes of the good life were not just the prerogatives of bourgeois society, but those of a socialist society as well (Semashko 1929:85). He reiterated how it was that the relationship of an individual to these objects distinguished the petit-bourgeois from the socialist. 'A person not of the petit-bourgeois past but of the socialist future strives for cleanliness and a cultured life, but a clean suit is not the final goal for him but one of the means for the realisation of his rising cultural demands' (Semashko 1929:89–90). What was important was one's social work and relationship to society.

Writing in 1931, U. Dubniak pursues a *byt* reformist line in spite of recent Central Committee pronouncements to the contrary. Dubniak addresses the issue of decoration and the creation of *uiut* in less stringent terms, allowing for a measured preoccupation with household *uiut* and acknowledging that:

> Of course extra decoration requires more time while cleaning, otherwise dust, dirt and insects will accumulate: but beautiful things in the home, in the dormitory and in the club please the eyes and permit relaxation. Of course one should not preoccupy oneself too much with the decoration of the home. But some minimum in this respect must be observed. (Dubniak 1931:37)

Here housework regains respectability as it supports the creation of *uiut*, now seen as a legitimate goal of socialism.

The slogan '*nichego lishnego*' (nothing superfluous) effectively regulated the degree to which petit bourgeois consciousness could be expressed. A regulating value, '*nichego lishnego*' was used to express the qualitative difference of the new order of spare, rational socialist material culture. Due to the slowly developing socialist economic base, this rationalist modernist order had yet to be realised. It could only be realised using pre-existing objects while minimising the potentially hazardous effects of these material vestiges of capitalism. However, as these objects unmistakably resembled the products of bourgeois economic relations embodying its values, they were inherently flawed and dangerous, and were believed to perpetuate those values in the new socialist order.

Radical *byt* reformers and literary satirists like Maiakovskii wanted nothing more than to obliterate these vestiges of capitalist economic relations. Hence the searing scorn heaved onto these objects and their use in the creation of *uiut*. Since *uiut* and the material well-being of workers was a major element for the socialist restructuring of society it had to be reconciled with the perception that pre-existing material goods used to achieve *uiut* in the present were 'carriers' (in the viral sense of the word) of petit-bourgeois consciousness.

What was one to do? People had to use the pre-existing material stock to structure their lives because a new one from which *uiut* could be created on socialist terms was non-existent. Denotative understandings of Soviet material culture made the social negotiation of the material world utterly hopeless, as everything would be petit-bourgeois by definition. Herein lay the source of the shift towards the conception that what one did with objects denoted petit-bourgeois consciousness, rather then the objects themselves. Since material culture was unable to signify petit-bourgeois consciousness, the material components of *uiut* (such as all those stuffed armchairs, potted geraniums, canaries and gramophones) ceased to harbour the 'virus' of petit-bourgeois consciousness. People and their relation to the world determined petit-bourgeois consciousness, and not specific items of material culture.

A contempt for the trappings of petit-bourgeois domesticity came under increasing criticism with the growing campaign against Trotskyite 'left deviationism' following Trotsky's ousting and the consolidation of power in the Party by the Stalin faction. A. K. Toporokov in 1929 wrote about the origins of this animosity towards domesticity in Russian thought, tracing it to early nineteenth-century Romantics. The cultivators of domesticity at the beginning of the nineteenth century were members of the legal estate of *meshchane* or petit-bourgeois. This legal estate was considered 'philistine' in the eyes of Romantic era intellectuals who were critical of social inequalities and who implicated those members of society considered to be the most passive (e.g. the *meshchanstvo*) in order to question the prevailing social order. In so doing they challenged the *byt* predicated on that order. This prejudiced and diminished the importance of *byt* issues in the eyes of progressive nineteenth-century intellectuals, with the result that creative talent neither addressed itself to the problems of *byt* nor attempted to reform it in order to realise 'higher social goals'. Social changes, precipitated by the abolition of serfdom in 1861, added to the problem of intellectual contempt and neglect of *byt* issues as old village customs collapsed in the wake of emancipation. This resulted in the 'bohemianism' of late nineteenth-century intellectuals which Toporokov felt ought to be energetically resisted during the Cultural Revolution (Toporokov 1929:126–7): 'Artist-individualists and all manner of those individuals with "left" leanings strove to incite the indignation of the bourgeoisie, shock and startle it in order to avoid at all costs being petit-bourgeois' (ibid.128). The 'bohemian' critique of society ignored issues of *byt* central to socialist development. As a result '[the people] cannot value and love domestic comfort and the family hearth' (ibid.132). While calling for the industrialisation of *byt*, Toporokov petitioned for a reappraisal of *uiut*. He reasserted its importance for the domestic life of workers, denouncing the ascetic barrack-like dwellings workers were obliged to live in, where it was impossible to cultivate *uiut* (ibid. 134).

Toporokov's agitational piece reflected the emerging rejection of radical reformist practices influenced by leftist 'bohemians', while reappraising the previously maligned petit-bourgeois cult of domesticity. The shift away from more radical approaches and its identification with 'Trotskyite left deviationism' found official affirmation in the oft-cited 16 May Directive of the Central Committee of VKP(b) of 1930:

> In addition the Central Committee of the VKP(b) warns against the attempts of certain comrades to construct the new *byt* by forced administrative means: administratively separating children from parents, socialised dining, etc. The new *byt* must be built taking into full account existing material conditions, and in no instance must it run away and construct plans for the realisation of which there do not exist the means or the possibilities. (Osipovich 1931:69)

This new orthodoxy resulted in rather desperate attempts by some *byt* reformers to adapt their rhetoric and ideas; some rejected the more extreme attempts of Osipovich and others singled out for harsh criticism. This new orthodoxy accommodated long-standing popular resistance to *byt* reforms, providing a forum for officially sanctioned dissent against previous *byt* reformist efforts.

By 1931 the Party's position was firmly set, clearing away in one fell swoop the entire programme of socialist *byt* reform to date. Lazar Kaganovich's speech at the 1931 June Plenum of the Central Committee put the final nail in the coffin:

> At the present time it is difficult to discern those forms of *byt* that will result in the final achievement of socialism and fully developed communism. In fact it would be entirely unMarxian to determine now what the concrete forms of future communist *byt* might be. Marx and Engels themselves did not preoccupy themselves with any directives concerning the concrete forms of future communist *byt*. On the contrary they warned against such attempts. They understood that the proletariat will assume power, and that pragmatically step by step, in its own time, the socialist restructuring of *byt* will progress towards those concrete forms and realise them.' (Osipovich 1931:77)

The proceedings of the June Plenum further elaborated upon this new position. While railing against 'right' opportunists who inhibited the construction of socialism, it simultaneously denounced the 'left':

> which with the leaps of 'left' opportunist phraseology advocates all manner of abstracted (*prozhektirskimi*) suggestions (the coercive liquidation of individual kitchens, and artificial propagation of *byt* communes, etc.).
>
> The Party will give a decisive rebuttal, both to right opportunists dragging us back and attempting to disrupt our construction, as well as to those 'left' phraseologists who do not take into account the concrete conditions of our period and in so doing aid the right. (Osipovich 1931: 78)

The message was clear: the 'hearth' was to be left intact with its individual kitchens and heavily ornamented trappings of petit-bourgeois domesticity. The June Plenum unambiguously announced the cessation of hostility on the domestic front. It shifted the problem of socialist *byt* from the hearth to the public realm of streets and urban planning: 'the improvement of city services – that is the most important basis for the restructuring of *byt* on new socialist principles for the labouring masses' (Osipovich 1931:78). While shifting Party responsibility to the development of urban infrastructure, it moved responsibility from the domestic realm onto the individual and specifically women. By 1934, the distinctive role of women and their return to the maintenance of the petit-bourgeois 'hearth' was complete. This new role was clearly spelled out in the exemplary oath taken by the housewife N. Zaitseva to her husband featured in *Rabotnitsa*: 'I promise to create *uiut* in our apartment, prepare meals on time, keep your workclothes in order, and I require in turn that you do not lose a minute in your shock work and that there are no lapses in your work discipline and that you pass your technical examinations with your worker brigade with the highest marks' (Rabotnitsa 1934:#5,19).

Although a woman's role in social work was still encouraged, her primary obligation was to support her shock-worker husband, ensuring that everything was provided for the comfort of the male industrial worker in order that he might improve his productivity in the industrialisation drive. Rewards for married heterosexual men were clear: a clean, bright and comfortable home with an efficient wife cooking, cleaning and ironing. Male resentment at the loss of these domestic privileges at the hand of *byt* reformers was appeased. Stalin returned the 'hearth' with all its pleasures and privileges to the new upwardly mobile man of the First and Second Five Year Plan for his dedicated work and loyalty to the socialist enterprise.

The Narkomfin Communal House and the Material Culture of Socialism

Of all the various individuals and groups involved in the reform of daily life and the consolidation of Soviet socialism in the 1920s, architects were exceptionally prominent. The architectural innovation of *Dom Kommuny* (Communal Houses) represented the most complete attempt to realise *byt* reforms and consolidate Soviet socialism. The most influential architectural group in this area was OSA (Ob'edinenia Sovremennikh Arkhitektorov, or Union of Contemporary Architects), headed by M.Ia. Ginzburg, the architect of the Narkomfin (see discussions of Cooke 1995; 1983; 1974, Bliznakov 1993, Khan-Magomedov 1972, Lodder 1983, Hudson 1994, Willen 1953). Whereas other *byt* reformers attempted to insert *byt* reformist practices within the remnants of pre-existing pre-Revolutionary architectural forms, the OSA group (formed in 1925 by M.Ia. Ginzburg and the Vesnin brothers), commonly known as the Constructivists, attempted to address the issue of the new *byt* head on by creating an entirely new architecture and material culture based on communist relations of production and consumption. As this economic and material infrastructure was only just being realised, there was a great deal of room for discussion, innovation and experimentation.

However, the various groups of *byt* reformers, and architects in particular, were searching for the one appropriate and ultimate consensus on the problem of the realisation of the new *byt*. The spirit of Soviet political and revolutionary action was dictated by the Leninist principle of 'democratic centralism', whereby a plurality of opinions and approaches were actively encouraged within Party life until such time as a Party position could be formulated and a 'general line' or consensus

63

could be taken and uniformly applied without dissidence. This 'general line' in turn would be adopted and provide the dominant axis about which all subsequent action would be directed, discarding and rendering superfluous all previously offered solutions in its wake. The contentiousness of debates on architectural solutions to *byt* reform should not be underestimated (see Willen 1953, Hudson 1994, Cooke 1995; 1974, Bliznakov 1993). The many competing creative voices were vying with one another for recognition by their colleagues and Party functionaries for the most perfect resolution and enactment of socialist and Party principles in their proposals for *byt* reform.

OSA and STROIKOM

The OSA group emerged as the most successful of architectural groups in the realisation and adoption of their solutions to the problem of *byt* reform. From 1926 to 1930, their mouthpiece, the journal *SA* (*Sovremennaia Arkhitektura* or Contemporary Architecture), was the most prominent architectural journal in the latter half of the 1920s and the only one dedicated to architecture in the years of the First Five Year Plan (Cooke 1983:40). In 1928 the STROIKOM (Building Committee) of the Russian Republic commissioned M.Ia. Ginzburg and other architects from the OSA group to create standardised housing types. These were to establish the norms for all subsequent state housing for the entire Russian Republic (the results of the research were compiled in the STROIKOM guidelines for state housing in 1930; see STROIKOM, 1930). However, only six such projects were realised embodying the STROIKOM guidelines, the most notable being the Narkomfin Communal House in Moscow (see Buchli 1998 for a broader discussion of the debates surrounding *byt* reform and the Narkomfin Communal House in architectural circles).

However, as in other fields of *byt* reform, by 1929 there had emerged an unease and lack of confidence in the viability and legitimacy of *byt* reforms in architecture prefiguring the eventual crisis and demise of *byt* reformist practices. In architecture this crisis is more readily apparent in the changing nature of architectural debates (see Buchli 1998). The Party was restructuring the architectural curriculum to address the more immediate and pragmatic needs of industrialisation, sacrificing many of the profession's most influential theorists. The defensive position taken by OSA already in 1929 in response to these changes veered towards outright repudiation of OSA's *byt* reformist programme in 1930. The famous 16 May 1930 decision of the Central Committee of the

Communist Party 'O rabote po perestroike byta' was reprinted in *Sovremennaia Arkhitektura* in their number 1–2 issue of 1930, which was dedicated to the question of socialist settlements. The directive explicitly condemned the full socialisation of family life envisioned in the STROIKOM schemes for a *Dom Kommuny* a few months earlier (see Buchli 1998 for a discussion of this scheme and others like it). The Central Committee directive instead called for the reassessment of *byt* reform, rejecting full socialisation in favour of the partial socialisation of the domestic 'hearth'. It asked the SNK (Soviet of People's Commissariats) of all the Union republics to come up with proposals in fifteen days for the creation of worker settlements and separate individual houses for labourers (*Pravda*, 29 May 1930, #146), thereby entirely rejecting the idea of fully communalised living patterns. The petit-bourgeois 'hearth' was to remain intact. Only laundry facilities, dining rooms, bath houses, schooling and day-care were to be communalised. The segregated petit-bourgeois 'hearth', where nuclear families would live and rear their children, was not to be touched. Such attempts to socialise child-rearing and reduce the private sphere to the vestigial minimalism of the private cell of the STROIKOM *Dom Kommuny* were condemned as 'leftist phrase mongering' and 'opportunistic'. Following the expulsion of Trotsky and the subsequent attacks on *byt* reform, there was little doubt in the mind of Ginzburg and others at OSA that the Party was changing direction and repudiating their efforts.

The question for OSA and other *byt* reformers in the first half of 1930 was what to do in these considerably changed circumstances. Appropriately enough, the articles following the reprint of the Central Committee directive in *Sovremennaia Arkhitektura*, nos. 1–2, 1930, followed the heading '*Kuda idti?*' ('Where to go?'). This was an awkward attempt to come to terms with the new Central Committee directive. The only option, without compromising the entire socialist project, was to conform to the Party directive, in the spirit of 'democratic centralism', and adjust one's beliefs and rhetoric appropriately. As a result, the *Sovremennaia Arkhitektura* editorial repudiated the ideas expressed in earlier issues and echoed the criticisms of the Central Committee's 16 May directive (Sovremennaia Arkhitektura 1930,1–2:5).

Throughout these new discussions, the issue of pluralism and consumer choice stands out prominently, rarely having been discussed earlier. The accusations of 'directive measures' in the Central Committee directive sparked these concerns prefiguring Lazar Kaganovich's claim in 1931 that the pre-existing urban order was, *de facto*, socialist and no longer a 'vestige' of capitalist forms. As in other spheres of *byt* reform, the new emphasis on individual consumer choice in the architectural writing of 1930 reflected a similar shift away from a denotative to a contextual understanding of material culture. Pluralism in living arrangements, embodying both bourgeois and socialist patterns, which previously threatened to infect the socialist social body and inhibit the construction of socialism, as now seen as the essence of cultural progress.

Whereas earlier the domestic sphere was to be tightly regulated if not entirely obliterated, it was now quite suddenly presented by some of the most committed architectural *byt* reformists as the locus of individual growth, development and cultural progress (see also the Okhitovich article in Sovremennaia Arkhitektura 1930,1–3:7). Pluralism was to prevail and appropriate socialist living formations were not to be regulated from above by 'directive measures' but determined from below by individuals themselves, according to their own needs, taste and desires. The demand for energies to be devoted towards the industrialisation drive could not permit the total restructuring of the landscape and the disruption of existing urban infrastructures. With the advancing consolidation of the Stalinist state, the environment within the architectural profession was becoming increasingly and intolerably hostile for *byt* reformers. By 1930 the VKhutemas school of architecture, most intimately associated with OSA, was closed down and in 1931 the journal *Sovremennaia Arkhitektura* was shut in favour of the more centralised and state controlled journal *Sovetskaia Arkhitektura*.

Ginzburg's *Zhilishche* (1934, but written in 1932, see editor's preface (Ginzburg 1934:6)) was published after the demise of *byt* reforms and the Constructivist movement in architecture. In this text he distances himself from the entire project, casting the five-year undertaking of the now extinct OSA group in historicising terms as a period of 'experimentation' which 'suffered from extreme conclusions and schematic solutions' (Ginzburg 1934:7). Here Ginzburg himself joins the chorus of critics of *byt* reforms, calling for a shift towards pluralism and the re-evaluation and revival of the domestic sphere as the locus for the development of the socialist self as opposed to the commune. Ginzburg goes on further to criticise: 'In such a manner in these examples of *Dom Kommuny*, the life of an individual is split (*raskolota*) into two unequal spheres; the small individual sphere (to which only sleep is given) and the larger social sphere (to which everything else is given)' (Ginzburg 1934:142). Ginzburg reminds his readers that 'In the frenzy for the realisation of communism with *Dom Kommuny*, it was forgotten that the battle with animalistic individualism and the petit-bourgeois family is the battle for the liberation of the new socialist self, for the preconditions of that self's utmost and thorough development' (Ginzburg 1934:148). Ginzburg concludes that these experiments reflected the conditions of an earlier, entirely different time (only two years earlier). Since this period, Ginzburg states in veiled terms referring to the recent upheavals in the architectural profession and the rise of the Stalinist state, 'the scale of the problems has changed, as well as the organisation of their solutions' (Ginzburg 1934:144).

The Conception of the Narkomfin Communal House

Having placed the Narkomfin *Dom Kommuna* in its volatile historical context, we can now examine the specific project and its development in greater detail. The Narkomfin Communal House of 1928–30 was not designed as a fully fledged *Dom Kommuna*, but rather as a 'social condenser' of the transitional type which, while accommodating pre-existing bourgeois living patterns (K and 2-F units), was structured in such a way as to ease an individual's transition towards fully socialised life (in the F-units). The mix of units based on different social patterns, both bourgeois and communal, was not an expression of tolerance of any and all types of living patterns based on different economic systems. Rather, the Narkomfin Communal House – unlike similarly mixed and tolerant schemes advanced later on – had a specific teleology aimed at the realisation of full communal living in the F-unit through the edifying effects of the architecture on its inhabitants (see Buchli 1998 for a more detailed discussion). The transformative effects of the architecture were to be realised in a number of ways, (1) through the modulation of architectural volumes, (2) through the use of light and colour, and (3) through the programmematic use of space. All these architectonic elements were marshalled to induce individuals to move away from bourgeois forms of social organisation towards socialist ones. In such a manner architecture and material culture were believed to have an explicitly denotative and transformative power to represent and then produce a particular form of social organisation. According to this almost Giddensian understanding, a literal 'structure' would 'structure' passive agents, unable to resist the transformative powers of material culture.

The original programme of the Narkomfin Communal House consisted of four separate buildings to achieve these social goals (see figure 6). The main structure (B) – the living block – was a long horizontal

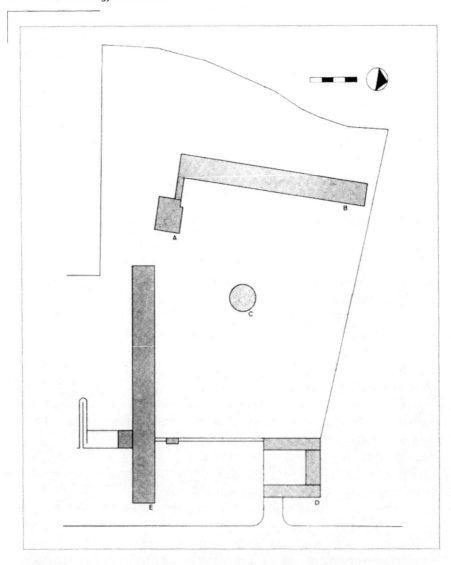

Figure 6 Author's drawing after original, MGINTA, folder 10024, document 102

building which accommodated all the living units of various types worked through the STROIKOM guidelines (F, 2-F, K, and dormitory units). The second structure, the communal block (A) was connected to the living block by a covered bridgeway. This building accommodated most of the socialised aspects of everyday life: the communal kitchen and dining room, the communal gymnasium, and the library. The third building, the *prachechnaia* or mechanical laundry building (D), housed the communal laundry facility, while the fourth and never built round building (C) was to have housed the children's crèche for the community (structure (E) was the second phase which was later realised by a different architect).

The rectangular mass of the living block was originally supported on the ground floor by a forest of pilotis (columns) and two entries (figure 7). There were a number of rooms in the entry that served at times as the living quarter for the concierge (*dezhurnyi*) as well as other rooms that variously served as a communal 'red corner' and library. The stairwell in the entries led up to the 24 F-units along the second corridor of the living block (see appendix). These were designed for an individual or couple without children. By the time one was living in an F-unit, one either did not have any children or gave them up after birth to the crèche. As the ultimate expression of socialised life and the new *byt*, these units had no kitchen. However, a small niche (see figure 8) was provided to accommodate a small stove for reheating of meals or making tea. If needed, these niches could be accommodated with Frankfurt- style minimal kitchen units (see Henderson 1996 for a broader discussion of Frankfurt kitchens). However, with the realisation of a fully socialist *byt* these would not be necessary and could be easily

Figure 7 View of the Narkomfin *Dom Kommuna*, early 1930s, Shchusev State Architectural Museum, Moscow.

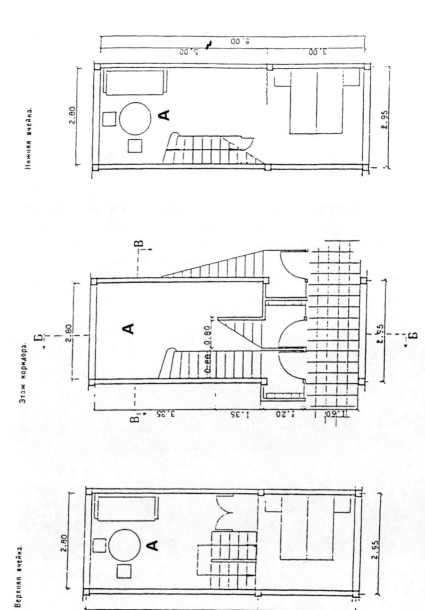

Figure 8 F-unit plans, STROIKOM 1930:58

removed at any time. The F-units could accommodate only the most basic functions of socialist daily life: sleep in the sleeping niches, personal hygiene in the shower cabin and private intellectual work in the spacious five-metre tall common room (room A, see figure 8). Eating, preparation of food, child-rearing and entertaining, formerly accommodated for in pre-Revolutionary housing forms, were factored out of F-units into the communal spaces of the complex.

The layout of the rooms ensured that the common room and sleeping niche were open to one another, visually and spatially. Ostensibly the reason cited by Ginzburg et al. was the hygienic circulation of air through the two rooms and the windows at either end. The only enclosed spaces were the shower niche and toilet. If required, a visual and physical separation between the sleeping niche and common room could be created using a curtain rod, as envisioned in one of the variations of the F-unit type (see figure 9 and Buchli 1998, Ginzburg 1934:127, 129).

More significantly the large windows and the thorough circulation of air ensured that the outside world of trees and daylight of the surrounding park was immediately and visually evident within the unit (Ginzburg 1934:92). The design of the unit ensured, as much as was

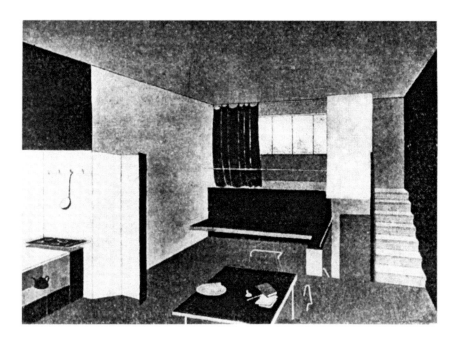

Figure 9 Interior of F-unit, STROIKOM 1930:56

physically and socially possible, that when inside one was not actually cut off from the natural and social world surrounding it. If the petit-bourgeois 'hearth' was characterised by *byt* reformers as striving as much as possible to sever its connections with the outside world, then the F-unit attempted to diffuse every possible element of the petit-bourgeois 'hearth' outwards into the commune of the Narkomfin with its communal spaces and further into the sylvan environment of the park surrounding the complex, thereby literally and metaphorically ensuring the maximal integration of the physical and social self inhabiting the F-unit with the socialist commune beyond and a more authentic relationship between the self and nature promised by the socialist revolution. (For further discussion of F-units see Ginzburg 1934:84, STROIKOM 1930:35, 55–61; for a more thorough discussion of the integration of the Narkomfin with the landscape see Buchli 1998.)

The 9 K-units along the first corridor of the living block were designed to accommodate pre-existing bourgeois domestic arrangements (see appendix). As such, these units were entirely self-sufficient and did not depend on the communal spaces of the complex for the maintenance of daily life as they contained a small but completely separate kitchen (see figure 10). Like the F-units, the K-units attempted to diffuse

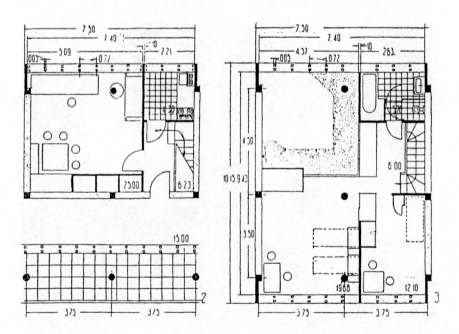

Figure 10 K-unit plans, Ginzburg 1934:105

visually and physically their domestic spaces outwards into the commune and park beyond. However, like F-units, they closed from view their respective kitchens, bathing facilities and toilets, as well as the children's bedroom. Both units pursue similar strategies for the ideal expression of socialist domestic space with a large common space for work and a niche for sleeping. Spaces which accommodated activities which should eventually be socialised, such as the separate children's bedrooms and kitchens, were literally hidden from public view.

Along the stairwells were arranged the 2-F units (see appendix). These were of two types: one with split levels (3 on the sixth floor) and the other all on the same level (3 on the fourth floor). Volumetrically, they were a combination of two F-units placed side by side (Ginzburg 1934:84) (see figure 11). However, unlike F-units these were fully independent self-sufficient bourgeois units and did not have the same spatial or visual qualities found in K and F-units linking interior space with the commune and park beyond. All the rooms, as in a typical pre-Revolutionary bourgeois apartment, were visually and physically separated from each other by full walls and doorways (see figure 11).

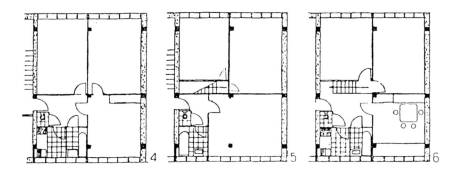

Figure 11 2-F-unit plans, Ginzburg 1934:104

Also along the southern stairwell were what I have called two articulated K-units. These units were never described in the STROIKOM guidelines or in any of the literature by M.Ia. Ginzburg or by any of his students or commentators. I have called them articulated K-units because of their formal similarities with other K-units. They differ in that they are significantly larger, accommodating an extra toilet and separate dining room on the first floor and large semi-circular balconies (see appendix).

On the roof of the living block was what can only be called a penthouse, which shares many common features with the articulated K-units. Designed by the client of the Narkomfin, Commissar Miliutin, for his family, the apartment has remained unaltered throughout the occupancy of the living block, carefully preserved by the Miliutin family resident there until the apartment was abandoned in 1975 when the family moved to the United States (see Buchli 1998 for a more detailed description).

On the roof, in addition to the penthouse, were dormitory units derived from analogous prototypical units of the STROIKOM (STROIKOM 1930:50,53) and Miliutin's own prototype living cells for linear cities described in Sotsgorod (Miliutin 1930:83). The dormitories are unique solutions, employing collapsible wall-beds and shared showers between units. At the end of this row is a rather spectacular glass-enclosed semi-circular space; described in oral histories as a communal area that served at various times as a common room, kitchen/dining room, bath and even at one stage as an apartment (see appendix).

The communal block stood independently, only connected to the living block by an enclosed bridge (see appendix and figure 6). As originally constructed the communal block consisted of two main storeys, each storey being of double height containing a mezzanine each (see figure 12). The first storey was to be the sports-hall with the area below the mezzanine containing the showers, toilets, dressing and storage room. The mezzanine itself was a resting area and observation platform over the sports-hall. This in turn connected directly with the bridge between the communal block and living block leading straight into the second floor corridor of the living block and onto the K-units and the outdoor terrace (see appendix). The second floor housed the communal dining room with the area below the mezzanine devoted to the kitchen and related service facilities. The mezzanine accommodated a rest area and reading room.

Ginzburg noted in 1932 (Ginzburg 1934:84), that the communal block was originally intended to have movable and detachable glazing on the entirely glazed north elevation of the building facing out into the park. In such a way all the communal activities in times of warm weather could be open entirely to the greenery and air of the park. For reasons of cost most of the fenestration had to be fixed. However, this statement does reveal Ginzburg's intention to further diffuse the activities of the communal block (like the domestic interiors of the K- and F-units) with its large open spaces out into the Arcadian setting of the park outside, further articulating the concept of a diffused socialist

Figure 12 View of communal block from roof garden, 1931, Shchusev State Architectural Museum, Moscow

Arcadia where social and economic formations are contained and in harmony with the natural order (see Buchli 1998 for a more thorough discussion of the building's relationship to the landscape).

The mechanised laundry or *prachechnaia* was one of the few aspects of the programme fully realised. It was situated in the original site plan as a sort of gatehouse facing out on Moscow's Garden Ring Road (see figure 6). Ideally, one would have passed by car under the archway formed by pilotis towards the living block along two roads at acute angles to the body of the main building cutting a tight swath through the trees of the park.

Of all the original aspects of the programme, the children's crèche was never realised. It was to have housed the children of the community participating in the construction of the new socialist *byt*. They would have spent their days and nights there (Ginzburg 1934:82) under the watchful eye of a professionally trained staff, leaving their parents, living near by, unencumbered to pursue their work and realise their public and socialised lives. The actual design for the crèche, however, went no further than a large circular footprint in the centre of the park on the site plan (see figure 6). The idea of the children's crèche, however, was retained to a limited degree. In the communal block, the gymnasium, rest area and summer dining room were given over to a makeshift children's crèche (Ginzburg 1934:82–3; Narkomfin Dom Kommuna Oral History, hereafter NDKOH) which was used by the children of reform-minded parents during the first few years after construction (NDKOH).

The Narkomfin Communal House, however, was only the first phase of two housing projects for the site (see figure 6, structure (E)). A second block of housing was designed by Ginzburg and Zundblatt. It was to be situated perpendicular to the Narkomfin Communal House along the southern edge of the park and was to house the Second House of the Soviet of Ministries (Ginzburg 1934: 107–11, Miliutin 1930:105; and see Khan-Magomedov 1972: 108–9). Despite architectonic similarities with the Narkomfin Communal House, the Second House of the SNK was based on radically opposed forms of social organisation. The Narkomfin Communal House was a 'social condenser' working to transform as yet bourgeois Muscovites into good socialist citizens living in fully socialised F-units. The Second House of the SNK was distinctly bourgeois, composed of rather luxurious individual D-units designed to accommodate nuclear families with separate kitchens.

However, in the wake of the Central Committee directive of May 1930, and the upheavals of the previous year in the architectural profession, the Narkomfin at the time of its completion in 1930 must have already appeared somewhat archaic. Already the 1929 proposal for the Second House repudiated the transitional nature of the first phase in favour of fully socialised F-units. By 1930 the idea of a 'transition' from bourgeois K- to socialist F-units and the fully socialist STROIKOM *Dom Kommuna* was losing ground in favour of bourgeois K- and D-units. The completion of the Narkomfin Communal House must have seemed a triumph for *byt* reformists steadily losing ground in the face of the rising Stalinist *apparat* and the restructuring of the architectural profession. By 1932 at the time of Ginzburg's writing of *Zhilishche* (Ginzburg 1934) and the scathing review of the building in the highbrow arts paper *Literaturnaia Gazeta* (Literaturnaia Gazeta, No. 36, 11 August 1932), the Narkomfin Communal House had already been relegated to the dustbin of history as a peculiar and archaic manifestation of a bygone era.

Stalinism and the Domestication of Marxism

The consolidation of power by the Stalin faction during the First Five Year Plan was founded on the creation of a new class of administrators or cadres mostly recruited from the working and peasant classes. They held different attitudes towards the domestic sphere from their Revolutionary seniors; a difference which I would like to describe as emphasising the interiorisation of social life over its exteriorisation earlier. These ascendant individuals developed a different understanding of the Soviet good life which prevailed over that of the 1920s *byt* reformers. Although this new domesticity grew to enjoy official support (as had the *byt* reformers a few years earlier) it was less alien to the aspirations of the majority of Russians and represented a liberalisation of the domestic realm, allowing popular tastes to flourish. Entrenched divisions of class and education were less palpable in the 1930s. Soviet media and statistics concurred to demonstrate that a large part of the new elite aspiring to and gaining predominance in Stalinist society were really no different from the rest. Apocryphal accounts of peasant boy turning factory director abounded in newspapers and journals and could be confirmed in the admissions figures to institutions of higher education (Fitzpatrick 1992). The social backgrounds of the new men and women attested to the fact that a new type of administrator was indeed being created. Stewardship of the controls of the political and social apparatus was passing to individuals from the broader spectrum of Soviet society. At the same time, understandings of socialism became broader, more flexible, and 'fuzzier', in order to facilitate this expression and the interiorization of social life it required.

The Consolidation of the 'Hearth'

Regarding official attitudes towards the domestic sphere the changes are nothing short of radical. The war on the domestic front and domesticity ceased almost entirely. Journals such as *Kul'turnaia Revoliutsiia, Byt i Kul'tura* and *Sovremennaia Arkhitektura* (all major mouthpieces of the war on domesticity) no longer existed by 1932. Literature on the rationalisation of housework, and most theoretically critical household advice, also stopped being produced after 1932, as well as the numerous agitational tracts and philosophical inquiries into the problem of petit-bourgeois consciousness. Concern over the spectre of Soviet petit-bourgeois consciousness warned against by Maiakovskii, Trotsky, Lunacharskii and others ceased to be articulated. This body of criticism contradicted the new broader and 'fuzzier' socialism of emergent Stalinist cadres and denigrated their aspirations to the socialist 'good life'.

In Stalin's oft-quoted words, '*Zhizn stalo luchshe, zhizn stalo veselee*' ('Life has become better, life has become more gay'). Stalin proclaimed socialism achieved, the proletariat victorious and life, at long last, to be enjoyed. To facilitate this new official *joie de vivre* of Stalinist socialism, the Party and the state apparatus began to pursue a conscious policy of retreat from the domestic realm. This policy freed a space within the four walls of the home and breathing room was created for the uninhibited expression of domesticity and the interiorization of social life. The *melochi zhizni* (trifles of everyday life) that once were tremendously infused with political significance by *byt* reformers were now being abandoned.

> The Party does not interfere or create norms for the trifles of the everyday life of a communist: it does not insist on rules of behaviour of every member of the Party for every aspect of a member's life. But the Party does require from every member such behaviour in private life that serves the interests of the Party and the working class. (Rabotnitsa 1936,#7,3)

Aspects of private life that held the Party's attention were organised religion, the stability of the nuclear family, drunkenness, and education. The 'hearth' of the petit-bourgeois nuclear family was reinforced, yet the pursuit of domesticity within went unmolested. Changes in family law in 1937, severely restricting divorce and reinstitutionalising impediments to abortion, further reinforced the consolidation of the 'hearth' by overturning the work of *byt* activists and feminists in the 1920s.

Regarding the minutiae of daily life, the Stalinist motto that 'cadres determine everything' prevailed in the regulation of domesticity. Party members, for example were called upon to 'live such that one's life is an example for those non-Party people living around you' (Rabotnitsa 1936,#7,3). Whereas previous *byt* reformers attempted to establish 'objective' (that is, fixed) rules with which to contain and regulate the domestic realm, the Stalinist empowerment of cadres avoided specific norms. Instead power to invoke normative sanctions was transferred to cadres themselves, to the new upwardly mobile men and women forming the bureaucratic and professional elite. They could use the 'example' set by themselves, without direct Party interference and within very broad parameters (such as those against religiosity), thereby determining the norms of behaviour permitted to flourish under Stalinism.

Housing Law Changes

The power of individuals to effect arbitrary normative control over the domestic realm was further reinforced by changes in housing law. The bankrupted 'leftist' *byt* reformist co-operative housing movement was swept away by the 1937 Law on the Preservation of the Housing Fund and the Improvement of Housing in Cities of 17 October. This law effectively abolished the previous autonomously administered and financed housing co-operatives. It also recalled state loans, and in effect repossessed properties by transferring them to local councils and state industrial agencies (Sosnovy 1952:299; Hazard 1939:130–41). Housing stock was effectively administered by these bodies, which then appointed unsalaried housing administrators (Hazard 1939:136–7). The housing administrator in turn designated who, in a particular communal apartment, was to be responsible for the maintenance of the common areas of that apartment and ensured the observance of rules for internal order (ibid.136). In short, the housing administrator was empowered to oversee the 'responsible' use of socialist property.

By this time, housing had effectively become state property. The statement in Article 131 of the 1936 Constitution that 'persons attempting to violate public socialist property are enemies of the state' (*Constitution of the USSR* 1936:73) further emphasised the responsibilities of housing administrators before the state. This justified a system of state surveillance creating a disciplinary structure supervised by locally empowered individuals. Earlier housing co-operatives had elected administrators from within their community, making them solely responsible to the co-operative and no other body.

The powers housing administrators and their subordinates wielded were considerable and they enforced vaguely defined administrative rules and procedures, which thereby ceded to them considerable influence over an individual's daily affairs. 'The rules' were established by local Soviets, and varied greatly. In Moscow for instance, 'the rules' concerning hygiene verged on the draconian (see Hazard 1939:58–9). If any of these rules were 'maliciously' violated then the house administrator could arrange for prosecution under the Criminal Code and a court order to evict the offender. House administrators who were lax in their responsibilities could themselves be prosecuted (Hazard 1939:60). An administrator who carried out improperly these responsibilities could be prosecuted for failure to protect state property (Hazard 1939:56; see also Article 131 of the Constitution of the USSR (*Constitution of the USSR* 1936:73)). Eviction could be gained by a number of means: either by an individual's insinuations or by a state enterprise. Offences such as habitual drunkenness, brawls and general disorderly conduct were sufficient grounds for eviction. On the other hand, eviction was not limited to merely general 'abusive' and 'disruptive' behaviour. One could be evicted for using one's dwelling in order to gain 'unearned income' (Hazard 1939:98).

However, before housing administrators could invoke the Criminal Code to deal with violators, there existed several levels of coercion. *Stengazety* (wall newspapers or bulletin boards erected and maintained by the local housing administration) publicised warnings and shamed offenders (Hazard 1939:114). After public censure, more grievous or repeated offences could be brought before the 'comradely court' comprised of ten to twenty-five members elected from a general meeting of residents. The jurisdiction of the 'comradely court' was broad, encompassing anything related to the economic and social life of the building. The court usually dealt with offences of a 'petty' nature and could only level fines up to 50 roubles or one-fifth of an offender's monthly wage (Hazard 1939:114). If 'comradely courts' proved ineffectual, then the 'People's Courts' were approached where the Criminal Code could be invoked. Eviction also occurred whenever an individual was fired for whatever offence, since housing was provided as part of an employment package. Termination of employment entailed the loss of housing without any provision for alternative accommodation (Hazard 1939:120).

It should be noted that these rules and their interpretation were intended to regulate individuals with valid claims for housing either through inheritance, the local council, or state and industrial bodies. Housing was not perceived by the Soviet legal code as a right so much as a privilege of full citizenship. In the case of citizens of good standing, this privilege was generally maintained. However, not everyone was entitled to full citizenship under Soviet laws. Individuals of 'alien class background' or those thought to be enemies of the state were beyond the pale of socialist society and not recognised as full citizens, and were thereby denied access to housing. Anyone fired from a job, for conduct considered contrary to the interests of the state, immediately lost her or his housing privilege (Hazard 1939:73,76). One of the most immediate consequences of the Purges of 1934 and 1937 was the eviction of denounced individuals and their families, resulting in the homelessness of dependent spouses and children.

Women's Roles and the 'Hearth'

Byt reformers of the 1920s, despite their attempts to eliminate the domestic realm and realise the emancipation of women, shifted the locus of women's activities from the individual hearth to the level of the socialised 'hearth' of the commune or co-operative. The great public role women were encouraged to assume was in the maintenance of the communal socialist 'hearth'. Earlier, women's involvement in these activities would have been viewed as an accommodation to pressing circumstances by 1920s *byt* reformers. Yet in the 1930s, the maintenance of the communal 'hearth' was seen as intrinsically worthwhile. As one representative of the Central Council of the Red Cross, Comrade Moirova, said, 'Our Soviet woman is not only the housewife of her own hearth: she is the housewife of the entire nation' (Rabotnitsa 1936:#22,10). The maintenance of the individual 'hearth', the communal socialised 'hearth' and socialist society at large were the domains in which women were encouraged to labour and exert their authority and serve as the housekeepers of the greater Stalinist state: 'at first sight trifles, such as the exemplary maintenance of every apartment, room, kitchen etc., are identical with the exemplary maintenance of the city, as it is composed of the exemplary maintenance of every separate home, court, sidewalk and even the foliage by the gate' (Rabotnitsa 1936:#7,17). Women's *aktivi* (household committees of housing co-operatives) were encouraged to assume responsibility for the greater socialist 'hearth' by the maintenance and repair of dwellings, the landscaping of courts and neighbourhoods, and even civil defence (Rabotnitsa 1936:#7,17; Rabotnitsa 1936:#22,10–11).

This new public role as the 'housekeepers of socialism' expanded the arena in which most women could extend their influence. However, this was a far cry from the ideal pursued by *byt* reformers, which saw the public role of the housekeeper as transitory until the 'hearth' was eradicated and full equality achieved. The use of unpaid socialised women's labour in the domestic sphere (formerly considered an undesirable but necessary expedient) was now a virtue in and of itself. Nonetheless, the unpaid 'socialist housekeeper' of the building committee created positions of power and opportunity for individual women under the peculiar conditions of daily life in Stalinist society.

The 'comradely courts' of earlier housing co-operatives were retained after the 1937 housing law change (Hazard 1939). The courts, the *aktiv domokhoziaiek* (housewives association) and the housing administration with its appointed administrators gained considerable powers under the new laws. The women's magazine *Rabotnitsa* in 1939 ran an article about the creation of an *aktiv domokhoziaiek* at no. 24 Probrazhenskii val. When the *partkom* (Party committee) of the Transformator factory took over the direction of the apartment house following a recent reshuffling of ownership, the situation of housewives in this building changed radically. An *aktiv domokhoziaiek* of twelve women was formed, empowered by the *partkom* of the factory to oversee the supervision of the apartment house. A *stengazeta* (wall newspaper) was hand written by these women describing the requirements for *kul'turnyi byt* (cultured daily life). This served as a community noticeboard of events and information which changed three times a month. In addition, the editorial group of the *aktiv* organised 'raids' with a team of fifty individuals of the 384 apartments. During these 'raids' they would gather information to determine renovations required of individual apartments in order to keep them in proper order. These 'raids' revealed those who were the 'uncultured inhabitants, neglectful of their duties to communal housekeeping'. The results of these 'raids' were revealed to the community at large in three subsequent *stengazety*.

The *aktiv* at no. 24 extended their activities to the prevention of fire hazards and civil defence. They made provisions for the creation of a laundry facility, gas lines and landscaping. The author concluded incredulously, 'are those the same women who not too long ago were isolated in their narrow private lives? A year and a half has changed them unrecognisably. The women matured politically, their world view expanded, they spread their wings, feeling the gusts of air of our great epoch. They have become true participants in the construction of socialism' (Kogan in Rabotnitsa 1939:#13,13).

The role of housing administrator was ideally suited to the non-waged wife, empowering her with considerable potential influence on her surroundings. An article in *Rabotnitsa* describing the work of Marina Ivanovna Bleskina, at no. 1/27 Pervovo Smolenskovo in Moscow, describes this new ideal role and the opportunities it provided for her (Rabotnitsa 1939:#25, 10–11). Gradually in her capacity as housing administrator, she was able to *ochishchat'* (purge) the apartment house of undesirables: 'frauds and speculators'. That is, she facilitated the eviction of 'alien' class elements, rendering these men and women with their families homeless and jobless. In such a manner, Marina Ivanovna made it possible for deserving *udarniki* (shock-workers) to move into the former apartments of *déclassé* occupants. In addition to cleansing the building of 'alien' class elements, she organised childcare for newly installed shock-workers, and turned what was described as a bar on the premises into a *krasny ugolok* where the 'comradely court' of the community would meet.

Marina Ivanovna's efforts as an expert 'housekeeper' of the socialist 'hearth' opened great opportunities for her. She was elected three times as a deputy in the Moscow Soviet. She worked for nine years as a community leader in the Cultural and *Byt* Section of the Moscow City Soviet, overseeing the repair and maintenance of city properties and the enforcement of hygienic standards in housing and in stores. The message of such a success story was clear to the mass readership of journals such as *Rabotnitsa*. Women, in their traditional roles as redefined by the requirements of the Stalinist state, received mandates which not only assured their participation in the formation of Stalinist socialist society, but offered 'real' – as real as one could imagine within the confines of a patriarchal society – opportunities in the exercise of power in their own lives and over others. The image of Marina Ivanovna as housing administrator (the socialist housekeeper *par excellence*) was one of power to maintain physical, moral and social hygiene. So empowered she could broadly interpret draconian housing policy required to cleanse the socialist 'house' of vermin, both biological and human. The image of Maria Ivanovna was one of considerable influence previously unattainable to the majority of women.

Stalinist Consumerism

Stalinist femininity entailed a strikingly different attitude towards domesticity than the fiercely antagonistic stances of *byt* reformers during the 1920s. The joys of domesticity were revived and were reminiscent of the pre-Revolutionary celebrations of the bourgeois 'hearth'. However, the clear identification of the maintenance of the domestic 'hearth' with the well-being of the community, the city and the state validated the pursuit of formerly superfluous and endangering domestic pleasures as an affirmation of the socialist order. *Uiut* and hygiene took on new meanings as affirmations of the socialist order whereas previously they were seen as mutually exclusive. It was generally understood that *uiut* could not be achieved without some sacrifice of hygienic standards. Also greater investments of time and energy were required of women to maintain it, prohibiting their entry into the public sphere of socialist labour. However, as women's public roles became increasingly associated with the larger project of socialist housewifery, such a preoccupation with the interior pursuits of domesticity became entirely appropriate.

Stalinist housewifery was further enforced by the legal changes in home ownership triggered by the abolition of housing co-operatives. One's house was no longer one's own, as under the old co-operative system. Housing now belonged to the government, Party or enterprise – in short the state. Consequently, one's relationship to one's home was the same as for any other form of state property and one could face criminal charges if that property was damaged and neglected. Individual action in the home was intrinsically linked to state interests. However, those interests were determined and expressed contextually according to an individual's own local understanding of that relationship. Nevertheless, a refusal to maintain hygienic standards and pursue *uiut* represented an affront to the state and contempt for the maintenance and celebration of socialist property, as one errant apartment house was criticised by L. Veselova on the pages of *Rabotnitsa* in 1941: 'in this house with all its comforts, there is no order, no loving relationship to state property . . . concerns for culture in *byt*, for the preservation of the state housing stock are discarded' (Veselova in Rabotnitsa 1941:#16,9). She blames this sorry state of affairs on the failures of the local sanitation commission to educate and organise the women of the housing block towards a more caring relationship to state property (ibid. 9).

The interiorisation of social life, the sanctity of the home and the legal protection of domestic pursuits were assured in Stalin's Constitution of 1936 whereby private property within the domestic realm of the individual household was explicitly protected (Hazard 1939:36) Article 10 of the 1936 Constitution stated that: 'The personal ownership by citizens of their income from work and savings, home and auxiliary economy, of objects of domestic and household economy as well as objects of personal use are protected by law' (*Constitution of the USSR* 1936:41). Hazard noted that the sovereignty of the individual in the domestic realm was tested in court cases. Evictions of temporary tenants from homes built at personal expense had been upheld, affirming one's right to enjoy personal property as one saw fit (Hazard 1939:36).

Housekeeping, Accommodation and Coercion

The cultivation of *uiut* served as an expression of hope for the success of Stalinist socialism. Linked with localised and interiorised domestic strategies, *uiut* served effectively to accommodate both state and local individual interests. Not to cultivate *uiut* was not to participate; it was an expression of apathy and contempt for the socialist order. The decoration of the home, like the decoration of the workers' club, and the street parade worked in concert to affirm the 'spontaneous' and 'popular' expression of people's support for the state. Consequently, there was a marked shift in official attitudes towards dust, filth and dirt in general. If in the 1920s dirt was associated with petit-bourgeois consciousness, it was now considered an expression of contempt for the Stalinist state.

However, to speak of coercive forces in the regulation of household affairs in the 1930s is problematic. The housing laws and the surveillance of housing administrators and housewife *aktivi* were powerful coercive devices for the maintenance of hygiene and *uiut*. Yet, unlike the 1920s, a specific model for the achievement of this new domesticity was obviously lacking, resulting in a certain freedom of interpretation, which allowed a limited populism to prevail in these matters. What was important was that people attempted to pursue *uiut* as best they could. How that was achieved was left to the people themselves, who were empowered by broad laws and regulations informed by prevailing local custom, personal idiosyncrasies and a very limited stock of material culture with which to give expression to socialist domesticity.

The Party and the state simply required that one keep house. How one did that was not one of the 'trifles' the Party actively involved itself in. Authority was devolved to individual housewives, *aktivi*, housing administrators and local communities. Consumerist acquisitiveness was cultivated in order to encourage locally administered domestic activity. To quote Stalin in 1935, 'Socialism can only be victorious on a highly industrialised labour base, much greater than under capitalism, a base that is abundant in industrial products and all manner of consumer goods, on a base of a prosperous and cultured life for all members of society' (Rabotnitsa 1939:#15,18). An editorial in *Rabotnitsa* picks up and elaborates:

> The regeneration of cultural needs, the rise of salary, the many forms of savings at banks demonstrate that our people have all the means to obtain beautiful things, decorate their apartments comfortably (*uiutno*), set their tables beautifully, and dress themselves in good taste. Our industrial production is obliged to satisfy these demands of the masses completely, and industry will make good this task, working with Bolshevik tempo, realising daily the Stalinist attention and concern for that which beautifies the daily life (*byt*) of the Soviet citizen. (Rabotnitsa 1938:#23,2)

The Stalinist good life at home was facilitated by the limited production of coveted prestige goods (furniture, radios, phonographs, porcelain, cameras and electrical appliances) (Rabotnitsa 1938, #23, 2; 1939, #15,17–18; 1940, #8-9,5; Nove 1982; Zalesky 1980:753–4). Such prestige items were extremely expensive and difficult to come by. One way of procuring such goods was as a bonus for diligent labour, or in some cases for heroism (Hazard 1939:20, see also Siegelbaum 1988, Kotkin 1995 and Fitzpatrick 1979). The *vydvyzhentsi* and Stakhanovite movements offered such material perks to encourage 'socialist competition', and reward hard-working and loyal cadres. Stakhanovite workers were awarded 'free' Crimean vacations, better furniture and better accommodation (Hazard 1939:18). Exemplary women from housewife *aktivi* were rewarded with watches, dress material, silk shawls, embroidery and trips to sanatoria in the Crimea (Rabotnitsa 1936:#22,10–11).

Recipients of these goods were given a mandate to deploy and use these scarce consumer goods as they saw fit. The Stakhanovite or *udarnik* enjoying his or her home was an image for society to aspire to: 'With their example, Stakhanovites and *udarniki* inspire their colleagues at work. That is why Stakhanovites must be the spearheads of cultured life in their *byt*' (Semashko n.d.: 2). The Stakhanovite at home, however, was generally left to her or his devices to establish what these norms might be with minimal state interference. Stakhanovites were empowered by goods inaccessible to the rest of the population, variably establishing their local and contingent norms of use. What was significant was not how domesticity was pursued but that it was pursued and by how much.

Nowhere is this process of Stalinist enfranchisement of the deserving worker more obvious than in the allocation of a new apartment to a deserving cadre. The process of moving into a new apartment, the *novosel'e,* exists as a distinct genre of Stalinist socialist realist mythology. It is endlessly retold in magazines, newspapers and movie clips. A typical movie plot consists of the family of a deserving worker, usually Stakhanovite, moving with its belongings old and new into a gleaming apartment house recently built by the Soviet regime after having lived in a communal apartment or *izba* (village cabin). These *novosel'e* were a confirmation of the state's promise to raise the standard of living of Soviet citizens and ensured the confluence of state interests with individual gratitude and advancement (see TsGAKFD SSSR Nos. 1-2277; 1414; 14445 and 4240-VIII for excellent period newsreels of *novosel'e*).

The Stalinist Domestic Interior

Although the manipulation of space within the Stalinist domestic realm was left mainly to the inhabitants themselves, a certain uniform competence of spatial use is discernible which cannot be attributed to any official literature. The competence that emerges from film clips and period photographs and ethno-historical evidence is identical with the 'uncultured' competence of domestic spatial use reviled by 1920s *byt* reformers. The unhygienic, irrational, vulgar and 'uncultured' interiors that had characterised 'petit-bourgeois' interiors of the 1920s were now the 'cultured', *'uiutno'* and hygienic interiors of the Stalinist 1930s. However, Stalinist competence facilitated interiorisation and elaborated the domestic realm even further, with the introduction of new socialist and state produced prestige goods such as radios and gramophones. It usually describes the overcrowded one-family single room of a communal apartment (Trotsky 1972:139, Hazard 1939, Sosnovy 1952), typically occupied by four family members: husband, wife, elder relative and child. It is similar in size and occupation density to the pre-Revolutionary peasant *izba* and in many degrees represents a continuation of some of the spatial and symbolic features of traditional *izby* (Budina and Shmeleva 1989), such as the table around which the household gathers and the red corner.

The Table and Red Corner

The table with its chairs, located centrally within the room under a large lampshade, is the focus of the household about which all items of furniture relate in a centripetal pattern. It serves as the locus about which all family activity takes place, such as eating, resting, reading and working (see figure 13) carrying over a pattern from peasant *izby.*

Figure 13 'In the apartment of a milling-machine operator', Moscow 1954, TsMADSN, no. 0-17908

The household's relationship with the world outside the domestic sphere was facilitated by the red corner, which was further mediated by new state-produced technologies. State-controlled transmissions through *tarelki* (single-channel radios), as well as phongraphs and newspapers, brought the socialist order of the outside world into the world within. These were often located in the red corner alongside representations of Soviet political figures, namely Lenin or Stalin, along with the household's collection of Marxist texts (see figure 4).

The Bed

The bed, typically made of metal, was usually placed along the edge of a wall. The more desirable ones had large shiny bulbous posts, and an elaborately decorated coverlet with embroidered fringes along the bottom and the rails. The decorative focus of the bed, however, was a mound of three down pillows (*gorka*), placed in order from largest to smallest. Sometimes a particularly enterprising woman might devise an embroidered coverlet that would drape over the entire *gorka*. The *gorka* was an important signifier of the wealth of the household and a point of pride displaying a woman's skills in housekeeping and embroidery.

Invariably, alongside the bed would hang a small rug or *kovrik* against the damp and draughts. Rugs had an additional decorative purpose and were highly valued objects in a household's inventory and prominently displayed (see figures 13, 14). The rugs could be machine-made or artisan-made, and in some instances were imitated in paint on wood or cloth (Chizhikova 1979:62–3). The designs on these *kovriki* would invariably be figurative landscapes; typically a stag in the forest or a swan on a lake (or in some cases exotic subjects like camels, pyramids and palm trees). Rugs from the central Asian republics or Ukraine and the Caucasus would also serve as alternatives to figurative landscape designs.

The Takhta

The *takhta* (which is similar to a *divan*) was also placed along the wall about the family table (see figure 15). Used for seating during the day, the *takhta* also served as a sleeping platform. It was often covered with embroidered cloths and cushions but no *gorka*. A *takhta* was distinguished from a *divan* by a shelf covered with an embroidered cloth on top of which were displayed various sorts of figurines, particularly the ubiquitous line of seven white elephants (*sloniki*). These figurines were crafted from a white-coloured material (usually marble, calcite, earthenware or porcelain) (see details of figures 13 and 15) and were considered good luck charms that promoted and signified the well-being of the household.

The Buffet/Commode

The other major element of the Stalinist interior was the buffet cabinet or commode. This item of furniture was intimately associated with petit-bourgeois consciousness and condemned by *byt* reformers in the 1920s who actively strove to eradicate it. They were elaborately carved, with glassed-in shelves for the display of elaborate tea services. Thus they were negatively associated with competitive social display and unacceptable in a classless society. Usually these buffets were conspicuously placed along the wall facing out onto the central table (see figure 13). More often than not they would be adjacent to the red corner or placed at an angle in their own corner creating a separate focus for the room. So prominently placed, the buffet, like the red corner, visually and

Figure 14 F-unit interior, 1992, Author's photograph

Figure 15 'A lathe operator in a new apartment, Moscow Oblast, 1952', RGAKFD, no. 0242408

physically engaged guests and household members alike, displaying treasured family serving pieces, as well as photographs and certificates of achievements by members of the household.

The commode served a similar function to the buffet and its surface was covered by elaborate embroidery that set off valued perfume bottles, mirrors, photographs, porcelain figurines and vases. Often the commode also accommodated the display of *sloniki*. These two items of furniture were the primary vehicles for displaying 'secular' objects which displayed the private day-to-day prosperity of the immediate household, further expressing the interiority of the domestic realm.

Etazherka

The *etazherka* (etagère or shelves) falls within the 'sacred' realm of the household's red corner. As the primary vehicle of display for the components of the Soviet red corner – and the world outside – it held the household's collection of Marxist texts and the *tarelka* (radio). Directly above the *etazherka*, or on it, would be the family's images of Lenin and/or Stalin as well as other representations of the Party pantheon. Often the individual shelves of the *etazherka*, the tops of the books, and the *tarelka* would be covered with embroidered cloths (see figure 15). Ostensibly protecting them from accumulating dust, the covering emphasised the objects visually as well as the surfaces they protected.

Embroideries

The various types of embroidered cloths (*salfetki*), used to protect and cover surfaces from radios to *gorki*, were significant aspects of the Stalinist interior and one of the means with which to express interiority. Earlier *byt* reformers condemned these embroidered cloths as superfluous 'rags' harbouring dust and infections. However, as a decorative element they were essential to the creation of Stalinist *uiut*, at times covering virtually every imaginable surface (see figures 13, 14 and 15).

It is significant to note that this embroidered work was exclusively executed by women continuing a female peasant tradition. Embroidery was typically home-made, created by the women of the family for the decoration of the family home. Embroideries were important expressions of the needlework skills of the household's women as well as signifiers of their commitment to the creation of *uiut* in the home (see Parker 1984 for a broader discussion of women's embroidery). Sewing circles were commonly formed in workers' clubs and community red corners, where women could gather to exchange ideas and techniques for embroidery. They would then leave these sewing circles and continue work in their homes, working out ideas and techniques learned in these groups, spreading fashions and technical innovations. Of all workers' club and red corner activities these were the most popularly attended by women of the community (Central Committee of the Communist Party (Bolsheviks) of Ukraine 1929). Particularly skilled women could sell their work outside the home to other women and households, through informal networks or at local markets. Soviet law allowed the sale of individually produced goods on the free market, so long as they were produced without hired labour. Urban Stalinist women, much like their peasant predecessors, thus had a means at their disposal outside their unpaid domestic labours to earn extra income.

Besides just being an extra source of income, embroidery was virtually the only way in which domestic space could be appropriated, made individual and interiorised. Despite official rhetoric advocating acquisitiveness in a climate with constant shortages, the dearth of consumer goods was phenomenal in the 1930s (Zalesky 1980). Very little physical material was actually available for people to appropriate and fashion in order to meet the conditions and aspirations of their daily lives. Furniture was expensive, rare and of little variety. The opportunity to exercise taste and choice was severely curtailed. One of the only ways an individual could exercise a certain degree of control over the physical environment was through the creation and deployment of these embroideries. These artefacts were produced entirely under the direct control of individual women, each one exercising her own taste in the design, production and deployment of these decorated articles in her home (NDKOH).

Wallpapers and Stencils

Interiorisation was further expressed with decorative wall treatments. Aside from needlework the only other means independantly to manipulate one's physical surroundings was by the papering and stencilling of walls. When available, wallpaper could be hung, using one's own labour and without the approval of housing authorities (see a model lease in Hazard 1939:128) (see figures 13 and 15).

Similarly, stencilled decorations and *trompe-l'œil* were used to great effect (particularly where wallpaper was unavailable). Such decorations only required paint and individual hired labour, resources more or less available. When professionals were not at hand, these treatments could be executed by members of the household. These wall treatments took on a variety of designs, but were usually in imitation of segmented panelling, surmounted by a decorative border at the ceiling. In some instances, these stencils imitated wallpaper (see Chizhikova 1979:62 for the use of stencils in rural dwellings). The area within the panels could be additionally decorated with palmettes, geometric patterns or gradations in colour further modulating the surface of the wall (see figures 14, 17 and 18 [bottom]). In skilled hands considerable complexity and nuance could be achieved in the modulation of the wall surface. Such wall treatments represented a particular form of unofficial decorative art. Neither designs nor techniques were recorded or published, but they presumably passed from master to apprentice, evolving locally within communities according to the tastes, fashions and desires of individual craftsmen and their clients.

Figure 16 F-unit interior, 1992, Author's photograph

Figure 17 F-unit interior, 1992, Author's photograph

Figure 18 F-unit interiors, 1992, Author's photograph

The Second World War

The Second World War represented a hiatus in the Stalinist pursuit of domesticity. The privations of wartime, the destruction of the housing stock and evacuations (not to mention the stupendous numbers of lives lost) made it unrealistic to pursue domestic pleasures and expressions of interiority. The war was not, however, a period of repudiation. As soon as it was over and the process of recovery began, the cultivation of the 'hearth' vigorously resumed. The need to rebuild, regain normalcy and forget the horrors of war quickened the pace of post-war acquisitiveness. People moved back into their devastated homes, or found new ones. Reunited families took stock of who survived, was divorced or still unaccounted for. Families gradually attempted to rebuild themselves and their homes as they sorted out the wreckage of the war.

The 'hearth' was substantially more important than ever for the rebuilding of families and Soviet society in general, and its regenerative powers were keenly cultivated by the state. The suffering endured by every Soviet family during the war allied disparate segments of society towards recovery. The cultivation of the hearth became everyone's goal, and the state was there to provide the means both materially and morally to realise these aspirations. The war had provided a powerful common focus for the first time in the Soviet period, undercutting former social tensions. For the first time in its history, the state had virtually unequivocal public support, having vanquished an enemy common to all of its citizens. As the State was the sole provider of employment, housing and material goods, the recovery of every family – every reunion, every apartment, every rebuilt home – was to be facilitated by the state's monopoly of social and economic life.

The 1920s *byt* reformers attempted to eradicate the domestic realm in order to create an entirely public socialist society devoid of a competing petit-bourgeois private realm. The Stalinist state, on the other hand, harnessed the 'hearth' brought it under state ownership and control, and leased it out to individuals for use. Rather than destroying it, the Stalinist state effectively appropriated it to serve state interests. Then with the war (better than any campaign from the Cultural Revolution) the 'hearth' was destroyed a million times over in both human and physical terms. The new 'hearth', just like Stalin's new intelligentsia, could be restructured completely according to the needs of the state. The reconstitution of the 'hearth' after the war was effected entirely by the grace of the state with the tools and materials it alone provided. There was never any ambiguity regarding the intimate linkage of people's personal post-war reconstruction with the interests of the socialist state. At the time of Stalin's death in 1953 these interests had at long last become one and the vast majority of Soviet citizens earnestly mourned him. Thus the interiorisation of social life, the recovery and the legitimacy of the Stalinist state were never more tightly intertwined. In the following chapter we will look at this process as it worked itself out amidst the community of inhabitants at the Narkomfin Communal House.

The Narkomfin Communal House and Marxist Domesticity

Everybody's lives are closely examined by the others. Everyone lives in a communal apartment as if they were under a magnifying glass. There are no secrets. Everyone knows what someone has brought with them, what is cooking, what you wore yesterday, what you are wearing today. But however strange that may be, that does not exclude the fact that some of the inhabitants of the communal apartment lead a mysterious, even secretive existence. They are treated with suspicion, myths grow up around them, often totally untrue and inaccurate. Thus, many people are certain that in the second room from the door lives a legendary wealthy millionaire and in the seventh from the kitchen – a German spy; beside him a terrible bandit and so on. (Kabakov 1989:52)

The modernist Constructivist understanding of the landscape of the Narkomfin site changed rapidly with the planning of the Stalinist apartment house for the Council of People's Commissariats by the architect Leontovich between 1933 and 1935 (see figure 20). This construction replaced Ginzburg's earlier proposal for a second apartment building (Ginzburg 1934:107–11; Miliutin 1930:105; see figure 6). A 1949 photograph of the radically altered park attributes its design to Leontovich. Most of the trees of the nineteenth century park had been removed and new ones were planted according to a more formal geometric plan. There were two avenues of lime-trees that led up to the two entries of the main living block. These avenues were aligned with bordered grassy areas and manicured bushes. A formal garden lay in front of the heavy classical facade of the new Stalinist apartment building. In keeping with a formalist 'taming' of the

Figure 19 Expanded K-unit interior, 1992, Author's photograph

Figure 20 'View of Narkomfin Park, 1949', Shchusev State Architectural Museum, Moscow

previously free-form nineteenth-century park, an asphalt road was placed alongside the Narkomfin living block. Old trees, so carefully accommodated in the original construction, were removed, pushing back the tree line away from the house, which was now separated by a low border of fencing and shrubbery.

The Buildings

Every element of the complex's original programme was realised, with the exception of the childcare centre. The second phase was built, although unrecognisably in the form of Leontovich's Stalinist structure. The incomplete realisation of the complex set it out of balance, radically affecting the realisation of the programme in only a few years to come (Ginzburg 1934:82).

One section of the living block to undergo considerable change was the ground floor. *Zhilishche* noted that the ground floor contained only one apartment (Ginzburg 1934:86). By 1936, however, the entire open area between the pilotis was filled in with extra apartments (see appendix). The bridge, in turn, ceased to be. A portion of it was turned into a long bathroom with tub and sink. House records and numerous oral histories also make references to a dormitory being there (NDKOH).

The roof – where the Miliutin penthouse, dormitory and solarium were located – hardly changed during the Stalinist period. The Miliutin penthouse remained in the family without any alterations to the interior. The dormitory continued to function, although its curved glass-enclosed common room was turned into an apartment sometime after the war (NDKOH) (see appendix). The solarium remained as is, but the roof garden was constantly used to dry laundry by the local inhabitants.

The communal block was the most significantly altered. Sometime between 1930 and 1934, ownership of the Narkomfin building was transferred to the Council of People's Commissariats. During the construction, Miliutin ceased to be Commissar of the Narkomfin in July of 1929. At the time of occupation a shift in the building's management occurred, from the reform-minded Miliutin to the concerns of an expanding and dynamic Stalinist bureaucracy. Coinciding with the first wave of purges, a shift in programme was to be expected and, indeed, did come about.

Details of this new programme on the part of the Council of People's Commissariats are very sketchy, however. Ginzburg, writing in 1934, describes the communal block as having to fulfil simultaneously all the functions of the originally projected block, including the unrealised childcare centre. Consequently, all that could be achieved was the communal kitchen. However, the dining room it served no longer functioned as such, as most inhabitants took the kitchen's prepared meals back with them to eat in their apartments (Ginzburg 1934:82, NDKOH). In addition the sports-hall appears not to have been realised; photographs dating shortly after construction (before 1934) show it converted into an architect's atelier. What remained of the structure was given over to the childcare centre (Ginzburg 1934:82). However, the overall appearance and internal arrangement of rooms were not affected by changes in programme for most of the Stalinist period.

The remnants of the original Ginzburg programme did not survive the change of management to the Council of Ministries sometime after 1934. The double-height ground floor of the main fenestrated mass of the structure was walled up sometime between 1949 and 1951. Instead of a communal centre, a number of other operations were accommodated there during the Stalinist period, including a printing shop for the Council of Ministries.

The *prachechnaia* or laundry building was one of the few aspects of the programme to be fully realised. Built as planned, the mechanised laundry functioned as such for some time. Oral histories refer to the laundry functioning well into the 1950s whilst still under the management of the Council of Ministries. It fell out of use presumably around the time of the complex's appropriation by the Moscow City Council in 1961, after which the *prachechnaia* was administered separately (see also TsGARSFSR, fond 403, opis 1, list 25).

The dismantling and segmentation of the original conception of the site (already underway by 1934) continued throughout the Soviet period. Funding, combined with a lack of commitment to issues of *byt* reform such as childcare, conspired against the original programme. All of this in turn placed an extra burden on the existing facilities, disrupting the efficiency of Ginzburg's programme (Ginzburg 1934:82, Khan-Magomedov 1972:107–8). The transfer of the complex to the Council of People's Commissariats of the Russian Republic (in the wake of Stalin's consolidation of the state apparatus) worked to repudiate those aspects of radical *byt* associated with the older Bolshevik elite. Miliutin, though not purged, lived in fear of it (NDKOH). His quick succession of jobs in the early 1930s suggests an unstable period in his career leading to his position as head of the Motion Picture Commission where he wielded less power, but was much safer from the Terror (Miliutin 1939:11). Individuals like Miliutin could no longer influence the future of the complex and its social programme. Thus the Narkomfin Communal House lost its original patronage and ceased to represent the future of Soviet housing. It became just another building belonging to the Ministry of Soviets.

Because of the building's high profile as the representation of the new *byt*, it was not void of significance and entirely neutral. The building was vigorously expressive of the recently discredited social and political campaigns of *byt* reformers. Vilified in the press a mere two years after construction (Literaturnaia Gazeta, No. 36, 11 August 1932), the building must have become an embarrassing reminder of discredited 'left' and 'Trotskyite' thinking to its new owners, the Council of People's Commissariats (later renamed the Soviet of Ministries in 1946). The second half of the project, the unrealised 1933 second *Dom Kommuna* planned by Ginzburg and G.A. Zundblat, failed (see Ginzburg 1934:107; MGINTA, folder 10024, document No. 102; Miliutin 1930: 105). The Soviet of Ministries opted for an architecture more appropriate to the prevailing climate, and built the ornamented and classicist

Stalinist design of Leontovich (MGINTA, folder 257, document No. 2) (see figure 20).

The conflict between two architectures representing the aspirations of competing bureaucratic elites is most poignantly highlighted by the realisation of the second half of the residential programme in the new Stalinist classicist idiom. There is reason to believe that, due to the negative political implications of the Narkomfin Communal House (in the turbulent environment of the years leading up to the first wave of purges in 1934), people found it expedient to leave their apartments in the complex. Regrettably, the household registry only dates from the time internal passports were issued in 1932. In the first book of the household registry, the first third of entries are lost; some surviving records do note that people moved across the park into the new Leontovich building. However, oral histories have suggested that by the time the Great Purges occurred in 1937, not that many people in the Narkomfin were affected. The occupants of the Leontovich building suffered more severely. Individuals living there occupied more powerful bureaucratic positions; as a consequence they were more likely to be purged. It was remarked that those who had influence and political savvy could arrange to be moved into the Leontovich building, since its apartments were more luxurious than the spartan units of the Narkomfin. Individuals with the proper means could in this way disassociate themselves from the discredited ideology believed to be embodied in the material culture of the Constructivist Narkomfin, and embrace the ascendant ideals represented by the material culture of the new Stalinist structure designed by Leontovich.

Unrepentant *byt* reformers, such as Ginzburg and Miliutin, remained at the Narkomfin. These individuals did not adapt very well to the new political climate, which was so antithetical to their goals and aspirations of the past ten years. By political acumen and luck, some managed to avoid arrest and execution (Ginzburg 1934; Miliutin 1930). Both Ginzburg and Miliutin attempted to reconcile their *byt* reformist positions in their writings within an increasingly hostile climate. Their careers, however, suffered, and they were forced into other positions with lower prestige and less influence. Ginzburg's editorship of the influential journal *Sovremennaia Arkhitektura* ceased in 1931, along with the journal itself. The rest of his career was spent creating sanatoria in provincial southern Russia and Ukraine, in a very spartan but decidedly neo-classical idiom (Khan-Magomedov 1972 :146–69). Others, like Semashko, managed to adapt to the political climate, but not without considerable personal and political compromise. Semashko left his first family living at the Narkomfin in order to establish a new family with a second wife in a Stalinist building on the present day ul. Semashko, closer to the Kremlin.

Though still a building of the bureaucratic elite, the Narkomfin did not house individuals of sustained high-status, like those in the Leontovich building. Moreover, as the communal block ceased to function and supplement the activities of units in the living block, life without these facilities became more uncomfortable, particularly to the vast majority of inhabitants in F-units which were not self-sufficient. Hence those who had independent self-sufficient K-units were not as affected by the dissolution of communal services as those in the F-units.

Though somewhat forgotten in the new political climate, the building was not forsaken; housing was in too short supply to consider abandoning it. Yet the social programme it represented was most definitely rejected, as witnessed by the loss of the communal facilities in the early 1930s. As a building of the well-funded Council of People's Commissariats, however, it was meticulously cared for by a staff of gardeners, doormen and gatekeepers, while the floors of its communal areas were given gleaming parquets and carpeted with runners.

The Development of Households at the Narkomfin Communal Complex: Performing Socialism

It is only partially true that the discourse on *byt* reform disappeared with the ascent of the Stalinist state. The discourse on socialist hygiene certainly disappeared where it was related to *byt* reform. However, this rationalising discourse was to reassert itself with terrifying consequences throughout the course of the Terror or *chistka* – the literal 'cleansing' of the Communist Party of 'undesirable', 'alien' and 'impure' elements. The language of the Purges and of *byt* reform was the same, but the sphere encompassed by this 'hygienic' and rationalising discourse shifted. If domesticity and the feminine were previously problematic, the public and the masculine became the key issues during the Terror. It was on the basis of the successful performance of these public and masculine roles that socialist social competence was judged, often with terrifying consequences. Men, as a result of their dominance in public roles, suffered most; while women suffered relatively less by virtue of their association with the domestic realm, which was no longer the focus of socialist rationalisation. Women enjoyed a qualified respite, in spite of the suffering they would endure as a consequence of their male partners' successful or unsuccessful performance of public socialist roles. (See Holmgren 1994 for an excellent discussion of this retreat in terms of Soviet literary criticism and the relatively safe spaces women found within Stalinism.)

The Purges, as a higher order of socialist hygiene, also involved a certain restructuring of the items of material culture associated with the domestic realm according to contextual understandings. Cleaning out 'alien class elements' literally involved cleansing the apartments of purge victims with their belongings, furniture and books. These in turn could be redistributed without any adverse effects through their radical appropriation, without being 'infectious' as modernist denotative understandings would have required. That is, objects associated with class enemies could at the time of arrest or investigation be used as proof – by virtue of a contextual relation with an 'alien social element' – of their 'alien' status (see Kotkin 1995). On the other hand, the moment the determining 'alien' element was removed (i.e. the person who was arrested) these objects could be redistributed either by appropriation (by those individuals who performed the arrest) (NDKOH) or via restricted second-hand stores run by the NKVD (People's Commissariat of Internal Affairs) (NDKOH). The objects remained literally the same, yet a contextual understanding of material culture permitted them to be reused without threat of 'infection' or contradiction by 'proper' Soviet citizens – those individuals still believed or believing themselves to be adequately performing socialism. This was facilitated by an understanding of socialist performance as being determined by an individual's actions, rather than one's ability to realise abstract ideals according to modernist denotative understandings. However, certain objects were far too clearly associated with 'alien' social elements such as books, whose authorial signatures directly linked them with the consciousness of the 'alien' element. At the Narkomfin, children were instructed by worried parents not to play near books confiscated from the apartments of purge victims piled up at the building's columns. These parents rightly feared that their children might sell the books at an antiquarian shop for ice-cream money and be traced back to their families and implicate them as 'alien' social elements as well (NDKOH).

The Performance of Stalinism

The issue of performance is central throughout these discussions of competing understandings of the material world. This emphasis on performance and competitive differential competence is something Clifford Geertz focuses upon in his study of the nineteenth century Balinese state. Geertz describes Bali as

> a theatre state in which the kings and princes were the impresarios, the priests the directors, and the peasants the supporting cast, stage crew and audience. The stupendous cremations, tooth filings, temple dedications, pilgrimages, and blood sacrifices, mobilising hundreds and even thousands of people and great quantities of wealth, were not means to political ends; they were the ends themselves, they were what the state was for. (Geertz 1980:13)

Political action resulted in 'stagecraft [as] a thespian art' (Geertz 1980:120). This understanding of the performative 'theatre state' – with its accommodation of personal bodily sacrifice in the form of immolation and other acts of self-destruction – strikes a certain chord with the Terror under Stalin. The Party subjected itself to blood-letting and 'self immolation' on an unprecedented scale in its search for the ultimate expression of socialist piety. Just as the widows of Balinese princes, assisted by relatives, serenely threw themselves into funeral bonfires in the most 'perfect' expression of their understanding of Balinese cosmology (Geertz 1980:98–102), Bolsheviks denounced neighbours, spouses and themselves in their individual attempts at the most perfect realisation of socialist principles in the enactment of the socialist state.

Boris Groys, referring to this point, describes the Stalinist state as the full realisation of the universalist strivings of the modernist avant-garde. Stalinism was not an aberration but a logical conclusion, if not the most perfect expression, of the 'total' aesthetic project devised by modernist avant-gardists to achieve the demiurgic restructuring of the material world. Socialist realism, and the Stalinist state and its society, represented the fullest expression of this modernist urge towards 'total art'. The translation of the avant-garde into Stalinism is argued by Groys thus:

> By its own internal logic, the artistic project becomes aesthetic-political. Because there are many artists and projects and only one can be realised, a choice must be made; this decision is in turn not merely artistic but political, since the entire organisation of social life is dependent upon it. Consequently, in the early years of Soviet power the avant-garde not only aspired to the political realisation of its artistic projects on the

political level, but also formulated a specific type of aesthetic-political discourse in which each decision bearing on the artistic construction of the work of art is interpreted as a political decision, and, conversely, each political decision is interpreted according to its aesthetic consequences. It was this type of discourse that subsequently became predominant and in fact led to the destruction of the avant-garde itself. (Groys 1992:21)

Consequently, whilst in the service of the Stalinist state 'as party bureaucrat the Soviet artist [was] more an artist, more a creator of the new reality, than in the studio in front of the easel' (Groys 1992:52).

In this respect the nineteenth-century Balinese and the twentieth-century Stalinist states are comparable. State ritual in Bali, as under Stalin, was turned into a 'lexicon of carvings, flowers, dances, melodies, gestures, chants, ornaments, temples, postures and masks - rather than into a discursively apprehended, ordered set of explicit "beliefs".' These understandings resulted in 'state ceremonials [that became] metaphysical theatre: theatre designed to express a view of the ultimate nature of reality and, at the same time, to shape the existing conditions of life to be consonant with that reality; that is theatre to present an ontology and, presenting it, to make it happen – make it actual.' (Geertz 1980: 104). The parallels with the representative strategies of Soviet socialist realism become apparent if one considers the Constitution of the Soviet Union of Writers, which states that socialist realism 'demands from the artist a true and historically concrete depiction of reality in its revolutionary development . . . combined with the task of educating workers in the spirit of Communism' (quoted in Bown 1991:90). Or, if one considers the statement of Andrei Zhdanov, the leading Party theoretician on art: socialist realism 'must be able to show our heroes, must be able to glimpse our tomorrow' such that the artist becomes an 'engineer of the human soul' (Bown 1991:90). Just as a lexicon had been established in the creation of the Balinese 'theatre state', so too a lexicon was formulated in the case of the Stalinist state so that a 'change [in] the existing conditions of life [could become] consonant with that reality' (Geertz 1980:104).

Moreover, Stephen Kotkin has suggested the notion of 'speaking Bolshevik' (Kotkin 1995) in an attempt to understand the dynamics of Stalinist society. 'Speaking Bolshevik' was part of a performative strategy to enact socialist principles required of every Soviet citizen, through which a 'totalising' social project (the creation of the Soviet socialist 'theatre state') would be realised. Following this line of reasoning the

Purges were not so much an aberration, but a logical expression in light of prevailing contingencies: a belief that socialism, whatever it was, was better than capitalism. Thus, encirclement by overtly hostile capitalist and fascist countries made possible the belief that under such conditions 'enemies within' could most certainly exist. This, combined with a precondition of unswerving orthodoxy required by the Party in all matters, made the conditions that fanned the flames of the Purges possible. In this respect Kotkin echoes Groys's position that this quintessential expression of Stalinism, like socialist realism, was in keeping with a logic inherent to the Stalinist state and its historical circumstances. Thus Geertz, Groys and Kotkin together suggest that rather than necessarily being anomalous, 'monstrous' and 'tragic', the Terror and its culture was a logical and integral part of the original demiurgic totalising project that was the creation of Soviet socialism.

Underlying Geertz, Groys and Kotkin is an understanding of social action that emphasises performance and theatricality and in which issues of appropriate action, aesthetics, unity of vision and consistency of execution – in short, style – become very important. To quote Bourdieu:

> Since the history of the individual is never anything other than a certain specification of the collective history of his group or class, each individual system of dispositions may be seen as a structural variant of all the other group or class habitus, expressing the difference between trajectories and positions inside or outside the class. 'Personal' style, the particular stamp marking all the products of the same habitus, whether practices or works, is never more than a deviation in relation to the style of a period or class so that it relates back to the common style not only by its conformity . . . but also by the difference which makes the whole 'manner'. (Bourdieu 1977:86).

Style is integral to an agent's successful negotiation of a prevailing habitus; and in the case of socialism proper, style became integral to the successful performance of Soviet socialism.

Bourdieu further elaborates with particular relevance to Soviet society:

> If all societies and significantly all the 'totalitarian institutions', in Goffman's phrase, that seek to produce a new man through a process of 'deculturation' and 'reculturation' set such store on the seemingly most insignificant details of dress, bearing, physical and verbal manners, the

reason is that, treating the body as a memory, they entrust to it in abbreviated and practical, i.e. mnemonic, form the fundamental principles of the arbitrary content of the culture. The principles em-bodied in this way are placed beyond the grasp of consciousness, and hence cannot be touched by voluntary, deliberate transformation, cannot even be made explicit; nothing seems more ineffable, more incommunicable, more inimitable, and, therefore, more precious, than the values given body, made body by the transubstantiation achieved by the hidden persuasion of an implicit pedagogy, capable of instilling a whole cosmology, an ethic, a metaphysic, a political philosophy, through the injunctions as insignificant as 'stand up straight' or 'don't hold your knife in your left hand'. (Bourdieu 1977:94)

Like Groys's 'total art', and Kotkin's 'speaking Bolshevik', Bourdieu's understanding of the totalising and diffuse nature of habitus, with its attendant demands on performative competence, becomes particularly relevant to the performance of socialism.

Thus, in light of the totalising enterprise conducted by the Communist Party in the spirit of 'democratic centralism', the socialist habitus (to follow Bourdieu) comprised a broad field of doxic knowledge. However as Kotkin pointed out, not everyone actually knew what comprised socialist doxa or the nature of the socialist habitus (Kotkin 1995). (Kotkin neglects to point out, however, that this was not for want of trying; rather it was a unique attribute of the Stalinist state that deliberately inhibited this process.) Yet because of the totalising nature of the socialist enterprise, everyone ought to have known. This impulse towards doxic certainty was what created a climate wherein legitimacy was anchored in the mastery of a habitus. Yet, no one was completely certain of it. In fact, the rise of Stalinism ensured that it was uncertain, whilst nonetheless retaining the impulse towards certainty. Thus in contrast to Bourdieu's understanding of the totalitarian state, absolute power was not ensured by the explicit restructuring of habitus according to a fixed and knowable set of doxic assumptions. Rather, power was ensured by demanding doxic certainty without the certainty of a mediating habitus. Thus, the supreme authority of the Communist Party, as embodied by Stalin himself and his appointed agents, could arbitrate the habitus appropriate to realise socialist doxa, contingently, locally, and with devastating authority.

A certain element of 'fuzziness' therefore becomes necessary for the participation of society as a whole in the enactment of social performance. This relative 'fuzziness' of performative strategies, in

Bourdieu's words, would 'allow one to introduce just enough logic for the needs of practical behaviour, neither too much – since a certain vagueness is often indispensable, especially in negotiations – nor too little since, life would then become impossible' (Bourdieu 1990a:73; see also 1990b:13,87). Similarly, as in the case of Stalinism, the terms by which socialism could be performed were deliberately 'fuzzy' in order to permit a greater deal of social participation which empowered individual agents locally and contingently, at the expense of the fixed denotative doxic knowledge characteristic of the modernist Leninist state. Elsewhere, John Bowen argues in the case of Gayo ritual in Sumatra that such 'fuzziness' ensures social cohesion wherein a myth of social egalitarianism predominates (Bowen 1994:86). As regards the Stalinist state, this requirement was paramount to state legitimacy based on the enfranchisement of the proletariat.

As Kotkin points out, the industrialisation drive and capitalist encirclement required the strictest adherence to and actualisation of socialist doxa. Yet no one was allowed to develop a consistent and dominant habitus towards this end, which meant it could be anything. However, doxic certainty required that a habitus must be something particularly defined, especially under such stressed conditions. Within such a climate, the need to demonstrate one's mastery of socialist habitus (that is, perform socialism as best one could) was imperative. How that was achieved was fundamentally arbitrary. There were no attempts at guidelines as during the Cultural Revolution. Socialist performance had been made 'fuzzy' to permit the ascendancy of Stalinism and ensure maximal social participation, thereby securing state legitimacy. Yet whatever habitus it was, paradoxically it had to be performed correctly and singularly; and herein lay the key to Stalinism's extraordinary and horrific control over social action.

In this way we might be able to understand the denunciations of colleagues, neighbours and family members; the fervent expression of socialist piety in the light of brutal interrogation; the 'confessions' to 'crimes', all the while asserting one's devotion to Stalin and the socialist enterprise (even when it became clear to the bewildered and confused victims of this process that they had failed to perform socialism properly despite their earnest personal belief that they were being successful). Ironically, the totalitarian nature of the Stalinist state was not realised by recourse to what would appear to be a totalising discourse. Rather, absolute authority was achieved by harnessing an urge towards such a totalising discourse. This was coupled with the arbitrary actions of the state as personified by Stalin and state agents who determined erratically and wilfully what appeared to be an appropriate expression of that urge as local contingencies required.

The performance of socialism permeated every aspect of political and daily life: ideology, work, speech, family relations, dress and the domestic interior. What might have appeared as a retreat in favour of popular aspirations (Fitzpatrick), or a co-optive 'big deal' (Dunham), was in its technical effect more like an extraordinarily elaborate means of keeping the terms of socialist performance uncertain ('fuzzy'). This ensured popular participation until the state and its agents chose when to exercise arbitrary certainty in these matters, and exert crushing power over individuals with the bloodiest of consequences. The 'axiological urge' and its yearning for consensus was subtly and cynically exploited under Stalinism with devastating consequences.

The state retreated in its attempts to rationalise the domestic sphere and the feminine and instead focused its rationalising efforts upon social 'hygiene' in public roles and the masculine. However, the constitution of the domestic realm could be invoked at will by virtue of contextual understandings of material culture used to describe an 'alien class element' as 'anti-Soviet', thereby implicating every aspect of an individual's domestic life by association. Two identical domestic strategies of socialist performance could be considered at once 'alien' and 'Soviet', depending upon whether the agent was a designated class enemy or loyal Party member. In essence, everything was determined by the socially and variably constituted role of the agent, which in turn determined the context by which domestic strategies would be evaluated.

As noted earlier, the sphere of socialist performance shifted from the domestic realm, where it had been during the Cultural Revolution. The new sphere of performance focused instead on the physical bodies of Soviet citizens in the public realm; on those constituted as 'kulaks', 'Trotskyites', 'class aliens' and 'wreckers'. The language of hygiene used to eradicate petit-bourgeois consciousness (as embodied by 'dirt' and 'vermin' in relation to furniture, design and domestic life) shifted with devastating results onto human beings themselves. In this respect, the case of individuals and their families during the Purges was of particular significance. The demiurgic process of socialist construction shifted from material culture to human 'material'. It rooted out 'alien' elements and attempted literally to create an entirely new human stock for the realisation of socialism.

Changing Social Structure at the Narkomfin

Ground-Floor Units

Occupation of the ground floor occurred shortly after the initial settlement of the Narkomfin. At the time the building belonged to the Soviet of Ministries and the profile of the occupants of the ground floor was more heterogeneous. Often, households that considered themselves members of the intelligentsia shared facilities with households that were decidedly proletarian. Single households of professionals were often converted into communal apartments for labourers. For instance, before the Second World War one apartment was originally occupied as a single household by a scientific consultant, who was later purged in 1937 (see appendix). Subsequently the apartment was shared by three households, whose heads were registered as labourers with the building management of the Soviet of Ministries. The geographic origins of these inhabitants were also quite diverse – from beyond the Russian Republic, from within Moscow, and from the deepest rural villages.

K-units

House records and oral histories confirm that the original inhabitants of K-units were well-placed individuals, such as a Kremlin physician; a Narkomfin administrator; a professor of art; or a ministerial executive (see to appendix). When the Leontovich building was erected in 1934, household records and oral histories show that some families with influence arranged to move to these more spacious Stalinist apartments (NDKOH). Despite this fact, the profile of K-unit inhabitants as elite bureaucrats remained. Those who had left were replaced by similarly well-placed bureaucrats, yet obviously with less influence than their predecessors (NDKOH).

The construction of Building no. 10 and the purges of 1934 and 1937 were two events that had profound effects on the continuity of occupancy of these units in the pre-war years. One of the first families to occupy one of the K-units moved into the new no. 10 building in 1934, after which the Narkomfin unit became communal and was occupied by three households headed by bureaucratic officials. In 1934 the original household of one of the K-units was purged, leaving another family headed by a Narkomfin official to move in. One of the communal K-unit households was purged and apparently the extra space was apportioned to the remaining two households. Another was purged and made communal with two households, one headed by a chauffeur and the other by the widow of the purge victim. One unit, originally appearing as communal, headed by various professionals and bureaucrats, was cleared out by 1937 (almost certainly purged) and became a single household unit headed by an official of the NKVD. Yet another, the single household of a bureaucratic administrator, was purged in 1937 and replaced by a single household headed by an administrative consultant. The original inhabitants had all been employees of the Narkomfin, or individuals with a particular interest in the social programme of the building. Households replacing those that had moved or been purged consisted of employees of the recently formed Soviet of Ministers of the Russian Republic. Even though these new households were headed by individuals of relatively lesser rank, they were for the most part comprised of bureaucrats and professionals like their predecessors. However, these individuals came from the wider professional and social base of the Soviet of Ministries of the RSFSR and were far less homogeneous as a group than the original settlement of Narkomfin administrators and reform-minded *byt* enthusiasts.

With the evacuations of the Second World War and post-war resettlement, K-unit households - particularly communal ones – became even more heterogeneous. Evacuated elite households were quartered with non-elite households such as a delicatessen worker or a secretary and her family. In the majority of these instances, wartime non-elite households remained; the evacuees never returned. Occasionally a returning family had to share the unit with non-elite wartime residents. The post-war period was no longer subject to such disruptive events. Households within these communal units came and went for more conventional reasons when children grew up, in-laws moved in or older people died. Single household units, though far more stable than communal households, would also experience similar changes.

F-units

Among the 24 F-units, occupancies after 1934 suggest the arrival of new households after earlier ones moved out. Moreover, registries dating from the beginning of the 1937 Purges suggest that many of these newly arrived households moved in after the previous one had been purged. The social profile of these units is consistent with other Narkomfin households. For the most part they were headed by high-ranking officials of the Narkomfin and other agencies. For example, of the 10 units, 5 were headed by senior male officials of the Narkomfin, three of whom were of urban origin and two of rural backgrounds. Two households were headed by staff members of the NKVD of rural origins. Only one of these households was headed by a woman with her own last name, who was also a Personal Pensioner (a title held by a retired high ranking Communist Party member).

The post-1934 households were of similar rank to the group of ten households that remained. Three of the eight post-1934 households were headed by professional women, such as a physio-technician, architect or administrative secretary, all with their own last names. The other five households were headed by men of higher professional standing; such as a Narkomfin executive, a Gosplan (State planning) executive, and the head of a state directory. Of the households that took up residence in the wake of the 1937 Purges, all three are of similar rank. All household heads are male: a Gosplan executive, an administrator with the Soviet of People's Commissariats and a Communist Party executive. The wives of these male household heads pursued careers, but of significantly lower rank. One was a secretary using her own name; another an accountant using her husband's; and the other was a dependant of her husband with his name.

Of the 24 units only 8 became communal from 1933 onwards, for a number of reasons: the purges; wartime evacuations; the loss of *zhilploshchad'* (the status-linked legal norm of square meterage an individual or family could claim when housed) due to the death or departure of a registered member of a household or the loss of civil rights following arrest. Like other units, these became communal as a result of unforeseen contingencies disrupting the original programme and settlement of the building.

Stairwell Units

Stairwell units, like K-units on the first floor, originally housed some of the most elite families. However, oral histories recall that when they moved out, the newcomers from the late 1930s and into the post-war period represented low- and middle-level office workers. Although bureaucrats, they did not represent the managerial elite as had the first occupants. Not only were these new households headed by people of relatively lower status, by virtue of their reduced access to *zhilploshchad'*. They also tended to originate from rural backgrounds: they were part of the influx of newly promoted workers of lower management comprising the Stalinist bureaucratic machinery.

The Impact of the Purges at the Narkomfin

Ground-Floor Units

Only one of the seven units comprising the ground floor lost a household to the Great Purges of 1937. Details regarding the purge of this particular individual are not known. Yet it is important to note this incident and the impact it might have had on the other six households, their interrelationships and the tensions involved in everyday life. This must be considered in light of the heterogeneous composition of these households, often living on top of one another in crowded communal apartments. For example, one contained the household of an official of the secret police (as did a neighbouring apartment). This neighbouring apartment was additionally occupied by the households of an administrator of the Narkomsovkhoz Bureau and an engineer and Party member. Both the administrator and the engineer were household heads with professional backgrounds typically victimised by the Great Purges. The opportunity for agents of the state to identify and eliminate victims and their households was particularly enhanced by overcrowded conditions. The sharing of kitchens, bathrooms and toilets conspired against privacy (Boym 1995; Kotkin 1995; Kabakov 1993). Living in a communal apartment with two other families - one of which was headed by an NKVD official - opened up otherwise unseen quotidian activities, conversations, and comings and goings to observation by representatives of the state.

K-units

The Great Purges of 1937 had a particularly significant and traumatising effect on the lives of K-unit households. They were more affected than on any others at the Narkomfin. Of the nine K-units, only three did not lose a household to the Purges (see appendix). Oral histories from surviving households on that corridor all refer to the sweeping and cataclysmic effect of the Purges. Individuals recall that the entire house was purged and that every night someone would be taken away screaming and crying. Records, however, show that the entire building was not swept clean as some individuals recalled. However, amongst the community of K-units sharing the second-floor corridor, the sense that everyone around them had been taken away by the Purges was literally true.

In 1937, it was certainly the case that either one's apartment or a neighbouring apartment lost a household to the purges. The change in the composition of the community of K-unit inhabitants was keenly felt and remarked upon. All oral histories from K-units and other units comment on the fact that a new group of people moved in, people with different ideals from those of the community preceding them. They were bureaucrats of the same ministries, but middle-level and sometimes described as 'careerists'. They were not committed to the pursuit of social ideals embodied by the building and pursued by the original community (NDKOH). In some instances it seemed as if the actual perpetrators of the purges took over the apartments of their victims. One unit, for example, was reoccupied in 1937 by an official of the NKVD, rumoured among surviving inhabitants to have been one of those who arrested people in the building (NDKOH).

For the post-war period until Stalin's death, there were two registered officials of the KGB at the Narkomfin. One of these men was known to some inhabitants, knowledge of the other is uncertain. One lived in a single household unit, whereas the other lived in a communal unit. The latter shared the unit with at least two or three other households. The presence and knowledge of these individual officials of the KGB show that while K-unit inhabitants were very much aware of the devastating impact of the purges on their immediate community, they were also aware of the presence of individuals directly connected to the state agency responsible for the arrests of their neighbours. Whether those individuals were actually involved is not relevant. They were perceived as representatives of the awful power of the state, in the very midst of the community of K-unit households.

The Stairwell Units

Considering the high-ranking individuals living in the stairwell units, the number of Purge victims here is relatively small (see appendix). Only two instances are recorded, most notably the entire Karklin/Pure family. Of all the families purged in the Narkomfin, the case of the Karklin/Pure family is by far the most tragic. In January 1938 Martin Martinovich Karklin, a widowed Latvian and high-ranking Party member (Head of Council of the Central Committee of the Directory of Affairs) was arrested by the NKVD. He was living at the time with his common-law wife Paulina Pavlovna Pure, also a high-ranking Party member of Latvian origin and member of the Supreme Court of the Russian Republic. Pure was spared at the time of her partner's arrest. Karklin's two children from his previous marriage, Iskra and Kim, were taken by the NKVD to the Danilovskii Monastery Children's Home.

With their biological mother dead and their father arrested as an enemy of the people, the children were officially without guardians in spite of the presence of their father's common-law wife. Legally, they were considered orphans in the eyes of the state and taken to this grim facility, managed by the NKVD, which dealt with orphans of 'enemies of the people' (NDKOH). In the meantime Paulina Pavlovna Pure did something considered very rash in those days – she remained in the apartment. The widows of purge victims typically fled their homes to live elsewhere with friends or relatives until it seemed investigations were over, for they were often the next in line to be arrested in the course of an investigation (Holmgren 1994, NDKOH). Paulina Pavlovna Pure possibly felt immune from the investigation as she was not legally Karklin's wife. She also probably felt secure within the legal system, seeing herself as a keen defender of the fairness of the Soviet legal system being a member of the Russian Supreme Court. However, seven months later in August, she too was arrested by the NKVD and taken away. The apartment was emptied. Two months afterwards it was occupied by the high ranking family of the Deputy Head of GOSPLAN RSFSR (the state planning agency of the Russian Republic).

In the community of the six Northern Stairwell units, the atmosphere of fear and threat of surveillance was not only fuelled by tragedies such as the purge of the Karklin/Pure family and others, but by the presence of employees of the NKVD living amongst them as well. As in other parts of the building, the stairwell units had their share of NKVD staff. In the case of the Northern Stairwell units, the head of one household was an employee of the NKVD. They arrived in May 1938 (following the departure of a high-ranking Jewish family quite possibly as a consequence of the Purges) and stayed there until 1947.

Similarly, in the community of five Southern Stairwell units, there was one known Purge victim (NDKOH), directly under whom lived the family of a staff member of the NKVD. He remained there through the Stalinist period until 1955, when he moved to another address in Moscow while still an employee of the secret police.

Amongst the community of 23 F-units, there were five confirmed purged households. In addition, there were two households which were almost certainly purged since new families settled there in 1937 and 1938 respectively. One unit – after it was purged – was actually replaced by an NKVD household in addition to two other NKVD households already living at the Narkomfin. As with other sections of the house, families moving in were of arguably lower rank yet certainly culled from the broader social base of the Soviet of Ministries. As for other sections of the house, the impact of the Purges was indeed palpable, affecting one's closest neighbours. Similarly, the presence of the NKVD was acutely felt, with three interspersed households heightening the sense of fear, and possible surveillance and denunciation.

In the stairwell communities each unit could count at least one household in five or six as known victims of the Purges. Despite this, most of the inhabitants interviewed felt that the impact of the Purges on their immediate community was not so great. This was certainly the case in comparison with the second-floor community of K-units, where over half the households were purged. Rather, oral histories consistently acknowledge many more victims in the adjacent Building No.10, where individuals of even higher rank were housed.

Before the Stalin era, the state attempted to rationalise and directly control the domestic realm through the manipulation of material culture. The Stalinist state's retreat from these rationalising attempts permitted spontaneous and differential performances of socialism in the domestic sphere by rendering it transparent to observation and interpretation, as well as to the potential activities of state informants and agents in the highly public domestic lives of communal apartments. Furthermore, the Terror did not function systematically but highly erratically (Getty and Manning 1993:6). This compounded a sense of fear that anyone could be an informant; an instrument of state control possessing the power to create and eradicate the state's – as well as one's own personal – enemies, anytime, anywhere and for any reason. Within a group of households all sharing the same entrance and the first immediate point of spatial and social contact, everyone becomes familiar with everyone else's face, daily movements social contacts and domestic activities (see Kabakov 1993). The realisation of a household's purge and a knowledge of neighbours working for the state organs perpetrating the purges could only instil the deepest fear in the fearful, or intensify the suspicions of the venal informant. Thus the increasingly performative nature of socialist social life required under such transparent circumstances that individuals 'perform' socialism as best they knew how. It was imperative to speak as they thought one ought, to carry oneself as they thought one ought to and conduct one's daily life in an exemplary socialist fashion with the hope that one was getting it right. As the terms of socialist performance were 'fuzzy' – locally and contingently understood – individual aspirations merged with the agent's perceived aspirations of the state thus legitimating and implicating one another.

It has often been remarked how remarkably similar to one another various domestic strategies were in the Stalinist period in the absence of any normative proscriptions. An explanation lies partly in the persistence of certain rural norms which were not subject to modernisation under Stalin, as well as the dearth of material goods that limited the expressive nature of prevailing domestic strategies. When these factors were combined, the result was a certain uniformity. However, the intense transparency of domestic life under Stalin, abetted by overcrowding, meant that a certain ontological security might be achieved if there was a consensus of domestic performative strategies amongst a given population. It was from amongst that population that one could be denounced, spied upon and informed on (see Kotkin 1995, Boym 1995 and Viola 1993). Thus, if one performed socialism in the domestic realm in a manner similar to one's visible neighbours, one could achieve a certain modicum of security against accusations of improper performance so long as one adhered to local understandings. At the same time, this process ensured a particular identification with socialism by condoning local, individual and unrationalised expressions of domesticity. A person was left to his or her own devices to interpret and perform socialism. Simultaneously one realised in personal terms the demiurgic project of socialist construction in an identification with state goals, as well as one's own contingent and personal needs. Desires and ambitions were legitimised in this joint project of individual and state performance of socialism, thus realising Groys's 'total art of Stalinism' and the modernist avant-garde's ambitions of the previous decade in new and unexpected terms.

New Stalinist Women

The choice of spouse had a significant impact on the forms of socialist performance pursued at the Narkomfin (see Bourdieu 1984 for a discussion of similar strategic choices of spouses in French society). As women's roles were so crucial to an understanding of petit-bourgeois consciousness and the object of *byt* reform, a correct choice of a femininity was crucial for the competitive performance of socialism for women as well as for men. Women's oral histories would relate with admiration how some high-ranking male officials from the original inhabitants demonstrated a loving commitment to the women they married prior to the Revolution by staying married to them, unlike many other men similarly positioned (NDKOH). These women were described as being from the 'old school'. They were housewives without careers, who pursued neither social nor Party work. They were 'believers' instead of atheists; they kept icons hidden from view in their closets and trunks (*sunduki*). Seen as presences of petit-bourgeois consciousness in the lives of otherwise communist men, such women would have been considered a hindrance to a husband's career as a Communist Party official. Upwardly mobile men during the 1920s and at the height of the Cultural Revolution were known to divorce such wives in order to further their careers. The Party encouraged men to marry women who were more acceptable to *byt* reformist practices; women who had their own careers and public lives pursuing Party activities. In many respects, wives of the original community of inhabitants tended to present themselves in accordance with the demands of *byt* reformist femininity as evidenced in the household registries.

Amongst the original inhabitants were several households headed by women. These women had independent careers, some of a rather high status: such as a medical doctor; a member of the Supreme Court; an economist; a high-ranking Party official; and an architect. Similarly, in households headed by men, wives tended to be professionals with independent careers who asserted their public independence by choosing to keep their own names upon marriage. The women of these households represented the exteriorised Bolshevik *byt* reformist ideal of liberated women: freed from the chains of bourgeois domesticity, pursuing public roles in the construction of socialism. Because of their high rank and double incomes, these households could afford *domrabotnitsi* (live-in maids) to take care of the onerous tasks of daily life that still encumbered women of lower rank. In some instances at the Narkomfin, when resources were tight and paid female labour unaffordable, a single household adopted two competing feminine roles for its female members. One female member pursued the public careerist role advocated by *byt* reformists, while another female member – typically a woman's mother, mother-in-law, sister or sister-in-law – would take over the maintenance of the domestic 'hearth' and assume a more interiorised, 'petit-bourgeois' role.

New households moving in after the original inhabitants were composed of rather different women. The heads of these households tended to be male of lower managerial status and rural origin. Their spouses, too, tended to be housewives of similar origin. When they did work outside the house, they had lower-status positions as, for example, secretaries or schoolteachers. These jobs were not so much professional careers as low-level white-collar work to supplement the family income. These women were less likely to be able to afford *domrabotnitsi*, especially as their unpaid domestic labour was duly harnessed towards the maintenance of the 'hearth'. They bore the 'double burden' that began to characterise urban Soviet women. Not only did they work at full-time jobs, they were also responsible for shopping, cooking, childcare and housework. These women were far more implicated in the management and elaboration of the domestic realm than the careerist women of higher social status of the original community of inhabitants. These new Stalinist and arguably more populist women's roles were in the ascendant as women pursuing *byt* reformist roles were systematically disenfranchised as a consequence of rapid downward social mobility caused by the purges (NDKOH) and as wives of 'enemies of the people' – as in the Karklin/Pure family.

These new women were favoured through the demiurgic process of the social engineering of the Purges. They tended to assume their husband's name and play less prominent public roles. When a woman worked solely as a housewife her main activities and concerns were the maintenance of the household. This was no mean feat, considering the difficulties involved in procuring food, services and goods during the Stalinist period. Women employed in low-level jobs were additionally burdened with such duties. Prestige and feminine fulfilment were considered more in terms of the pursuit and maintenance of the domestic realm and less in the public realm of employment. Women working in low-level jobs were inclined to identify with more traditional and familiar roles associated with the maintenance of the domestic 'hearth'. The stress on socialist performance along with an increasing transparency in all aspects of daily life to state agents favoured such women and men in their performative strategies.

At the Narkomfin, however, these new women found themselves in an architectural setting ill-suited to the revival of domesticity. Apartments were equipped with extremely small kitchens (now well below prevailing norms) or, worse, none at all. Large windows were unyielding to brocaded window treatments; while bare fibrolit floors, monochromatic walls, lofty ceilings and open floor plans were impossible to make cosy or '*uiutno*'. Stalinist 'homemakers' found themselves in an environment that required a great deal of work to bring these spaces into line with understandings of domesticity now open to free expression. Needless to say, these Stalinist homemakers were not daunted by the task and ingeniously effected the appropriate transformations.

The Apportionment of Space

The Ground-floor Stalinist Units: The Reintroduction of Pre-Revolutionary Spatial Patterns

In the wake of the 1937 Purges, certain understandings of material culture gained favour. This was particularly apparent at the Narkomfin in new uses of space to express socialist domesticity. The addition of seven 1936 ground-floor units in between Ginzburg's pilotis articulated a return to pre-Revolution bourgeois spatial patterns. This inclusion, on its own, entirely undermined the position of the building, which was originally viewed as a raised volume suspended within the landscape (see Buchli 1998, and figure 7). In addition, the fenestration of the units followed conventional pre-Revolutionary practice. The windows were not arranged, as in the rest of the building, as horizontal ribbons of glass to maximise the hygienic penetration of light within.

Their plans also diverged significantly. These Stalinist units were typically composed of three rooms with kitchen, bathroom and toilet clustered together. The provision of an individual kitchen for each unit clearly illustrates a return to segregated self-contained households for nuclear families. In addition, the clustering of the toilet, bathroom and kitchen deviated from earlier hygienic norms. Together these new Stalinist units illustrate a return to spatial practices previously condemned by modernists for sociological, political and hygienic reasons.

The first households to occupy the ground-floor Stalinist units were rather varied. However, with the exception of two units, all were communal with two or three households living one to a room. Here husband, wife, children and extended family were often crammed into a room of 15.6–9.22 square metres. A family of three would have 3–5 square metres per person (well below the accepted minimum standard of 9 square metres). Conditions were little better than in traditional peasant *izby* as reported by Soviet researchers at the time (Edelman 1993:15). In addition, over half of these units had a *domrabotnitsa* who would probably have occupied the approximately 7-metre square area of the entry hall.

K-units

As discussed earlier, K-units were envisioned as abbreviated bourgeois units for nuclear families, built to ease the transition to fully socialised F-units. These became associated, however, with the more elite families of the complex because of their spaciousness, amenities and greater *zhilploshchad'*. Here space was apportioned in approximation of the architect's original plans. As housing was scarce, single-household K-units accommodated increasingly more crowded households composed of several generations of an extended family, with the consequence that the open spaces of K-units were eventually divided to accommodate these large households. This was typically done by erecting two thin partitions from the upstairs gallery balustrade up to the ceiling which sealed off the main common room from the rest of the unit (see figure 21). One could then pass from any room into a circulation space and remain entirely separated from the common room, visually and physically. These minute, strategic interventions effectively reversed the earlier exteriorising spatiality towards one of interiorisation, emphasising the domestic realm over the public.

The Stairwell Units and Miliutin Penthouse

2-F-Units. The 2-F-units turned out to be the most in demand (Ginzburg 1934:84). Their anomalous nature raises some interesting issues in the discussion of the Narkomfin. Socially, these were the most hetero-geneous: occupied at one end by some of the most elite members of the Bolshevik Soviet bureaucracy and at the other end by some of the poorest and most disenfranchised households. The socialist ideal of bourgeois families evolving into communards was not facilitated by the architecture of these stairwell units. Occupying the most private and least visible areas of the building, they embody the contradictions of a highly heterogeneous society in flux. In addition, there were two makeshift units, created at the initiative of the local administration. These were carved out of existing public spaces (from a makeshift hairdresser's formed in the corner of a stairwell and another unit carved out of the second corridor communal kitchen (see appendix)).

In the southern stairwell, the 2-F-units were each originally communal apartments occupied by two families. By contrast, in the northern stairwell, all the 2-F-units appear always to have been single-family households. Their transformation from single-family to communal households was achieved effortlessly with minimal arch-itectural manipulation requiring no effort to realise interiorised strategies of spatial use.

The Expanded K-Units. The most elaborate units of the entire complex were the three expanded K-type units. All these units began as single-

Figure 21 K-unit interior, 1992, Author's photograph

family apartments. However, as time went by, only the Miliutin pent-house remained a single-family household, whereas the others became communal as the original household dissolved.

Expanded K-units could be modified into a communal apartment in the same way as regular K-units by enclosing the mezzanine above the common room. In addition, a second kitchen was installed in the corridor of the second floor to provide separate kitchens for discrete households, one on each floor. One unit, however, ingeniously split the 5-metre high common room in half horizontally, creating two rooms, one on top of the other and joined by an internal staircase (see figure 19). With plenty of ceiling height to spare, the floor space of the unit was doubled without any increase to its legal *zhilploshchad'* of 26.31 metres.

The F-Units

The F-units represented the apex of exteriorised communalised life within a *Dom Kommuna*. Yet, for the most part, they endured fewer radical alterations. However, the rather minimal alterations that were carried out substantially altered the spatiality and social programme of the unit. In many respects its limited size and volume restricted the range of possible interventions. One of the most significant and ephemeral of these was to convert what was previously one volume suggesting two spaces (e.g. a common area and a sleeping area) into two, sometimes three, distinct and physically segregated rooms (see figure 16). The modernist exteriorising plan, designed to explode the domestic 'hearth' into the socialised world without, contracted inwards. This withdrawal was a requirement for the Stalinist sense of *uiut*: moving away from the public realm of socialist action inwards.

Transforming the Material Culture of the Narkomfin

These subversions of the cosmological order of the Narkomfin were effected in a number of ways. First and foremost they resulted because of new people manipulating space with different understandings of how material culture functioned in socialist society. They were required by the state to celebrate and perform their newly affirmed domesticity, locally, untutored and on their own terms unconstrained by state-approved normative understandings of spatial use.

However, the material culture of the Stalinist 1930s was rather difficult to manipulate. It was expensive to procure, and freely available only to well-connected and elite families. Very little was actually produced (Zalesky 1980, Nove 1982). In addition, the means for individual production of necessary goods were severely restricted. Peasant handicrafts and markets were eliminated as a consequence of collectivisation (Fitzpatrick 1994). Non-state production was restricted to a small number of individual craftsmen who sold and produced their own wares without employed labour amidst a dearth of raw materials (see Kotkin 1995 for conditions in Magnitogorsk).

Yet, some materials were available, and certain types of individual production could be pursued to create the material conditions necessary for transforming the domestic environment. These were paint, thread, fabric and wood; in short, the raw materials of homecraft. Thus, as individual skill would allow, one could paint walls in an original design, construct shelves, and sew and embroider fabrics to cover unappealing furniture, and create anything from wall hangings, pillows, borders drapes, tulles, tablecloths, needlepoints and tea cosies. A vast array of artefacts traditionally associated with feminine domestic labour (Parker 1984) could be deftly employed by female homemakers in defiance of the *byt* reformist material culture at the Narkomfin, and create the local conditions necessary for Stalinist *uiut* and the interiorisation of social life.

Creating the Illusion of Petit-Bourgeois Uiut

The retreat from the socialist realm of public action to the 'hearth' was facilitated by a number of ephemeral yet highly strategic manipulations, which effectively reversed the explosion of the 'hearth'. These manipulations consolidated the 'hearth', and effectively overturned the exteriorising modernist cosmology inscribed within the Narkomfin. The primary agents of these subversions were the new Stalinist women of the Narkomfin, who were given a mandate by the state to manipulate scarce resources in their individual and local domestic performances of Stalinist socialism.

*Stencilled Wall Decorations (*Trompe l'œil*).* Stencilled wall decorations (commonly known in Russian as *'alfreinaia rabota'*) used techniques of *trompe l'œil* to subvert diffused, exteriorised modernist volumes. They reversed the direction of spatiality back inwards by suggesting pre-Revolutionary panelled rooms in imitation of brocade and panelling through the modulation of light in gold and silver paint. The result was a contained space with articulated surfaces and boundaries drawn inwards. With a few strategic brushstrokes the outward and socialist modernist volumes disappeared, to be replaced by a radically different spatiality, with an entirely different relation to the world – one that was inward, focused, private and domestic (see figures 13, 16, 17 and 18).

Drapery. Drapery was similarly deployed over openings to further segment space, to create 'rooms' instead of 'areas'. Drapery further consolidated space inwards, away from the socialised public and natural realm. Large expanses of glazing were covered with heavy tasselled drapes that matched the curtains segmenting the F-unit into rooms, further articulating a unified and differentiated space approximating the *stolovaia* (dining room) of pre-Revolutionary days (see figure 18).

Flooring. The uniform floors of *fibrolit* (a composite linoleum-like material) were similarly subverted by turning former 'spaces' into differentiated 'rooms'. Wood parquet (typically oak) was installed at the individual expense of inhabitants whose technique of installation required a delineation of discrete quadrilateral spaces. These floor areas helped to delineate the appearance of newly constructed 'rooms' such as the *stolovaia* in the front, an intermediary 'kitchen' in the middle area of the shower cabin, and the rear 'bedroom' (see figure 16).

Embroidery. The process of interiorisation was further accommodated by the creation of various sorts of embroidered cloths. These *salfetki* were draped at times over every imaginable surface: divan cushions, shelves, radios, buffet cabinets, gramophones, pillows, beds, tables and even entryways. *Salfetki* further differentiated interior surfaces and consolidated space inwards away from the outside public world. They were literally 'fluffed' and 'nested' in an attempt to withdraw even further from the public realm of socialist action. This withdrawal was precisely what *byt* reformers decried and what oral histories acknowledged as the socialist 'immorality' of such activities. This 'privatisation' and 'withdrawal', facilitated by the deployment of privately embroidered cloth, served to 'individualise' space by altering the appearance of socialist and industrially produced consumer goods including the state-built buildings themselves, further consolidating the domestic 'hearth' inwards. (See also McCracken 1989 and his related discussion on 'cosiness', and Miller 1994:211–12 on his observations of similar 'internalising' strategies in Trinidad.)

Creating Modernist Byt

In the remaining modernist *byt*-inspired households during the Stalin period an altogether different strategy towards the domestic realm is evident. Rather than pursuing strategies of conspicuous display, these households pursued a strategy of conspicuous austerity. Decisions were hardly arbitrary or ill-thought-out, but deliberate and highly normative. Individuals reported that they only had as much as was needed and did not accumulate unnecessary items. Such statements revealed a highly sensitive and calculated understanding of the use of domestic space that was not in the least bit unconsidered as their statements would have one believe otherwise.

This appearance of austerity could only be realised by highly placed and established single households with sufficient *zhilploshchad'* and reliable access to resources. These families did not have to hoard goods. Furniture was accessible by family inheritance or through one's employer. Families could also store furniture for a later purpose as many householders had access to storage in a dacha. So, even though families might be saving or even hoarding household items, this would not be visible in their homes. In addition, some families could shop at the restricted commissaries of their enterprises (the Narkomfin and Soviet of Ministries of the RSFSR) or patronise expensive, well-stocked food stores (one family for instance had their groceries delivered from GUM on Red Square in the 1930s). Furthermore, nearly half of the households at the Narkomfin had a *domrabotnitsa* in the pre-war period. One of her principal duties was to shop for the household. Hoarding was not necessary since there was always the *domrabotnitsa* who could be sent away on long shopping trips to track down scarce goods.

For non-elite families occupying one room in a communal apartment or overcrowded unit, the conspicuous hoarding of goods – such as furniture and food – was unavoidable. Due to their lower status as evinced by access to less *zhilploshchad'*, these families had low priority (if any at all) for furniture from their employers. They had to obtain what they could when they could, and then simply keep it until the time it was needed. Such families had neither access to restricted commissaries nor the means to buy food at expensive food shops that could deliver groceries to their homes. They had to find what they could and store whatever was non-perishable. The waged housewife did not have access to a *domrabotnitsa* who could shop for her. Hence the dreadful overcrowding of one-room households so offensive to earlier reformers stuffed with superfluous 'unnecessary' furniture and goods – blocking out air and gathering dust.

Austere domestic strategies were pursued most effectively in elite single household units. These controlled the visibility of their domestic environment by admitting only those individuals they wanted with significantly more ease than a household in a communal apartment. There, one was always exposed to neighbours with whom one had nothing in common, while constantly and uncontrollably exposed to their visitors. Consequently, single-household units could engage in local domestic strategies that differed considerably from those of communal households. Most individuals from single-household units could only recall other apartments similar to their own. They seldom visited apartments that were any different and never remembered visiting the communal apartments or dormitories of the Narkomfin.

Individual households exposed to communal units would have been more susceptible to the comments, observations and behaviour of other individuals inspiring a tendency to conform to local conventions. In such units, injunctions on the part of neighbours and household administrators to conform to a celebration of Stalinist domesticity were likely to have been keenly felt – particularly in light of the fear of denunciations and reports to state authorities. Domestic life in these units was in a sense far more theatrical; appearances were vital and susceptible to virtually continuous observation and comment. Conversely, families occupying single-household units that were inspired by and identified with modernist 1920s *byt* reformers could continue to pursue their austere and decidedly unStalinist domesticity, safely observed only by intimates and peers. Thus they could rest secure in their commonly held ideals and their local understandings of socialist performance, against the onslaught of newcomers with different local performative strategies.

Strategies of interiorisation were pursued when modernist ambitions were forsaken, or units became overcrowded. By segmentation and the creation of barriers, inhabitants pursuing interiorising strategies instantly withdrew themselves to the best of their ability from the surveillance of neighbours – a visibility strategy essential to survival during the Terror - and simultaneously repudiated modernist norms of exteriorisation. The pursuit of interiorising domestic strategies at once gave expression to contingent, individual and local understandings of the domestic 'hearth'; affirming the Stalinist socialist order while at the same time staving off as best one could possible agents of state surveillance.

Petit-Bourgeois Consciousness and the Material Culture of Distinction

A heightened sense of alienation affected the original community as it found itself rapidly dwindling and no longer amongst its peers. A sense of distinction emerged, particularly amongst households affected by the Terror, distinguishing them from those who settled in the wake of the Purges and the war. The distinctions established were cast metaphysically in terms of degree of 'spirituality' or *dukhovnost'*, which had its material correlates in discussions of the use of space within these units. The original inhabitants were characterised by their possession of a high degree of *dukhovnost'*, which in the pursuit of modernist exteriorising strategies eschewed materialistic pursuits in favour of social work and public life. Those who arrived later were not in possession of *dukhovnost'* to the same degree. The evidence of that was seen in the attitudes these new families had towards their domestic environment, their cultivation of a private domestic sphere and their use of household space employing strategies of interiorisation.

This connection between *dukhovnost'* and one's attitude to the domestic sphere affirmed the values and denotative understandings of material culture of 1920s *byt* reformers. One individual recalled how her father and uncles felt that paying attention to one's interior was 'petit-bourgeois'. It was important to eschew all exterior appearances and devote oneself to one's work. She described the interior of her childhood home as very puritanical with 'nothing superfluous, everything was purely utilitarian and related to one's work'. As a result she preferred a room that was messy, 'but where it was visible that a person had an "inner life"'. Everyone in her family was 'too busy to occupy themselves with the interior'. As a result they did not look after the apartment, they 'didn't really know how to live'. Only the *domrabotnitsa* took care of the house. She recalls specifically the interiors of other high-ranking families as being 'strictly utilitarian'. There was no 'attention to interior or exterior appearances' and no 'frivolous objects'. These attributes she recalled as being characteristic of the families she knew in the Narkomfin during the Stalinist period.

One individual echoed this perception in her description of the family of the former Commissar of Health for the Russian Republic Semashko in a 2-F-unit. Despite their being *'inteligentnye liudi'* (members of the intelligentsia), a sort of 'war communism' prevailed. Their apartment was completely empty with a minimal amount of furniture: 'they were never interested in any sort of *byt*, or decor, or *meshchanstvo*. They were very modest.'

A former occupant of a K-unit expressed similar sentiments. The creation of an interior ('*oformlenia interiera*') and the accumulation of beautiful things were, particularly in relation to one's neighbours, not acceptable ('*ne bylo priniato*'). She said that people had lived modestly, with only a minimum amount of things that corresponded to their immediate needs. As for according attention to one's *byt*, she said that people back then 'lived according to new ideas and lived those ideas, they took them to heart.' Within these new ideas they raised their children. Their lives as a consequence were rather spartan ('*spartanskii*'). Only the nanny took care of the children, prepared food and saw to the housework. Referring to the wallpapering of rooms and the use of *trompe l'œil*, she responded that in the days before Stalin's death, the apartments she knew and visited never used wallpaper, not even in the 1950s (when wallpaper was cheap and widely available). Walls were merely painted. She attributed a lack of concern for decorated walls to those who were more concerned about the peace of the family, the well-being of the children and a general regard for more warm and spiritual relations between family members. Consequently, she maintained, they did not preoccupy themselves with the creation of an interior – such an interest was simply 'not acceptable' amongst the families she associated with.

In addition, a woman from an expanded K-unit described the apartment of her husband's family as devoid of any interest in creating an interior.

> One was too involved in one's own work to engage in machinations and procure something. We simply did not set such things as one of the goals of our lives, it was too hard to do, but some people simply lived for such things and managed. These people create a 'cult' of furniture, a 'cult' of their apartments, of hygiene, rearranging furniture, buying new and better, more fashionable furniture. There are people who have a certain petit-bourgeois style, which is all for show. In our family this was not the case. We had spiritual values. We had many friends, and lived in an 'open house'. Our furniture and things were for other purposes.

When asked if there were any people who did not possess such spiritual values, who were petit-bourgeois, she responded that: 'There were probably some people here, no doubt, who were petit-bourgeois in the building, but we simply did not know such people. At least amongst the people we socialised with there was no one we could describe as petit-bourgeois.' Their families mostly socialised with Bolshevik elite families intimately associated with the pursuit of *byt* reformist ideals. They did not socialise with many others and thus had no idea of the sort of people living in the dormitories of the building. They acknowledged that originally the occupants of the Narkomfin Communal House were rather homogeneous, mainly members of the intelligentsia. However, later on the population became more dissimilar: 'liudi byli vsiakie' (there were people of all sorts).

Exteriorisation is given its metaphoric expression in these descriptive statements by *byt* reformist inhabitants through their emphasis on 'openness' and movement outwards from the domestic 'hearth'. Individuals described their homes as an 'open house', in the sense that people from their social circle frequently came by at any time to meet and pass the time. Their doors were literally and figuratively flung open to their world. The material props for such 'open' socialising were porcelain services, crystal glassware, and serving vessels that were usually prominently displayed in buffet cabinets and *stenki* (modular cabinets). In the eyes of their owners, however, these were not mere petit-bourgeois artefacts used for denoting consumerist accumulation and household wealth. Rather these objects functioned as vehicles facilitating socialisation beyond the level of the nuclear family and the 'hearth'; they facilitated a sort of communal *stolovaia* of friends and associates, aspiring to a community of like-minded socially committed communards of the 1920s. Such 'open-house' activities also coincided with the exteriorised set of values proclaimed by modernists who felt that public roles were more significant than domestic ones. Their 'higher', 'social' goals were expressive of a greater degree of expansive 'spirituality' that was also exteriorised, moving beyond the narrow confines of the petit-bourgeois 'hearth' and encompassing the realm of public and socialist action.

However, changes in the composition of the community of householders wrought by the Purges and the Second World War brought in a new and different set of people. These new households had a different understanding of material culture and the importance of the domestic sphere that emphasised interiority. This difference was best illustrated in one of the expanded K-units. In 1945 the marriage of an Academician living there breaks down as a consequence of the pressures brought on by the Purges. The first family remains in the old dining room and study as the apartment becomes communal. Two other families move in: one headed by a factory director into the large downstairs common room and the other into the two mezzanine bedrooms. Hence three families reside whereas previously there was only one. Accordingly, in order to create the segmentation typical of a communal K-unit, the mezzanine was sealed up. The factory director's family divided the 5-metre-tall room horizontally in half, creating two separate rooms connected by an internal staircase

The factory director's household's understanding of domestic space was markedly different from that of academician's household. Upon their moving in, the walls were immediately decorated with elaborate stencilled patterns (*alfreinaia rabota*) (see figure 19). A large ornamented mirror flanked by a portrait of Lenin was placed in the corner. Heavy drapes trimmed the windows, and portraits of Gorkii, and Esenin were arranged along the other walls. A *gorka* (a variant of a buffet cabinet) was prominently placed along the periphery of the common room. It contained the household porcelain and figurines such as the ubiquitous little elephants. The factory director's grandchild fondly recalled the *gorka* with all its household wares and figurines, and the overall decoration of the apartment as representing a 'petit-bourgeois well-being' typical of the times. These objects and decorations connoted that everything in the family was 'in order' ('*v poriadke*'); that everything was fine in terms of employment. The *gorka*, 'like a display cabinet in a store, not that this is a fashionable shop or that it is rich, but it shows that everything is here'. It conveyed the public message that everything was well. Referring to the disparaging connotations of petit-bourgeois consciousness in reference to such displays of material well-being, the grandchild stated 'I find that *meshchanstvo* is not derogatory, but a normal word . . . a kind of family, a kind of spirit.' He countered his statements in a mocking official tone that 'a worker should only have that which is necessary, no superfluous things, none of those ribbons, only necessities, only useful things, the very bare necessities.'

The contrast in attitudes and appearance between the *byt* reformist interior *par excellence* of the academician and the new Stalinist petit-bourgeois interior of the factory director's family could not be more pronounced. Here we can see how during the Stalin years with the rise of new men and women within the state bureaucracy, and the ensuing retreat from *byt* reform on the domestic front, a new understanding of social action emerged. This understanding involved a certain retreat from action in the public realm and a return to the domestic 'hearth'. This shift was facilitated by new contextual understandings of material culture that privileged the agency of the individual at the expense of objective denotative understandings. This facilitated a dynamic of interiorisation in physical and social terms opposed to the understandings of the modernist Leninist state.

By relinquishing 'objective' (denotative) knowledge' for 'fuzzier' (contextual) understandings, state legitimacy and local individual strategies became intimately linked; each legitimating the other in the common realisation of socialism. In this way, the social contract enabling the totalising enterprise of socialist construction could be realised. This explains the ease and sincere appropriateness with which images of Lenin could be accommodated within the factory director's and other households during this period. In terms of material culture, however, only a few and highly ephemeral changes occurred. Yet these strategic interventions had effects on a cosmic scale, reversing entire spheres of social action with their concomitant understandings of family, gender, self and public life. Within a few years following Stalin's death, as we shall see in the next chapter, this dynamic would come to experience a repeat reversal; a move towards exteriorisation with the revival of modernist *byt* reforms during the 'Thaw'.

De-Stalinisation and the Reinvigoration of Marxist Understandings of the Material World

The years following Stalin's death resulted in a convulsion in the architectural establishment unparalleled since the victory of Stalinist Classicism over Constructivism. The modernist principles of the 1920s were in the ascent once more. The cease-fire on the domestic front was lifted with Stalin's death and hostilities resumed anew. The domestic realm was once more problematised and *byt* became an issue of paramount importance. The spectre of petit-bourgeois consciousness and its threat to the realisation of full communism in a late-socialist society was raised again. Within seven years of Stalin's death, a new Cultural Revolution was waged based on the principles of the first Cultural Revolution of the 1920s. Now, however, it was occurring unencumbered on the foundation of a fully industrialised urban society.

This second Cultural Revolution continued throughout the 1960s and decelerated in the 1970s when reformist fervour subsided in the general malaise affecting Soviet society in the Brezhnev years. This malaise is referred to by Millar (1985) as an aspect of the 'little deal' under Brezhnev. This took hold, resulting in the final gasp of socialist reformist fervour: the Perestroika of Mikhail Gorbachev from 1985 to 1991.

The Twentieth Party Congress in 1956 and its Consequences

Khrushchev's 'secret speech' to the Twentieth Party Congress in 1956 exposed the horrors of the Stalinist system and effectively swept away the events of twenty-five years and the experiences of an entire generation. This no doubt came as profound relief, particularly to the intelligentsia savaged by the Terror under Stalin's rule. The negation of the past twenty years was extraordinarily destabilising and called into question the goals of the socialist project. This period of reassessment – commonly referred to in the west as the 'Thaw' (and in recent years as the precursor to *glasnost'* and *perestroika*) – was often perceived as a period of liberalisation. Some Western observers saw this as a period when the stirrings of 'free' and 'open' civil society could be felt. However, this was a period of striving to legitimate the socialist project, while recoiling from the horrific excesses of Stalinism. Freedom in the liberal democratic sense was not what this period was about. Rather it was a search through to the roots of the socialist revolution to regain principles forsaken in the pursuit of the Stalinist state. In short it was the absolution of the Party, which could only be found in terms of the body of Bolshevik ideas existing before the Stalinist ascendancy. Hence the oft-quoted slogan, 'return to Lenin'.

In terms of this reorientation, we can see how the issue of *byt* regained prominence. It assumed a position in the debates of post-war *byt* theoreticians close to the debates on the eve of the 1930 Central Committee directive. In rhetorical terms, the discourse on *byt* in 1959 was virtually indistinguishable from that of 1929. It should not be seen as a liberalisation of attitudes towards the domestic realm but quite the contrary. It was the reproblematisation of *byt* and a period of intense state and Party engagement with the terms of domestic life, one that was highly rationalised and disciplined. If the Stalinist state was poised at the threshold of the 'hearth', the Khrushchevist state walked straight in and began to do battle. This offensive on the domestic realm was waged on two flanks. The first front, facilitated by the massive building campaign announced after the Twentieth Party Congress in 1956, was a *tabula rasa* whereby the new housing stock of the nation could be effectively inscribed with a new body of disciplining *byt* reformist principles. The second front was the pre-existing body of housing. It employed taste and household advice to regulate behaviour that would lead towards a realisation of *byt* reformist socialist goals. The two fronts in turn were co-ordinated by a new ideological tool in *byt* reform, namely the emerging concept of *dizain* (design).

Byt, Dizain and Socialist Ethics

While *byt* re-emerged as a problem – almost indistinguishable in rhetorical form from its roots in the late1920s – the field was by no means the same. The retreat from the regulation of the domestic realm under Stalin left its impact. An entire generation was raised in expectation of the joys of domesticity under terms of locally empowered action. In a recovering and rebuilding post-war society, these joys could not easily be denied. Neither could the idea of the individual independent agent. The rhetoric of reformers often echoed the hostile tones of earlier ones, often in direct contradiction of Party and government policy. An irreconcilable tension existed between the situation 'as built' and the 'as legislated' directives of Party and government. The discourses of *byt* reform relied upon *byt* reformist objectives of the Cultural Revolution as the only remaining legitimating socialist discourse on the domestic realm after the dismantling of the cult of personality. *Byt* theory and *byt* practice were at loggerheads. The only remaining legitimating discourse on domestic practices, aimed at the obliteration of the domestic sphere, was in direct confrontation with the expectations and aspirations of most Soviet citizens.

This tension was alleviated in two ways. Firstly it was alleviated by the understanding that Soviet society was experiencing 'high-socialism' in its penultimate phase before full-blown communism (in the 1960s that was expected to occur around 1988). Consequently society was in a transitional phase requiring an accommodation with existing conditions. This allowed reformers to understand behaviour not corresponding to *byt* reformist ideals as temporary, regardless of how strongly individuals felt. It was simply part of an ontological phase towards full-blown communism where there would be no room for domestic pleasures. Secondly, taste began to perform an important role in regulating pre-existing patterns of domestic behaviour which flourished under Stalin and were now increasingly perceived as petit-bourgeois. Taste encouraged more acceptable socialist behaviour. Consequently, taste and its arbiters could safely diffuse these contradictions by their regulatory functions. That is, the pursuit of domesticity could be accommodated if it followed certain rules that acknowledged this ultimate socialist ontology. The arbiters of taste could pick up those strivings for domesticity, redirect and contain them in a manner that would eventually see them whither away as full-blown communism was reached and the domestic 'hearth' completely obliterated. Much of the rhetoric therefore revolved around the rationalisation of what *byt* theoreticians referred to as 'irrational consumer behaviour'

(Zarinskaia 1987). Thus Stalinist superfluity could be adequately contained about this disciplining axis of regimented taste. Needless to say, in strictly design terms, minimalism was the operative word in the arbitration of taste (see Buchli 1997 for a broader discussion of *dizain* and its relation to Western design).

A number of institutions responsible for the socialist rationalisation of the domestic realm was steadily built up between 1956 and 1962. The foundation of GOSSTROI in 1955 (the state construction agency), and subsequent directives of the Twentieth (1956) and Twenty-First (1959) Party Congresses on *byt* established the physical infrastructure within which to realise *byt* reform. The *tabula rasa* was established upon which the first flank of the domestic front was fought. In 1962, a Soviet of Ministries of the USSR directive entitled 'Concerning quality improvement of the production of machines and consumer goods through the inculcation of methods of artistic construction' called for the rationalisation of the industrial process and the co-ordination of professional and industrial concerns to create a rational and centralised process of *dizain* for goods produced by the Soviet economy (I. Kosheleva in *Rabotnitsa* 1976, no 3, p. 25). The culmination of the rationalisation of the infrastructure necessary for *byt* reform was achieved with the foundation of the All-Union Scientific Research Institute for Technical Aesthetics (VNIITE) in 1962. Its mandate was to provide the expertise of architects, industrial designers, planners, sociologists and historians for institutions such as GOSSTROI and others responsible for the production of consumer goods.

The second flank of the domestic front dealt with pre-existing practices through the arbitration of taste. Literature on household advice revived with numerous books and pamphlets culminating in the Great Soviet Encyclopaedia's popular *Entsiklopedia Domashnego Khoziaistvo*, published first in 1958 and continuously through to the collapse of the Soviet Union. This literature was complemented by the journal *Dekorativnaia Isskustvo*, and various professional journals such as *Tekhnicheskaia Estetika* published by VNIITE. The concerns of *byt* reformists were given frequent coverage in popular women's journals such as *Rabotnitsa* and *Krestianka* as well as other popular media.

To further shore this flank on the domestic front, the institution of the *domkom* was revived with a vigour that could only be dreamt of by earlier *byt* reformers at the time of the first Cultural Revolution. In its new form, the *domkom* became the vehicle through which a community's Party members could actualise *byt* reformist principles at the most immediate point of contact on the domestic front, at the level of the individual household – through household 'raids', 'red corner' lectures and 'socialist competitions' for exemplary standards of *byt* between communities. Altogether the rationalisation of *byt* at the level of infrastructure and taste served to regulate the domestic sphere on every imaginable front. With the establishment of the VNIITE in 1962, this assault was given its final co-ordinated form which through the 1960s and early 1970s attempted to obliterate the domestic realm and vestiges of petit-bourgeois consciousness towards the ontological realisation of full-blown communism.

Eliminating the *Stolovaia:* Monofunctional versus Multifunctional Interior Plans

One of the most significant innovations of the housing boom was the introduction of a variety of open plans in apartment layouts to accommodate different family formations. These attempts were very similar to earlier work by OSA on *Dom Kommuny* emphasising flexibility. One of the most significant aspects of these new plans was the introduction of multifunctional zone planning. Stalinist-era apartment plans were characterised by interiorised single-function and spatially discrete rooms, reminiscent of pre-modernist pre-Revolutionary housing. In the 1920s such plans, categorically decried as petit-bourgeois, were designed to accommodate the segregated nuclear bourgeois family. Now the same monofunctional layout was rejected by *byt* reformers in the late 1950s and early 1960s as 'old-fashioned'. The old apportionment of space with furniture centripetally arranged around the perimeter of the room, focusing on the family, was exploded into a space divided up into functional zones (see figure 22).

The most significant aspect of this explosion was the elimination of the *stolovaia*. New apartment schemes accommodated dining in the kitchen, thereby relegating the family dining ritual to the 'mechanical' regions of the apartment where food was prepared and waste eliminated. The *stolovaia* lost its former spatial and ceremonial centrality in domestic life. If a kitchen was too small for dining, then family meals were accommodated by a folding table stored away and pulled out only when necessary. Permanently standing furniture was placed in a deep recess of the room along a wall; forming a separate functional zone, democratically situated with the other zones of the room with no particular spatial or symbolic emphasis (see figure 22).

Figure 22 'A room with a traditional arrangement [above]. A room with zoned spaces [below]', Merzhanov and Sorokin 1966:19

The Children's Corner

The only area to retain any spatial and symbolic significance was the corner by the window, because of its association with natural light. *Byt* reformers revived an old innovation from the 1920s, the *detskii ugolok* (the children's corner). Here in the most visually prominent and well-lit corner of the room a separate world in miniature reproduced the adult space in which it was embedded. Here the child was under constant display and observation as it imbibed the communist literary classics, surrounded by images of the country while representing the hope of youth and a reinvigorated communist future over the past.

Transformable Furniture

One of the significant innovations in the material culture of the interior was the development of transformable furniture. This was significant in two ways. Firstly, it physically minimised the number of artefacts (i.e. furniture), leaving one piece to function as two or three did in the past. This was part of the general process referred to by *byt* reformists in the late 1970s as the '*razveshchestvleniia*' (de-artefactualization) of the domestic sphere (Travin 1979): the gradual evanescence of physical objects supporting the domestic sphere, which like the state would whither away with the realisation of full communism. Secondly, transformable furniture served to mask functions considered inappropriate or secondary to the primary uses of certain rooms and furniture. These uses always referred to functions not normally considered appropriate to the common room: a couch or book-shelf could convert into a bed, a cabinet into a child's bed and desk, a buffet into a study and a sideboard into a dressing table (see figure 23). Most significantly, the dining table could simply fold up and disappear. Thus a single-room apartment could give the desired appearance of an integrated and spare common room (see Buchli 1997 for a broader discussion).

Household Advice

On the second flank of the domestic front, the regulation of taste was the most important tool for the rationalisation of *byt*. Taste served to regulate and modify pre-existing housing stock and domestic artefacts. Housing and consumer goods were still in shortage during the Khrushchev years – as in the days of the First Five Year Plan, one simply had to make do with what one had. Similarly, the pre-existing stock by

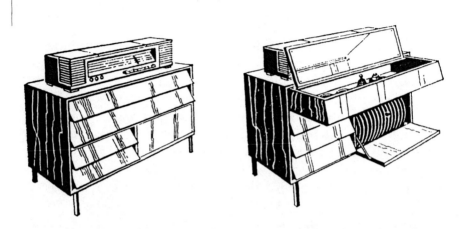

Figure 23 A commode that converts into a hi-fi and dressing table, *Kratkaia Entsiklopedia Domashnego Khoziaistvo*, 1962, vol. 2, p. 1041

virtue of its petit-bourgeois and now Stalinist associations contradicted the renewed ontological development of Soviet society. As before, the way to regulate these vestiges was through taste.

As much as authorities would have dearly loved for people to throw away their old furniture and buy new items designed according to *byt* reformist principles, people tended to only buy things when they needed them at specific life intervals. This meant that, much to the chagrin of *byt* reformers, whenever people moved into new apartments, they brought along with them much of the furniture they had before. As a result the new infrastructure was filled with material culture considered entirely inappropriate for its use according to *byt* reformers. Taste served to discourage the importation of vestigial material culture into these new environments. When that was not possible, household advice stepped in to provide guidance and physically alter pre-existing furniture to conform to *byt* reformist principles.

Exploding the Centripetal Plan

Household advice reinforced architectural attempts to explode the centripetal plan. In terms of the manipulation of material culture, this was by far the simplest way of achieving *byt* reform in the domestic realm: a basic rearrangement of furniture. It required no material inputs on the part of consumers or industry; one could simply break the nucleus of the petit-bourgeois 'hearth' by rearranging furniture, eliminating the *stolovaia* and creating dispersed zones of use in the room (see figure 22).

Elimination

The next step was actually to streamline the number of items of material culture within the apartment. The slogan of the 1920s *'nichego lishnego'* ('nothing superfluous') was constantly invoked by 1960s reformers. The aim was to eliminate as many items of material culture as possible that were associated with petit-bourgeois Stalinist domesticity. All but the most essential items were to be eliminated. This applied to furniture, particularly buffets and *gorki* as well as embroidered napkins, wall rugs, figurines, and various other knick-knacks that proliferated in Stalinist interiors.

Next to be changed were the walls, floors and window treatments. These manipulations required material inputs and were additive rather than subtractive (although their effect was more subtractive in appearance). However, the production of paints and wallpaper designed in accordance with new *byt* reformist aesthetics was sufficient that actualisation of these manipulations was affordable and within means. The elaborate *alfreinaia rabota* (stencilling) of Stalinist interiors was actively discouraged; instead uniform and light surfaces were advised along with appropriate wallpaper and paint products that ensured these schemes were realised.

As with earlier *alfreinaia rabota*, the manipulation of wallpapering and paint radically reconfigured interior architectural space. This achieved the most effect with the least amount of material and labour input. As the maintenance of wall surfaces was considered part of the tenant's responsibilities the cost of this most impressive of manipulations of interior architectural space was borne directly by the tenant, and not the city council or state enterprise. In addition *byt* 'raids' by members of the *domkom* often addressed the need for constant painting and wallpapering. Guides for *domkom* Party members suggested that walls be resurfaced every spring, ensuring on a regular basis the single most spatially significant alteration of domestic space. These injunctions to redecorate were timed to coincide with communist holidays such as May Day or the anniversary of the October Revolution. Thus, seemingly banal activities such as wallpapering served at once to reaffirm the pursuit of private domesticity and give concrete expression to the construction of socialism, thereby legitimating the Soviet state.

Even without the new and relatively costly inputs of *byt* reformist artefacts – such as the new furniture produced in the late 1950s and early 1960s – individuals were vigorously encouraged to realise many *byt* reformist principles with the minimum amount of material and labour inputs. As before, a cosmology perceived to be inscribed within the material order could be entirely subverted with a few strategic and ephemeral material gestures.

Ethics

Complementing the emerging literature on household advice was a new emphasis on ethics; focusing on petit-bourgeois consciousness, commodity fetishism and irrational consumer behaviour. If mere household advice could not induce desired *byt* reforms, ethical norms were marshalled to encourage a specific relationship with the material world that ensured the moral preconditions for *byt* reform. Petit-bourgeois consciousness once more became a problem in the eyes of theoreticians and ethicists. As always, petit-bourgeois consciousness referred to the vestiges of the past hindering the development of socialism. In its re-problematisation in the late 1950s and early 1960s, it served as a gloss for Stalinism as well. Thus the phenomenon of Stalin and the cult of personality was dismissed as the result of petit-bourgeois consciousness not having been fully rooted out of the collective Soviet psyche. Hence the heaviness, ornamentalism and 'superfluous pomposity' attributed to the monumental architecture of the Stalin period were rejected as petit-bourgeois. However, the equation of the Stalinist period with a time when petit-bourgeois consciousness ran riot was never explicitly stated. Certain superficial elements intimately connected with the period (such as those mentioned) served as the metonymic butt of criticism. It was not till much later under the Glasnost of Gorbachev's Perestroika that commentators such as Starostenko could make explicit this connection (Starostenko 1990).

The Revival of the *Domkom*

The *domkom* had survived intact up to the late 1950s, but had lost much of the radical autonomy it had when it was first founded during the 1920s co-operative housing movement. In the wake of the rapid rationalisation of the domestic sphere under Khrushchev, the *domkom* received an exceptional new mandate (see Buchli 1997 for a broader discussion). The Party revived an old self-supporting and self-financing institution that could effectively service and maintain the housing stock, while simultaneously ensuring the realisation of *byt* reforms. All housing blocks had their own *domkom*. However, from the figures presented by Aleksandrov (Aleksandrov 1968: 5–7), it is clear that only a minority participated to the full extent advocated by the Party. Though participation was limited, when realised it was very successful in introducing *byt* reform and communalism in daily life. The Nark-omfin was one of the first few hundreds of buildings which fully participated in the revival of the *domkom* in Moscow, and as will become evident in chapter 8, the effort was very successful.

Brezhnev: 'The Little Deal' and the Reassessment of *Byt* Reformist Practices

On 14 October 1964, Nikita Khrushchev was ousted from power and replaced by Leonid Brezhnev. From this date forward, historians and other observers refer to this period as the end of the 'Thaw' and the beginning of the '*zastoi*' or 'period of stagnation'. James Millar (1985:694–706) has referred to this new era as the time of the 'little deal' in contrast to Vera Dunham's 'big deal': her characterisation of the material accommodation between the Stalinist *apparat* and the Nomenklatura (Dunham 1976). This 'little deal' essentially slowed the strident pace of Khrushchev-era reform destabilising the status quo inherited from the Stalin period. It describes the efforts of the bureaucratic establishment to achieve stability in what was an increasingly threatening environment. This process has been similarly described by Victor Zaslavsky as the 'organised consensus' by which the Brezhnev establishment perpetuated itself through a series of complex social accommodations (Zaslavsky 1982). Under Khrushchev, wage differentials were low during the booming period of post-war recovery. At the time of Brezhnev's ascent, these small wage differentials were less satisfying to aspiring bureaucratic elites. Increased defence expenditure related to the Cold War along with gradually diminishing rates of economic expansion, resulted in fewer goods and services in circulation (Millar 1985:695). The systematic results of these accom-modations were increased wage differentials, a tolerance of quasi-legal perks for elites, and an official blind-eye turned away from low-level shadow economic activity (Millar 1985:697).

In terms of *byt* reform the contrast between Dunham's 'big deal' and Millar's 'little deal' is particularly apposite, as it conveys the spirit with which aspiring elites ensured their access to privileges against threats to their burgeoning authority and diminished access to resources. In terms of *byt* reformist literature, this involved a certain easing of the tone of debates in harsh 'objective' terms characterising the spirit of populist de-Stalinization under Khrushchev. Subjective notions of taste were reintroduced whose rules for application would be more easily controlled by those in greater possession of cultural and political capital (see Bourdieu 1984). This accommodation had its benefits. It justified contradictions between the materialist aspirations of the Stalinist period with revived *byt* reformist principles arbitrarily modulated by individuals in possession of sufficient political and cultural capital. Thus the Communist Party and state bureaucracy could control the appearance of contradiction through taste rather than by relying on intelligible, transparent and 'objective' criteria. In short, a guarded reprieve was in evidence – from the revived denotative understandings of material culture of the first and second Cultural Revolutions, wherein the attributes of 'petit-bourgeois consciousness' were fixed, clearly delineated and 'objectified', back to a more contextual and indexical understanding characteristic of the Stalin years. However, its social effects under these conditions were exclusionary rather than enfranchising as they had been earlier.

Dom Novogo Byta

This shift back resulted in troublesome and noticeable contradictions. This was nowhere more evident than in the controversies, a few years after Brezhnev's rise in the late 1960s, surrounding the *Dom Novogo Byta* (DNB or 'House of the New Lifestyle') movement. The DNB movement revived the *dom kommuna* of the late 1920s in the midst of the rapidly expanding industrialised housing stock of the 1960s. The first DNB proposal was submitted by N. Osterman et al. in 1964 to an open all-Union competition for collective housing for 2,000 inhabitants (see Meierson et al.'s proposal which won and N. Bant et al.'s proposal a year earlier (Gradov 1968:84–5)). Osterman's DNB was a literal translation of the more extreme fully socialised *dom kommuny* of the late 1920s. Osterman et al. had three unit types that were all without kitchens but included minor accommodations for 'episodic' cooking. People were expected to take their meals in a number of different communal dining facilities. This plan attempted to realise the 1961 Twenty-Second Party Congress objectives to return to Leninist principles: 'communal dining in the course of 10–15 years [that is, between 1971 and 1976] will become the dominant form of eating in comparison to dining at home' (Communist Party of the Soviet Union 1961:393). However, the DNB movement rapidly came under considerable criticism from within the Party establishment. It was decried as inherently elitist (echoing the resentment of elitist communards in the 1920s), and unfeasible in contemporary conditions despite its impeccable Leninist principles and the era of full communism rapidly approaching (in 1988).

The DNB movement also extended to planning where many of the disurbanist schemes of the late 1920s were reintroduced by architects in the mid-1960s. Schemes revolved around housing towers 87 and 100 storeys high. Children's dormitories, old-age homes, and communal dining and social facilities were immediately clustered within towers. Urban space was to be so concentrated and collectivised that the city would almost dissipate into nature (Gradov 1968). An illustration of this new landscape presents the viewer with an idyllic scene of lakeside trails and forests and not a building in sight (Gradov 1968:184). The result would be a 'higher socialised organisation of labour, daily life and recreation, a synthesis of Nature and technology, life in a natural setting - such are the main characteristics of the collectivised city' (Gradov 1968:184, see also Buchli 1998). For all practical purposes the classical city of bourgeois society would whither away, much like the state in Trotskyist and Anarchist projections (Kropotkin 1995), into a perfect realm of socialised human society merged with Nature: unalienated and without contradiction. This applied not only to buildings, but also to the world of goods within and the creation of the post-artefactual world.

Creating the Post-artefactual World

The revival of *byt* reforms continued unabated, despite conflicting Party rhetoric. When issues became public and were widely discussed in the popular press (such as the controversies surrounding the DNB), reaction quickly followed. However, within professional circles – far from the popular press – the issues of *byt* reform were vigorously pursued. One of the most salient and innovative aspects of the development of *byt* reformist thought was the *razveshchestvlenie* or 'de-artefactualisation of the material world'. This was the creation of a socialist utopia devoid of objects and the dangers of commodity fetishism.

Critical to the understanding of this concept of de-artefactualisation of the material world was the concept of the *material'no-veshchnaia sreda* (MVS) or 'the material object sphere'. The MVS served as a gloss for what can be understood as material culture; however, the Russian term conveys the understanding of objects in relationship to each other: an environmental system much like a biosphere within which human beings interact. The study of the MVS, therefore, came to be the focus of a number of disciplines: architecture, sociology, economics, design, archaeology and ethics (Travin 1979:7–14).

The rise in consumer goods with an appropriate rise in socialist consciousness (which would permit 'rational' and socialist use of these goods) was perceived as a problem of singular importance to the human negotiation of the MVS. In this respect Travin quotes Brezhnev at the Twenty-Fifth Party Congress: 'It is at once vital that the rise of material possibilities is continuously in line with the rise in the ideological, ethical and cultural level of the people. Otherwise we could be susceptible to the recidivism of philistine and petit-bourgeois psychology' (Travin 1979:11).

Thus to avoid slipping into petit-bourgeois commodity fetishism, the successful socialist negotiation of the socialist MVS would require its 'razveshchestvlenie' or 'de-artefactualization' (Travin 1979:99): '"De-artefactualization" in the full sense of the word denotes the disappearance of artefacts from the system of social relations, when the relations between artefacts will be entirely displaced by relations between people' (i.e. the pure state of unalienated social relations envisioned by Marx).

The creation of the post-artefactual world would involve the production of multiple-use goods rather than many single-use objects (such as the commode on figure 23). With the steady condensation of the material world on the basis of innovative and socialised technologies, human society would gradually approximate a de-materialised MVS. However, until that point was attained, the MVS would simple condense and evaporate as cities and the state apparatus would. Humans would exist in an unalienated state with each other and Nature: 'Removing the borders between the artefactual sphere of the household from the true sphere of nature, will become one of the key factors in the conception of the household of the future' (Travin 1979:112).

One means of realising this condensation of the MVS was A.B. Riabushin's concept of the 'zhilishche-teatr' or 'household-theatre'. (Riabushin 1976:325–53). Riabushin was critical of the multifunctional zoning of the 1950s. He argued that the condensational effect of multifunctional zoning, with its transformable furniture, was only palliative and predicated on what he called an 'artefactualist' orientation in the design professions (Travin 1979:107). Consequently, commodity fetishism was still a problem as 'herds of wooden Mastodons are released within the domestic sphere, where the consumer is humbled to the position of an observer in his own personal museum where he is no longer the master of his things' (Travin 1979:107).

The '*zhilishche-teatr*' posited by Riabushin would involve maintaining multifunctional zones in the apportionment of domestic space. Artefacts for the support of activities in these zones, however, would be stored in central places where they would be maintained and distributed as needed along a time axis, as opposed to those artefacts permanently residing in the domestic sphere. This 'extrapolation' of artefacts of domestic use would exploit the technologies of automation developed in the late 1970s and early 1980s. It would follow the centralising trend of the day, where services and maintenance were increasingly to be found and exploited in central places. Thus domestic artefacts could be delivered as needed into domestic settings from a central distribution network, realising certain 1920s *byt* reformist ideals. Travin quotes B. Kushner, a *byt* theoretician of the 1920s: 'The collectivisation of consumption will be facilitated not by certain kinds of objects, but by the possibility to replace certain specific and differing objects, continuously changing in their place in space, unavoidable for the different life processes (sleep, work, eating, rest) of human beings. For that we do not need beds, tables, sofas, and chairs to exist as objects' (quoted in Travin 1979:110).

However, theoreticians did not mean to banish individual material objects that served cultural or emotionally mnemonic functions. Such objects could be preserved: 'When we spoke of the expulsion of things, we spoke only in the first place of the overcoming of commodity fetishism and not of the obliteration of things entirely *per se*' (Travin 1979:113).

The condensation of material goods and the ensuing freedom of time would result in the liberation of the human spirit, freed from the friction caused by the negotiation of the physical world. Individuals would finally be able to realise and develop all aspects of their being. Quoting Marx and Engels, Travin writes that people 'will have true wealth - time not taken up by productive labour, but free for satisfying activity, with the result that people will be able to develop and act freely' (quoted in Travin 1979:113).

The conciliatory climate of the Brezhnev years evinced a certain degree of backtracking and accommodation in realising *byt* reforms, despite the existence of the requisite industrial infrastructure. A number of theoreticians made palliative gestures to certain aspects of reform.

One of these was E.M. Zuikova. Zuikova, writing in 1974, acknowledged the desirability of communal child-rearing and dining. She recognised that the nuclear family and the individual self-sufficient household under contemporary conditions could not simply disappear, as some of the supporters of the DNB proposed. Zuikova was more pragmatic and proposed a number of strategic interventions that would come close to realising *byt* reform principles. Without invoking the Taylorist principles of *NOT*, Zuikova advocated the rationalisation of housework, recalling earlier attempts to rationalise women's domestic labour in order to permit the entry of women into socialised life. As in the 1920s, the problem was with women's roles, and not with men's. Men in the 1970s were not seen as playing a role in the restructuring of the domestic 'hearth'. To involve men in the process could only be seen as counterproductive, dragging them down from public socialised roles into the unsocialised, individual, petit-bourgeois sphere of the domestic 'hearth'. Rather, Zuikova proposes *bytovye asotsiatsii* (*byt* associations) or household collectives (Zuikova 1974:70) instead of the DNB which she criticises in terms of the anti-Trotskyist rhetoric of the late 1920s (Zuikova 1974:79). According to Zuikova's estimates, these collectives would entirely collectivise and automate domestic functions by the year 2000 (Zuikova 1974:74) and effectively free women from the shackles of the domestic 'hearth'.

Men and Domesticity

Later in the Brezhnev period, the active role of men in the domestic sphere was considered for the first time. The reasons for this reassessment of gender roles are complex. Emerging post-war Soviet feminism may have combined with the overwhelming crisis of the 'double burden' affecting Soviet women to reconsider men's roles. In addition, the gradual ambivalence towards the domestic sphere suggested that, for better or worse, the 'double burden' would not disappear soon. As it became less pathologised, male involvement in this realm may have been perceived as less problematic. Household advice in the early 1980s began to urge women to include men in the negotiation of the domestic sphere. However, traditional gender roles were not to be violated; rather traditional masculine skills associated with the public socialist sphere were to be harnessed in the creation of the 'hearth' (see L. Orlova in Rabotnitsa 1982, no. 3, p. 30). Men could bring these skills into the 'hearth' and exert a rationalising influence. They could make furniture when adequate furniture was not to be had;

construct built-in closets when they were in need; and repair electrical equipment when repair services were lacking (Rabotnitsa, 1984 no. 11, p. 26). As one caption reads in an issue of *Rabotnitsa* 'Valia is busy in the kitchen, but Gena does the job of ten repair men' (Rabotnitsa 1984, no. 11, p. 27).

Perestroika, 'Rebuilding' and the Repudiation of *Byt* Reform

Mikhail Gorbachev became General Secretary of the Communist Party on 11 March, 1985, following the successive deaths of Yuri Andropov and Konstantin Chernenko. His ascent marks the period of Perestroika (rebuilding) through the ideological vehicle of Glasnost (openness). Gorbachev attempted to revitalise the Party and social life following two decades of an uneasy re-accommodation of Leninist principles. 'The period of stagnation' was broken by exposing the contradictions of this re-accommodation, through the policy of Glasnost, in order literally and metaphorically to rebuild (*perestroit'*) the socialist project and revive the classical Leninist principles which inspired it. However, established political and bureaucratic power bases were intimately implicated in this process. Perestroika would thereby challenge the legitimacy of the Party and government apparatus whose positions would be undermined by an objectivising reformist enterprise. This would disable local and arbitrary interpretations of the socialist enterprise upon which state legitimacy and socialism were forged.

In the course of seventy-odd years, the discourse of socialist construction legitimised the power of Party and bureaucratic elites through at least two cycles of empowerment and disenfranchisement. An attempt to invigorate the socialist enterprise a third time, however, fell flat. The project of socialist construction could not be sustained in light of three successive exposés of its contradictions. In short, the socialist enterprise itself became too uncomfortably implicated under Perestroika. The untenable climate of contradiction, revealed by Glasnost, introduced the possibility of alternatives provided by the West. Legitimating socialist discourses had simply been exhausted by this process. Hence the October coup of 1990, the discursive rejection of the socialist enterprise and the very dismantling of the Soviet socialist state.

The consequences of Perestroika for the process of *byt* reform similarly saw the rejection of the validity of the socialist *byt* reformist enterprise. This resulted in a profound reassessment of the 'hearth' and petit-bourgeois consciousness in a Soviet society which in the Russian Republic was rapidly beginning to see itself as 'Russian' once again. The popular media reflected the beginnings of a serious questioning of the official project of *byt* reform. The joys of the domestic 'hearth' were enthusiastically and unconditionally celebrated once more, and notions of petit-bourgeois consciousness changed. Attitudes, behaviour and artefacts that were once considered unquestionably petit-bourgeois were reconsidered in a positive light. Individuals came to reconsider their attitudes and behaviour as categorically and unproblematically petit-bourgeois (NDKOH).

Household advice for this period does an about-face. Advice in the late 1980s, once again, called for the radical restructuring of the existing base of material culture and architecture in order to accommodate changing needs. L. Shevtstova in an article entitled 'Tear down the stereotypes' (Rabotnitsa 1989: no. 1 p. 23) referred to the body of proscriptions characteristic of the Khrushchev and Brezhnev eras in a thinly veiled manner. Here she interviews a man whose hobby is homecraft and profession is the design of interiors. He calls for the radical restructuring of the existing stock arguing that 'the problem is that the size of furniture being produced now does not correspond with the size of our apartments'. Shevtsova vigorously urges the reader 'not to be afraid of walls – with the help of an architect you can knock out a niche or move a door'. In response to the previous two decades of household proscriptions Shevtsova urges 'as soon as we overcome all the many "forbiddens", and realise that everything is possible, everything, all that we desire, then our apartments will become comfortable and beautiful. But this is not the most important – that we free ourselves, and thrive within this outer comfort and experience inner. We will have ceased to have been slaves to our *byt*' (Shevtsova in Rabotnitsa 1989, no. 1, p. 23).

The New Role of Men in the Domestic Sphere

At this point it is vital to note the gender of the voices involved, and the gender of the agents performing Perestroika in the home. Throughout the entire history of the Soviet discourse on domesticity, men were conspicuously absent. As agents in the public sphere outside the home, their role was entirely insignificant in the problematisation of the domestic sphere; it was the woman/housewife who was the pathologised object of reform. Under Brezhnev this began to change and men were gradually incorporated into the maintenance of the domestic 'hearth'. Under Perestroika men figured prominently. Despite this fact, men's roles in the domestic sphere were quite explicitly described in accepted gendered terms. That is, they did not cook, clean, take care of children and the like. Rather they performed gender-appropriate tasks and built shelves, made furniture, painted walls, resurfaced floors and tore out walls. In short, men were the agents of Perestroika in that they literally as well as metaphorically *perestroili* (restructured) the 'hearth' and all that implied to facilitate new forms of family, social and political life.

All this knocking-out of doors and tearing-down of walls, however, was to realise the spatial arrangements of pre-Revolutionary petit-bourgeois interiors (see caricature in Shvetsova in Rabotnitsa, 1989, no.1, p. 23). Elaborate entries and parlours (*gostinaia*) were created, focused towards social display:

> At one time the *gostinaia* was the place where the face of the host could be seen. In it were the fireplace, piano, parquet floor, expensive chandeliers and *objets de luxe*. Our psychology has changed, our material base, and finally the amount of space. Everything has changed, except for the idea that there should be a *gostinaia* – the face of the owner of the house. (Rabotnitsa, 1989, no. 8, pg. 7)

Shevtsova above attempts to dismantle the petit-bourgeois stereotype of years of *byt* reform and revive the institution of the *gostinaia* as an integral aspect of domestic comfort and home life. The accompanying photographs show a standard Soviet apartment interior after renovations which create a *gostinaia* specifically for social display with an entrance way as a 'visiting card'. Here elaborate parquet is imitated in paint on the floors; the appearance of brocade-panelled walls is created with wallpaper and paint in the manner of Stalinist *alfreinaia rabota*, along with similarly panelled ceilings. The new male, and officially sanctioned, interventions in the domestic interior effectively subverted the original rationalist spaces of post-war housing with the same degree of power earlier interventions wielded in subverting Constructivist spaces at the Narkomfin (Rabotnitsa 1989, no. 7, p. 20; Rabotnitsa 1989, no. 8 pp. 6–7; Rabotnitsa 1989, no. 2, p. 20).

The new role men play in the domestic sphere within the confines of traditional Soviet gender roles is quite nicely summarised in this translation of a passage of household advice for women:

> If the men of the family are used to carpentry, it is easy to create a kitchen, for example, in the style of a Russian *izba* - one can create out of planks a massive table on heavy legs, with long benches along the side. And you [the housewife] can make drapes of linen, embroidered napkins, and arrange clay toys, [ ] and decorated plates on shelves. And don't be afraid of too many knick-knacks [after seventy years of communist battle against petit-bourgeois domestic clutter!], they only emphasise the beauty of the chosen style.
>
> According to your desire attempt to create in your kitchen a 'dacha veranda': a round table, wicker chairs, or stools painted light shades, embroidered napkins on the buffet and on the shelves, a light 'coquettish' table cloth on the table. (V. Burmistrov and M. Makeichik in Rabotnitsa 1988, no. 5, p. 7)

By invoking the traditional Russian *izba* (the embodiment *par excellence* of the pre-Revolutionary patriarchal order) and the dacha (the antithesis of *byt* reformist urban interiors) household advice literally sought to refigure the post-war stock of *byt* reformist housing. Traditional East-Slavic peasant roles were maintained: men worked with wood creating the carpentry, and women worked with cloth to create the elements of *uiut*. Illustrations mostly show men at work, while women take on a secondary role, creating the infill to achieve *uiut* with sole responsibility for its maintenance.

Similarly, radical changes in housing law and ownership gave a legal basis with which to assert individual autonomous housing at the expense of the vast stock of socialised housing. In addition the actual stock of material objects available changed considerably with the increasing proliferation of goods produced by new co-operative enterprises emerging under Perestroika. The informal non-centralised sector was legally formalised and an increasing number of foreign goods became available through thriving black markets and as wells as COMECON imports. Foreign sales catalogues and literature illustrating different bodies of domestic material culture and its uses, along with more frequent foreign travel, increased knowledge of the range of material alternatives. L. Ershova in 1988 writes about how impossible it is for anyone to realise good taste, frustrated by the incompatibility of state-produced industrial goods with people's desires. 'Objects ought to be beautiful, comfortable and fashionable. But for light industry these requirements have not been fulfilled' (Rabotnitsa 1988, no. 3, p. 28). In this climate, Ershova notes that the new co-operatives of Perestroika are able to provide goods that are more in tune with individual desires despite their high purchase prices.

Next, we will look at how these revived *byt* reformist ideals took hold after Stalin's death – how they were enacted at the Narkomfin and differentially deployed by individuals picking, choosing and combining them according to varying, partial and at times conflicting under-standings of how the material world is configured; thereby realising various changing and contingent domestic strategies with which to cope with the vicissitudes of social change culminating in the final collapse of the Soviet Union and the Soviet socialist project in 1991.

eight

The Narkomfin Communal House and the Material Culture of De-Stalinisation

Developments in the House in the Wake of Stalin's Death

The death of Stalin had little impact on the Narkomfin and its management. The Council of Ministries, which owned and maintained the Narkomfin, was unperturbed by his death, the subsequent interregnum and reshuffling of power within the Party hierarchy. Photographs and informants all report that the grounds were as well-maintained as ever with manicured lawns, tennis courts and fragrant lilac bushes (see figure 20). Repairs occurred regularly and promptly. Service staff such as the cleaners, janitors and doormen were retained and paid. The only change was the installation of an elevator along the southernmost stairwell, making life easier for an increasingly older community (see appendix). Most people look back on this period in the 1950s and 1960s as the halcyon days of the complex, when everything was in good order, functioned properly and was well-maintained. In physical terms, alterations to the site only occurred in the wake of very significant administrative changes. In 1961 the House was handed over to the ZhEK no. 6 (local housing administration). The remaining communal block remained with the Soviet of Ministries and was used as their printing press. (See Afanasiev Archive, document 32, p. 2).

As regards the *prachechnaia* (laundry facility), there is barely any documentary material. Presumably, along with the Narkomfin resid-ential building, it was given over to the ZhEK no. 6 in 1961. Today the *prachechnaia* is rented out by the local council to one of the new commercial enterprises which emerged after the collapse of the Soviet

Union. According to reports, the *prachechnaia* ceased to function as a laundry facility about the time of the 1961 transition. This would suggest that it was given over to the city council in the same year and put to some other use and reconfigured into offices for use by the city council, or for lease to other agencies (e.g. the TsBNTI, The Central Bureau of Scientific-Technical Information).

However this near-realised Arcadian idyll was belied by the fact that in the neighbourhood there were a number of homeless people. In 1964, there were 81 families (a total of 172 individuals including 7 children) who lived in cellars under very poor, dark and damp conditions. For 43 of these families, there was no glimmer of hope as they were not even on a waiting list for housing elsewhere. They did not obtain the legal right to domicile, and were invisible to the authorities and lost through the social safety net promised by the Party and the state. This was a galling issue under socialism and required special consideration. A member of the area's *domkom* was put in charge to monitor and help alleviate the situation of the homeless in the 1960s. (Refer to Afanasiev Archive document 15, p. 3; for more information concerning homelessness in the neighbourhood see the *Protokol* of the 8th. Session of the Krasnopresnenskii Raion Soviet of Labourers' Deputies of 10 March , 1970 [TsGAOR, SSSR, g. Moskvy, Fond 754, opis 1, delo 129, list 61–7].)

Almost immediately following the handover in 1961, the existing *domkom* began to take over the duties of management previously performed by the Soviet of Ministries. (See Afanasiev Archive, document 15, p. 6). Presumably the Soviet of Ministries deaccessioned its properties and their management to city councils as a cost- cutting measure (see Heller and Nekrich 1986:552–4,559; Nove 1988: 59–64, 77 for discussions of changes in the administration of the Soviet of Ministries). It devolved property and services to local communities which then had to bear the cost of labour and materials in the name of *byt* reform and the revival of voluntaristic socialist ideals, repeating the movement towards voluntarism in the late 1920s, when the goals of the Cultural Revolution were too expensive for enterprises to bear and were borne by groups of individuals themselves.

Changing Terms of Performance

With the 'Thaw' the terms of socialist performance had changed considerably, having exhausted themselves through the course of the Terror. The sphere of socialist performance retreated back to the domestic realm where it initially stood during the height of the first Cultural Revolution. The material expression of this performance also ceased to take the form of bodies of individuals purged in order to realise socialism. This is not to say that 'alien' social elements were not rooted out, imprisoned, tortured and executed. This process continued, but not with the same ferocity, as has been well documented in the dissident literature of the Khrushchev and Brezhnev years. However, the performative space and material had noticeably shifted back onto the domestic realm. Who people were was not so important as how they presented themselves through hygiene, dress and their manipulation of material goods, particularly in their use of domestic space.

The Social Profile of Inhabitants

Over the course of the post-Stalin period, there was a general tendency for successive occupations at the Narkomfin to be of decreasing social status. Earlier higher-status inhabitants – members of the administrative intelligentsia – tended to get other and better apartments in Moscow, particularly in the wake of the housing boom and the transfer of the building's ownership in 1961. For this period many communal units remained, only becoming single by gradual abandonment and in some cases entirely abandoned.

K-units

The K-units (being some of the largest and best appointed of the Narkomfin units) were often inhabited by households of rather high rank, particularly in the case of those continuously occupied by the same individual household. The fact that some high-ranking households could maintain continuous individual occupancy and others did not, would seem to reflect how well such families weathered the Purges, determining which units remained individual and which communal. Three of the ten did remain as individual households. However, two were occupied by individual households purged in 1937. They were reoccupied by single households again either by way of rank and connections such as the NKVD household. All the other post-Stalin communal K-units became communal after being reoccupied by lower-ranking households in the wake of higher-ranking individual households purged in 1937. Amongst these post-war communal K-unit households there was a marked tendency to resort to strategies of interiorisation; further withdrawing and differentiating space through the use of wallpapers, paint, curtains and partitions.

K-units remained occupied for much longer than one would expect because of their occupants' relatively high social rank. However, those units that became communal after the Purges were still occupied by white-collar workers, albeit of lower rank as evidenced by their right to less *zhilploshchad'*. However, in the post-war housing boom those who had the means left, and their units were occupied by households of notably lower status, such as those units headed by a boiler maker, mechanic and laundress.

2-F-units and Expanded K-units

As these units were of comparable in size and amenities to K-units (despite a difference architectonically and in plan), they were as a rule occupied by high-ranking households. All of these units remained continuously occupied after the death of Stalin and their households tended not to move into new post-war housing.

F-units

The social composition of the F-units remained essentially unchanged immediately after Stalin's death. The vast majority of F-units were headed by white-collar workers of the administrative intelligentsia. However, when given the opportunity to move to better apartments during the housing boom several years later, few remained. In many instances they were replaced by households of similar rank. However, just as often they were replaced by households whose heads were mostly male labourers. Throughout the 1980s a number of these units were vacated as conditions deteriorated and other apartments became available, eventually becoming entirely abandoned like the ground-floor units

Gender

It becomes clear, from looking at the registries, that *byt* reformist modernist understandings of femininity had truly begun to wane. Women began to represent themselves as dependants of their husbands, adopting their spouses' names instead of asserting their own. In most cases there were very few women registered as heads of households. Also, those registered as employed were typically in lower positions than their husbands. There were a few hold-outs amongst families of the original settlement but they were overwhelmed by new women, usually of rural origin, whose different understandings of femininity were more in tune with earlier Stalinist ideals.

With the resurgence of *byt* reform following Stalin's death it is clear, despite the rhetorical echoes of 1920s *byt* reformist ideals of femininity, that these were not acted upon at the Narkomfin. A tension is certainly palpable between those social roles envisioned for women and the actual conditions of daily life. There was a great diversity of contradictory social and domestic roles which heterosexual women assumed across a broad range. At one end there was the full careerist professional with her own name, head of household (with or without spouse), representing the pinnacle of *byt* reformist femininity. Further along the scale, there was the professional woman and household head who nonetheless maintained a social dependence on her husband and assumed his name, combining *byt* reformist aspirations with ascendant Stalinist norms. Towards the other end was the dependent wife with her husband's name, who laboured to supplement the household income instead of having a career. Finally, there was the dependent housewife carrying her husband's name who did not work in the public realm at all, and more than any other realised the ideals of Stalinist femininity.

The Apportionment of Space

Following the death of Stalin in 1953, the apportionment of space within ground-floor units remained extremely tight, with segregated nuclear family units excluded from the use of the communal facilities of the building. Considered undesirable because of their location on the ground floor, they were mostly vacated by 1977 once other housing was available (with the exception of one particularly low-status household which left in 1986).

K-units

All the post-Stalin era K-units experienced further segmentation of their original plans. This involved the sealing of the main room from the galleries on the second floor, which created three entirely discrete rooms in addition to the bath/toilet, kitchen and circulation spaces. In one K-unit, the main room was segmented horizontally to create two rooms on top of each other: a creative response to divorce and the impossibility of getting two new apartments, thereby creating two households out of the same *zhilploshchad'* .

Out of all the K-units only one retained the original *fibrolit* flooring in combination with oil paint. All the other units for which there is information were parqueted at the initiative of the inhabitants and retained to the present day. Four of these parquet-floored units were combined with oil-painted walls, while only two were combined with wallpaper. Of the K-units examined, none exhibited the distinctly high-Stalinist combination of parquet and *trompe l'œil*. Here the combination of high-status households performing *byt* reformist domestic strategies, to varying degrees, would indicate a reluctance to give expression to their domestic strategies in terms of high-Stalinist expressions emphasising segmentation and the hard separation of the domestic from the public realm. The modernist 'bourgeois' nature of these units might have already facilitated a certain degree of interiorisation, as evidenced by centripetal plans that did not require further interiorised arrangements as in other units not so readily predisposed (such as F-units).

The Stairwell Units and the Miliutin Penthouse

Of all the units in the Narkomfin, the stairwell units and the Miliutin Penthouse experienced minimal physical alterations. Only a third of them underwent segmentation in any way. Two of these were expanded K-units with walled-in common rooms. In one instance the main room was further divided horizontally, creating two rooms from the same legal *zhilploshchad'*. One 2-F unit was rather minimally segmented by the creation of a corridor so that the two rooms could be independently reached from each other. Of the extended K-units, a fair majority retained traditional Stalinist-era centripetal plans highlighting the autonomy of the nuclear family and its segregation from the public realm, while only three exhibited modernist sectional plans.

Among the 2-F stairwell units, floor and wall surfaces were extremely variable. Only one unit retained the original *fibrolit* and oil-paint combination. A fair number did retain the originally flooring in various combinations with wallpaper, *trompe l'oeil* and oil paint. The rest were redone in parquet at the initiative of the inhabitants during the Stalin years, and remained that way throughout the post-Stalin period. Of the parquet-floored units, the majority were combined with wallpaper. Only one was combined with oil paint while another had the very high Stalinist combination of parquet and *trompe l'œil*. The rather heterogeneous occupancy of these units entailed a broad range of domestic responses within their walls, relating to the varying degrees of interiorising and exteriorising strategies pursued.

F-units

All the post-Stalin era F-units experienced some form of segmentation. This was typically achieved in a majority of cases by the construction of a wall and a door creating an entirely discrete bedroom (see figure 16). Exceptions were four units which maintained the integrity of the original plan but accommodated a certain differentiation of space by the installation of curtains: a practice consistent with the architect's original intentions (see figure 9). When need be, the two spaces could be differentiated (see figure 18). This solution (though only carried through in four post-Stalin-era households) conformed to the architect's own suggestions and maintained the original exteriorising dynamic of these spaces.

The F-units were almost evenly split between traditional Stalinist-era centripetal arrangements and modernist sectional ones. Only four units retained the original *fibrolit* flooring. Despite the extreme durability of this material and its excellent preservation, the remaining units had parquet installed. The wall treatments in combination with the surviving modernist *fibrolit* floor are quite varied. They range from the originally conceived oil paints to wallpaper; and sometimes to the very unusual combination of *fibrolit* with Stalinist *trompe l'œil*. The rest of the units are more or less evenly divided by combinations of parquet with paper, parquet with oil, and the very high-Stalinist combination of parquet and *trompe l'œil*.

The Narkomfin *Domkom*

The Narkomfin *domkom* organised people to perform socialism according to local ambitions and requirements. The *domkom* stressed the correct socialist use of space, and suggested appropriate renovations at the occupant's expense. In short, each individual was encouraged in the performance of socialism. This was mediated by the rationalising actions of the *domkom* and its diffusion of a locally understood socialist spatial competence. The participation of inhabitants in these competitive performances of socialism was further facilitated by involvement in 'socialist competition' between communities. For example, the 58 apartments of the Narkomfin, with 178 residents competing, would sign documents to engage in socialist competition in *byt* with the 51 apartments of Corpus 10, the Leontovich building, across the park (Afanasiev Archive, document 15, p. 6). In this way the rationalising work of the domestic sphere was linked to public and communal action and renewed efforts towards the exteriorisation of social life and action, gaining momentum in the Khrushchev years.

The reorganised *domkom* of 1962 encompassed not only the territory of the Narkomfin but a number of surrounding buildings as well. At its head was a retired Party member who lived in one of the K-units of the Narkomfin. Various voluntary commissions comprised of residents in the territory of the *domkom* (*uchastok*) reported directly to him, such as the housing, library, landscape, sanitary, social welfare, and fire commissions. The most interesting of these for the purposes of this study was the housing commission. It would conduct mass-cultural work through lectures and meetings on holidays, interpersonal relations, the culture of *byt*, and the maintenance of the housing stock. This commission more than any other played the leading role in the local rationalisation of socialist performance in the domestic sphere. The housing commission was headed by an activist from one of the 2-F-units (Afanasiev archive, document 15, pp. 3–4). She was empowered to interpret *byt* reform for the Narkomfin and the *uchastok*. She co-ordinated the efforts of inhabitants towards the performance of socialism amongst themselves, and in socialist competition with other communities. She thereby established the local means by which the *byt* reformist exteriorisation of social life would be realised by the community.

The Organisation of the Narkomfin Domkom

The organisers of the Narkomfin *domkom* were volunteers and generally Party members. Work in the *domkom* was thus an expression of one's commitment to Party social work, and was inherently antithetical to the 'self-absorbed', private and non-social realm of petit-bourgeois domesticity. The activities of the *domkom* were essentially rationalising. Its purpose was to articulate the common good of the community, and organise itself and the community to realise this objective. The head of the *domkom* was a Party member elected by a vote of the assembled community. Although membership in the *domkom* administration was voluntary, participation in many of the activities it organised was to varying degrees mandatory. One was not necessarily required to participate in the photographers club, but the *subbotniki* (communal property maintenance) organised by the *domkom* was strongly encouraged as part of one's tenancy agreement (Directive of the Soviet of Ministries, RSFSR, 18 October 1962, no. 1390 in Afanasiev Archive, document 59, pp. 15–16). According to the same directives, tenants were required to open their apartments without hindrance to inspection by *domkom* appointees as well as workers of the housing commission (ibid. 16). Thus the compulsory rationalisation of the domestic sphere and its exteriorisation were ensured.

The *domkom* could on behalf of the community impose sanctions on individuals believed to violate norms of 'socialist community' (*sotsialisticheskaia obshezhitiia*). This took the form of reprimands or voluntary fines. The *domkom* could in turn take grievances to comradely courts. If this failed, the criminal code could be invoked if the *domkom* chose to file charges. There was one such recorded incident at the Narkomfin, where an inhabitant of one of the ground-floor units was prosecuted. The prosecution was brought forward by the head of the *domkom* on behalf of the community against him for repeatedly assaulting his wife while drunk and after the local police neglected to press charges following repeated arrests. The matter eventually was taken to the criminal court at the initiative of the *domkom* (Afanasiev Archive, document 57, p. 1 and document 58, p. 14).

The *domkom* could exert a great deal of power over the lives of inhabitants. It could apply pressure on them to participate in communal activities, as well as inspect households at its discretion without hindrance. Yet it could bring to prosecution cases of abuse when local authorities, such as the police, would ignore incidents of criminal domestic violence. In short, the power of the *domkom* was highly paternal and arbitrary. It could coerce and at the same time defend the interests of disempowered members of its community against institutionalised misogyny or the vagaries of homelessness.

In the climate of renewed *byt* reform in the post-Stalin period, the *domkom* at the Narkomfin had a unique heritage upon which to draw. Many of the buildings designed to realise the *byt* reformist principles of the 1920s were not under the control of the *domkom* (the *prachechnaia* and the communal block). However, the main living building, the park and other buildings in the second district were used to realise some of the original *byt* reformist objectives. As a result, in the course of the reintroduction of *byt* reform at the Narkomfin, a number of entirely new communal facilities were created. These were notably the communal library, the clinic and the photographic darkroom, as well as the knitting circle organised by a volunteer *domkom* official for mothers and grandmothers (Afanasiev Archive, document 15, p. 4) (she incidentally was also a Junior Lieutenant for the NKVD living in one of the F-units).)

Like everything else, the library, clinic and photographic darkroom were run on a voluntary basis. Funds, resources and labour were pooled from the community of the *domkom*. As state funding was lacking as well as direct state control, certain aspects of *byt* reform could reflect the local interests and talents of the inhabitants. In this respect *byt* reform at the level of the *domkom* in the 1960s (unlike the 1920s) probably reflected the interests and aspirations of the local population more directly. However, local reform represented the interests of that segment of the population which cared to participate in *byt* reform, usually the more elite inhabitants of the Narkomfin and Leontovich buildings.

The library was located within the group of rooms on the first floor directly to the left of the entry (see appendix). Together these rooms were referred to as the *krasnyi ugolok*. This was the communal locus of the Narkomfin, where meetings took place and 'comradely courts' convened. The library was run by a woman (Afanaseiv Archive document, 15, p. 4) who was also in charge of the clinic on a voluntary basis (Afanasiev Archive, document 53, p. 1). The *krasnyi ugolok* also housed the darkroom that was used by the inhabitants and equipped with their donations (Afanasiev Archive, document 49, p. 3). The holdings and activities of the library and other institutions in the *krasnyi ugolok* served as a statistical indicator of *kul'turnost'* (degree of culture) which was annually quantified in official reports by the *domkom*. They were a public expression of the extent to which *byt* reform was achieved at the Narkomfin that involved the co-operation of the state and local private interest.

The clinic ran ten months of the year out of a room of an articulated K-unit appropriated by the head of the *domkom* housing commission (see appendix). The clinic was staffed by doctors and nurses from the local hospital as well as by volunteers from the community. Between them, the two groups of medical professionals treated 508 patients in 1967 (Afanasiev Archive, document 53, p. 1).

Byt reformist activities were organised and managed relatively equally by men and women, and ultimately co-ordinated by a retired male Communist Party official (Afanasiev Archive, document 15). Time-intensive duties were performed by either women or retired men. These individuals were in one way or another relatively excluded from full and active public roles, choosing to assert their involvement in the public sphere by the pursuit of *byt* reformist activities. Quite probably for many of the women involved this was an opportunity to initiate public works in an expression of *byt* reformist femininity denied them in their professional roles by the persistence of a 'glass ceiling' inhibiting their advancement to more responsible positions. These organised activities could give expression to women's frustrated public ambitions (as well as undoubtedly those of a retired male Party official).

Attempts were made to realise a number of other communal facilities, but did not come to fruition. These were a geological cabinet in the Leontovich House and a children's crèche. Both spaces were to have been created following the resettlement of individual households. The crèche was to be in No.1a (see appendix), a ground-floor apartment, while the geological cabinet was to be accommodated in a recently vacated basement room in the Leontovich House (No. 10).

In terms of communal childcare, a kindergarten (or children's group) was in operation in the late 1950s headed by a former *domrabotnitsa* who lived in No. 10. She worked privately, charging between 15 and 20 roubles per child (which was not considered expensive in those days). She was not sufficiently 'cultured', according to some of her former employers, but she was considered very good with children (NDKOH). Again, those families that could afford to, were able to realise this aspect of *byt* reform, which allowed parents to engage more fully in public, socialist life.

The agitational *byt* activities of the *domkom* climaxed in anticipation of the fiftieth anniversary of the October Revolution in 1967. This anniversary was particularly important in the post-Stalin period as an occasion to vindicate Soviet socialism by offering an opportunity to reinterpret and express the principles of revived Leninist socialism. The Narkomfin, with its impeccable Leninist beginnings, offered a great deal of inspiration to the active members of the *domkom* for these celebrations. Preparations for the fiftieth anniversary celebrations were the duty of the 'Komissiia po Kul'tmassavoi Rabote' (the commission for mass-cultural work) headed by the local *Partorg* (party functionary). One of the concerns of the commission was the preparation of the house, apartments and courtyard. It was important to sustain established *byt* reforms such as the clinic, crèche, library, darkroom and geological cabinet. The earlier leading role the Narkomfin played in *byt* reform movements inspired the *domkom* to go further and realise as much as possible the original programme of the complex.

A number of agreements were signed between the Narkomfin *domkom* and the *domkomy* of other *uchastki* to engage in socialist competition for the improvement of *byt*, in order to 'worthily celebrate the fiftieth anniversary of the Great October Socialist Revolution' (Afanasiev Archive, document 72, p.1). These competitions would set out to facilitate local performances of socialism and would

> Develop the spirit of socialist competition amongst the inhabitants to realise the exemplary maintenance of the home, apartment, housing territory and landscaping.
>
> Determine needs for the renovation of apartments – painting, white-washing, wallpapering and others – strive that the inhabitants in 1966 at their expense and their labour renovate their apartments and updated their electrical wiring.
>
> Conduct cultural-enlightening work amongst the inhabitants through meetings, lectures, and the house library. (Afanasiev Archive, document 73, p. 1)

as well as

> Not to ignore instances of immoral behaviour such as drunkenness, hooliganism and other violations of morality intolerable in our society. To take measures involving social coercion against those individuals who stoop to immoral misdemeanours. (Afanasiev Archive, document 70, p. 1)

Thus the *domkom* strove to interpret locally new state norms for *byt* reform and rationalise daily life. This was achieved by the regulation of moral conduct, the exemplary maintenance of domestic space and participation in communal activities. Renewed forms of exteriorised social action could thus be facilitated according to local understandings developed through these competitions.

In the ultimate bid to revive the original programme of the Narkomfin and overcome the interiorisation of social life under Stalin, the head of the *domkom* solicited the Soviet of Ministries to give back the buildings it had expropriated from the community. His letter is worth translating:

> To the Head of Khozupravlenia Upravlenia Delami of the Soviet of Ministries RSFSR, Comrade Goriachev, N.N.,
>
> In our letter of 13/5/66 we the inhabitants of asked you to move 4 metres back from our building the fence that surrounds your parking lot because it prevents light from reaching the windows of the first floor. To this request you did not even reply.

With regard to the upcoming fiftieth anniversary of the October Revolution we call upon you to facilitate better living conditions for our inhabitants. What is required?

1 Move back the above-mentioned fence.
2 Give the ZhEK-6 your building-site storage facility, and we will organise there a red corner, as no one building in our *uchastok* has a place to conduct cultural work. The materials for your construction site would be easily accommodated in your garage.
3 Or return the part of the communal block that is occupied by your printing press, where we used to have a gymnasium and communal dining room. There we will house all that we need to conduct cultural work and sport, as well as revive the communal dining room.

The head of the *domkom* of the second *uchastok* ZhEK-6,
The secretary of the *domkom*
21 February 1967
(Afanasiev Archive, document 32, page 2)

The results reported by the *domkom* appeared impressive: 'In the course of work for 1964, the consciousness of the inhabitants was raised even more. They maintain their apartments better, along with the communal spaces and landscaping. They increasingly renovate their apartments at their own expense and labour and the rooms and places of communal use. They participate more actively in communal organisations, and mass actions (*meropriatiiakh*)' (Afanasiev Archive, document 15, p. 6).

The Impact of Perestroika

The legal status of the Narkomfin as part of the second district of the ZhEK-6 did not change from the Brezhnev to Gorbachev periods. However, the out-migrations of a critical number of individuals saw the gradual dissolution of the *domkom*. The construction of the new American Embassy next door in 1981 destroyed much of the old park, leaving the remaining inhabitants too severely demoralised, in their rapidly diminishing numbers, to attempt any remedy for the destruction. One woman remembered how the inhabitants fought for every tree when the builders ravaged the park, struggling with the authorities to prevent the park from being entirely destroyed. The effect was nerve-shattering: 'I don't even look around, because what I see is just nightmarish, the house and everything, I see it and I do not see it any more.' She would recall a recurring nightmare from childhood that the house was crumbling and collapsing around her, while she desperately tried to escape.

In 1992 a faint semblance of the *domkom* existed in the form of a local house organisation at the Narkomfin, headed by a woman from one of the F-units who originally moved there because of the social experiment at *byt* reform it represented. She was an actress and former Komsomol member. Under her direction the *domkom* attempted to realise certain aspects of communal action and *byt* reform as best as it possibly could under stressed circumstances. Efforts were directed towards the most essential and pragmatic maintenance of the building. However, traditional gender roles were maintained throughout. The boarding-up of broken windows, elevator repair and various repair jobs involved the men of the households, while the women were recruited to sweep and clean corridors and stairwells.

Under Boris Yeltsin the house is eligible for privatisation by the inhabitants if they can organise a co-operative and pay for the cost of maintenance and repairs. However, this is outside their means as repairs would have to be performed in accordance with preservation guidelines for monuments of Russian architecture. Presently, only half the units are occupied, so they do not even have the numbers from which to collect funds with which to realise the terms for privatisation. The Narkomfin remains city property slipping even more rapidly into decay.

Changes in the Configuration of Material Culture

The shift from contextual to denotative understandings of material culture renewed the pursuit of exteriorisation with changing under-standings of petit-bourgeois consciousness. Furniture (and in particular, the problem of old furniture) was directly affected. This becomes evident in the confusion in the minds of some inhabitants as to why they find themselves valuing something they quite clearly recall having devalued earlier. They were at a loss to express their reasons for thinking so except in terms of their own perceptual failings. One inhabitant of a 2-F-unit found that with the years she has become more attracted to things she used to call petit-bourgeois. Now she would like such old, decorated handmade things but regrets that it is no longer possible to possess them. Recalling her mother's large collection of crystal vessels, she remembers how she and her sister thought it was 'horrible, laughable, rather petit-bourgeois'; 'we did not understand then that it was some-thing valuable'.

These shifting inflections are clearly linked to changing concept-ualisations of material culture between denotative and contextual understandings. During the 'Thaw' and the reassertion of denotative understandings of material culture, furniture that was associated with the Stalin era and the pre-Revolutionary era was believed literally to embody and denote petit-bourgeois consciousness. It was antithetical to, and in fact inhibiting of, the process of socialist construction under the 'Thaw'. Old buffets and massive ornamented pieces of furniture, previously reviled under the first Cultural Revolution, began to suffer under the second one again. Yet, this time there was an industrial infrastructure, particularly a furniture industry, in place with the capab-ility of producing new items of material culture to replace old ones.

Similarly, the housing boom created spaces that were inimical to the use of old furniture. People at the Narkomfin often remarked how it was impossible to move large old decorated pieces of furniture into the new smaller-scale apartments. New modernist spaces conspired against items of old furniture, as did new norms of taste. Hence such pieces were thrown away in great numbers. (There is unfortunately no way to gauge how much was discarded, but reports of this behaviour were consistent.) Revived denotative understanding, associated with a negative understanding of petit-bourgeois consciousness, served to facilitate what can be called nothing less than a restructuring of the material world and its perception on a global scale, facilitating renewed 'exteriorising' dynamics of socialist construction.

Individuals participated in this state-sponsored restructuring of the material world for a number of reasons. Young people wanted to differentiate themselves from their elders, to realise their own identities and world view. This larger social project provided a convenient vehicle. Thus one inhabitant of a 2-F-unit and her sister realised their aspirations through their contempt for their mother's crystal. Another from a 2-F unit facilitated hers by wallpapering in order to create a differentiation of space to 'realise her self'. Whereas a K-unit occupant's frequent wallpaperings served to distinguish her spaces from her mother-in-law's.

By virtue of the hegemonic control the state had over production and the difficulty for individuals to produce goods on their own, a multiplicity of choices was simply not available. One had to utilise what was to hand in order to realise one's goals, no matter how mutually contradictory the two might appear to be. There were private artisans with their products, but these were few and strictly controlled within state-run markets. They were also regulated by modernist norms of taste which strove to exclude such artisanal products.

People could, of course, attempt to make their own furnishings and other domestic artefacts such as embroideries. However, the material inputs for such activities were rare. In all likelihood these activities involved materials procured through the grey economy. Furniture was almost impossible to make on one's own, though some did, like the inhabitant of a 2-F unit who had access to the necessary materials through the grey economy. Embroidery, on the other hand, was easily sustained as the required materials would be readily procured, though also with difficulty (several individual reports attest to the resourcefulness necessary to acquire the humblest needle and thread).

However, the strategies of the individual and state were not necessarily at odds. The dissolution of the old material order in favour of a new one helped heal the wounds of the past such as the privations of wartime, the Terror and any number of related personal tragedies. They could be imaginatively linked through the emergent understandings of denotative material culture enabling a highly useful and therapeutic metonymy. That is, a buffet cabinet could justifiably embody and denote petit-bourgeois consciousness and its link with Stalinist excess. However, it could also facilitate the forgetting of those excesses; the forgetting of the pain associated with purged loved ones or the hardships of wartime, evacuation and hunger. Sometimes the growing attribution of denotative qualities to material culture made certain items dangerous, so that they had to be thrown away. Objects understood to denote affiliation with the wrong pre-Revolutionary class or association with a purged individual could provoke a comment by a innocent child, nosy neighbour, police official or KGB informant and put a household at risk. Objects could invoke metonymic associations dangerous to one's well-being. One inhabitant of an F-unit recalled how few objects were saved by her family in order to protect her from knowledge of their past, which would have thwarted her rise in the Komsomol.

When taste became rationalised and structured the material world denotatively, it could be marshalled against the old material world and direct an individual towards new rules and understandings to describe an entirely new order. According to these prevailing new rules, objects were literally encoded to reject and forget old objects and rules. As one F-unit inhabitant noted, modernist design norms were inimical to old objects: 'The new apartments were designed for new furniture. They could not accommodate in style and size the old furniture. The old buffet cabinets could not fit in with the low ceilings, the minimal floor space and the *stenki*. Everyone had this new furniture and wanted it, throwing out the old stuff or relegating it to the dacha' (NDKOH). She added that 'the new apartments meant a new life, a new skin, everything was thrown out and the past forgotten as well' (NDKOH).

Not everyone participated in this process; some individuals resisted these redefinitions and recontextualizations only to be vindicated later during the Gorbachev era. For various reasons (some too personal maybe to even articulate) they resisted this new material cosmology. The factory director's grandson living in an articulated K-unit resisted, asserting the positive familial aspects of *meshchanstvo* against modernist detractors. The inhabitant of an F-unit would acknowledge the anti-*meshchanstvo* campaigns of the 1960s and 1970s, maintaining, however, that 'beauty is beauty, particularly for women. For men, it might be a bit simpler.' Another F-unit inhabitant would say that 'they [the communist officials] always tried to interfere in something and what they involved themselves in changed all the time'; she did what she loved, not caring if it was considered petit-bourgeois or not. In short she said that 'if you love something sincerely it cannot be petit-bourgeois'. Yet, another F-unit household would also state that 'people are by nature petit-bourgeois and when they moved here [to the Narkomfin] they just made it petit-bourgeois as well'. One F-unit householder would say, acknowledging herself as petit-bourgeois: 'one wants to live better and more beautifully and that [dejectedly] is petit-bourgeois?!' Finally, the occupant of an 2-F household, in an inversion of conventional understandings of petit-bourgeois consciousness, argued that at one time people kept the furniture they had for life (a modernist sensibility applied to Stalinist material culture). In the 1960s she observed that fashions arose (the new *byt* reformist modernist designs) and people threw out perfectly good furniture in the pursuit of petit-bourgeois fashion. Of course, today these very same people regret having thrown out the old 'decent' furniture.

Under Perestroika the charges were reversed and a new contextualism, reminiscent of the Stalin years, shifted the burden from objective modernist universals of taste and the material world towards individual discretion. Social action shifted from strategies of 'exteriorisation' to 'interiorisation' once more. Individuals were empowered (as earlier under Stalin) to determine the appropriate qualities of material culture on their own terms. Old items of furniture could be reincorporated on the basis of individually determined strategies, and not according to an objective modernist understanding. Once more, those individuals with sufficient means, those with access to storage – typically in the form of a dacha – could participate more readily in this revival. Dachas were often the repositories for old pieces of furniture thrown away during the height of modernist *byt* reform. Whenever the time arose in which a new contextual understanding reliant on old pieces emerged, such items were retrieved from dachas and reinstalled in urban domestic spaces. Individuals without access to storage simply had to throw such items of furniture onto skips where they were lost, or sold to commission shops. However, with the re-evaluation of material culture under Gorbachev, such pieces had become valuable, expensive and difficult to procure.

The process of forgetting, facilitated by modernist denotative understandings, was effectively reversed into remembering by invoking contextual understandings. This permitted individuals to remember safely as rationalised unitary norms no longer held sway and individual discretion prevailed. Old pieces of a household hidden from view for several generations were safely incorporated within urban domestic spaces; invoking pre-Revolutionary class affiliations, a purged family member or a tradition of religious belief. One 2-F householder kept her icons hidden in closets and suitcases; now she has moved them into the display areas of her buffet cabinets (see figure 24).

Figure 24 2-F interior with buffet cabinet containing hidden icons, 1992, Author's photograph

Gender and Shifting Understandings of Petit-Bourgeois Consciousness

The gendered nature of petit-bourgeois consciousness is very strong. In the various Soviet discourses on petit-bourgeois consciousness, women figured problematically. As women were the gender directly implicated in domesticity and the shackles of the 'hearth', their double burden became critical. They were susceptible to the chronic socialist malaise of 'false consciousness', making the reform of women's roles all the more problematic. However, the gendered associations of petit-bourgeois consciousness were intersected by related associations with domestic and private social roles, in opposition to the public, non-domestic roles characteristic of communalised socialist society. Thus a man, too preoccupied with private ambitions, pleasures and domestic contentment, was petit-bourgeois as much as the traditional non-modernist housewife.

More important than gender was the degree to which an individual participated in private domestic roles at the expense of public social roles; that is, how one pursued strategies of exteriorisation and interior-isation to perform socialism. Because of the traditional association of women with the 'hearth', women were more implicated in petit-bourgeois consciousness. At the same time, however, women who could afford to realise modernist socialist norms of public life, often did. They could achieve this by virtue of higher social status and the monetary appropriation of lower-class women's labour through the hiring of *domrabotnitsy* or *chastniki* (part-time maids), or by the exploitation of the labour of female kin such as single aunts and elderly mothers. A man, traditionally favoured for such public roles, could similarly avoid an association with petit-bourgeois consciousness as well as by simply appropriating the labour of his female spouse as a 'housewife'.

The negative associations of petit-bourgeois consciousness were reversed when the domestic realm was re-evaluated during the late Brezhnev and Gorbachev periods. As public socialist roles became increasingly problematic, the private realm of the domestic sphere rose in importance and relevance. For the first time, men were implicated in the domestic realm and began to participate more fully in the increased interiorisation of social action. As soon as the domestic realm became a sphere of masculine involvement, the negative associations were reversed to positive ones. Petit-bourgeois consciousness assumed a positive association that persists to this day. Both men and women could participate positively in the domestic realm with its petit-bourgeois associations while under a new regime that validated the interiorisation of social action.

Not everyone of course followed this trend. As the examples presented suggest, individuals often resisted these transformations, choosing to retain old negatively charged connotations rather than embrace new positive ones. One 2-F-unit householder, somewhat bemused, observed that in the present-day petit-bourgeois consciousness is considered a good thing and the pursuit of *uiut* is desirable again. She, however, cannot get used to the idea that *meshchanstvo* is a positive thing and does not believe it to be right. She is indifferent to these discussions and will continue to live as she always has, adding, in a conciliatory tone, that ultimately everyone should just live according to their character.

Concurrently, earlier reviled strategies ascended in social worth. This empowered the previously disenfranchised or enabled one to assert one's self with an ascendant position to attain social legitimacy. Hence the confidence with which the grandson of the K-unit factory director affirmed petit-bourgeois values, as well as the F-unit household just mentioned. There exists, also, a quiet acknowledgement of these values by new couples establishing their own households in the present day. A young couple occupying one of the F-units recognises petit-bourgeois consciousness as a natural state of being, while others express this silently by their unabashed and strident expressions of domesticity.

Hygiene was differentially understood along this continuum of alternating positive and negative associations of petit-bourgeois consciousness. Modernist *byt* reformist domestic strategies were traditionally justified through concepts of hygiene. Frilly drapes, figurines, rugs and the like were rejected and thrown out because they 'harboured dust'. Yet those individuals who pursued such non-modernist 'petit-bourgeois' domestic strategies with the open display of frilly drapes and figurines, maintained – instead – that they were exemplarily hygienic since they cared for their households, diligently cleaning them and these items frequently. Rather it was the modernist *byt* reformist member of the intelligentsia 'who could spit on housework!' (as stated by an F-unit householder), who was dirty, who never cleaned and ignored personal hygiene precisely for the reason that they did not cultivate domesticity, *uiut* and pursue otherwise petit-bourgeois domestic strategies.

Exploding the 'Hearth'

While certain families continued to elaborate the domestic sphere and interiorisation, others attempted to explode the 'hearth' outwards and realise the exteriorisation of social action. The centripetal arrangement about the dining table could be exploded into sectional 'zones' of activity, differentiating space according to use while breaking the symbolic centre of the domestic 'hearth': the central dining room table. Amongst post-Stalin K-unit households, already designed to accommodate the nuclear family, the symbolic expression of the centripetal plan was generally retained. In the stairwell units with a mix of bourgeois-type expanded K-units and 2-F-units, five expressed the 'hearth' through centripetal plans while three chose segmented 'exploded' schemes. This suggested a tendency to retain the original interiorised arrangements. Of the F-units however, designed specifically to explode the interiority of the domestic 'hearth', eight retained interiorised centripetal plans while a majority of ten expressed the original modernist use of zoned plans emphasising exteriority. Clearly, despite the original spatiality of these units, they were often used to achieve different forms of spatiality over the years. A plurality of responses could exist expressing both exteriorising and interiorising spatial dynamics to varying degrees, despite the original forms of spatiality believed to be inscribed within these units.

Men and the Reconsolidation of the 'Hearth'

In the Gorbachev and post-Soviet years, there was a marked and strident reconsolidation of the 'hearth' in a number of households. As opposed to earlier years the primary agents were men. The domestic sphere and the interiorisation of social action became more acceptable. Such strategies were not subversive and petit-bourgeois as they had been when women performed them earlier. Now they were progressive and invoked the forward-moving dynamic of Perestroika. At the same time the sphere of consumer services, which once permitted an individual to hire a craftsman, decayed rapidly over the course of the Brezhnev and Gorbachev years. Individual households were left on their own with their men to perform the gender-appropriate tasks of carpentry and the like. In addition, the authority of the *domkom* (particularly at the Narkomfin where the once-robust community of inhabitants had dwindled considerably) no longer held sway in these times when the authority of the Communist Party was increasingly being eroded.

Though building codes remained and would only permit ephemeral changes such as painting and wallpapering, the decay of *domkom* and ZhEK management over the housing stock resulted in individuals increasingly having to realise repairs on their own. (Refer to Afanasiev Archive for the increasingly worse and chronic problems related to capital repairs to the site as well as local RaiSovet archives on the general decline of repair services for the Krasnopresnenskii Raion, see TsGAOR g. Moskvy, Fond 399, Opis 1, Delo 352; TsGAOR g. Moskvy Fond 399, Opis 1, Delo 391; TsGAOR g. Moskvy Fond 754, Opis 1, Delo 7.) Thus, male-gendered roles devoted to repairwork and carpentry that were once fulfilled by socialised public institutions (such as repair bureaux, the *domkom* and ZhEK) had to be performed by men within their own households.

So empowered, and in need, these men went to work. One householder illegally smashed through the wall of the neighbouring unit to double his household's *zhilploshchad'*. The *domkom* no longer performed its 'raids', the ZhEK no longer sent out its repairmen, and the neighbouring unit's inhabitants abandoned it in 1986. The man's household required more space and taking Perestroika to heart, appropriated the neighbouring unit and rebuilt a new apartment for his household and thereby realised his own 'restructuring' of socialist *byt*.

Other male householders did not go to such extremes. In 1992, one man appropriated the two rooms next to his common room on the first floor, by merely opening up the doors of the old communal apartment and subjecting its walls to a new unifying wallpaper and paint scheme. Another managed to appropriate a room to his unit after it was abandoned in 1981. In the end all the men of these households, using their traditionally gendered skills of carpentry and repair work, were able in strident and at times highly dramatic ways to reverse the exteriorisation of spatiality and public life towards the elaboration of the domestic 'hearth'. They did this with a confidence and vigour that were the traditional prerogative of Russian (and Soviet) males, deploying their gendered skills towards the realisation of ascendant and newly empowered expressions of spatiality and in this case a new legitimised interiorised domesticity.

Ambiguity, Partiality and Accommodation

It is clear from these discussions that an individual's relationship to the domestic sphere is fraught with many contradictions, discontinuities and multiplicities of meaning. The domestic sphere at the level of Communist Party and local academic discourse has been, and will continue to be, in post-Soviet Russian society a highly contentious arena. That it should continue to be so at the level of the individual household in greater complexity and contentiousness is not surprising. A multitude of interests (such as the more straightforward, slowly changing goals of the state) converge with a greater multiplicity of individual (more contingent and often times contradictory) local and highly personal motivations. All the while these interests negotiated the shifting exteriorising and interiorising dynamics of social action.

The Soviet domestic sphere is most certainly a 'scrap', to use Smith's apt term. That this should be the case is almost an unintended consequence of the modernising efforts of the early Soviet state. By asserting a denotative understanding of material culture, it attempted rather violently to contain the pre-existing superfluity of meaning within the domestic sphere in order to achieve a specific social and political goal. This embodied the interests of a particular dominant group, namely the Bolshevik intelligentsia, and with it the elaboration of an exteriorising social dynamic. Those who were disaffected had to find alternative strategies to counter this dominance and assert themselves. One way was to promote an alternative understanding of how the material world operated that would invalidate what had preceded it. Such a strategy was the Stalinist contextual understanding that facilitated interiority by disaggregating the unifying effects of denotative Bolshevik approaches promoting exteriority. This was reversed with the assertion of a reconfigured exteriorising and denotative vision of the material world under Khrushchev. Then, yet again, this later position was gradually rejected, and disaggregated by an alternative materiality in the late Brezhnev years.

At the level of the individual these conceptual tools were available, 'out there', permitting the aggregation and disaggregation of understandings of the material world in order to realise varying strategies of exteriorisation and interiorisation. However, they had differing claims of validity and effectiveness depending on time, generation, class, degree of social mobility, gender and personal ambition. The material world and the universe it embodied was destroyed, reconstructed and destroyed again utilising these conceptual tools as needed. The success of these manipulations very often depended on the particular effectiveness of a given strategy in light of which understanding wielded greater public political power at what time. Frequently individuals reckoned wrongly and suffered while others benefited. If they were not quick to rethink their performative strategies, they could be left behind as one of the 2-F householders – with her now defunct modernist understandings.

A number of informants' responses seemed confusing and at times contradictory, such as that of Elena Andreevna who lived in one of the F-units mentioned at the beginning of this book. She was the daughter of an upwardly mobile atheist Chekist and a devoutly Russian Orthodox mother. She possessed what once was a decidedly petit-bourgeois and now 'antique' buffet cabinet that dominated her apartment (see figure 3). This cabinet once belonged to her high-ranking senior financier second husband. It was repositioned in later years in the sleeping niche where, bedridden and ill, she spent most of her time. Earlier, it functioned as the secular repository of the artefacts of domesticity. It was a celebration of the household's newly prosperous status within the Communist Party hierarchy. As they were rightful recipients of socialist advancement, such expressions of prosperity by Elena Andreevna and her husband were indeed appropriate. This was part-icularly so in the waning Stalin years, when individuals were allowed to express socialism in terms of their new found material prosperity. Life, after all, for Elena Andreevna and her husband had indeed 'become better and more gay'. Following the death of her husband in 1963, the quality of her life declined precipitously. She no longer enjoyed the benefits of his high position and was reduced to the status of a pensioned widow at the age of 43. The 'Thaw' held few opportunities for middle-aged widows such as herself. Khrushchev's Secret Speech denouncing Stalin held out no chance for happiness and redemption. For her, in fact, it denounced the happiest years of her life; she did not believe a word of what Khrushchev had to say.

Instead, over the years she moved the buffet from the front room into the eastern corner of the back room. In her sleeping niche looking out over the remains of Ginzburg's Arcadian socialist idyll, Elena Andreevna contemplated her life and her impending death. Here, where one would normally find the traditional Russian Orthodox 'red corner' containing icons oriented to the rising sun (and the realm of God without) Elena Andreevna kept her thirteen volumes of Stalin's collected works. She took good care of them – periodically removing them, dusting them off and re-reading passages. Interspersed with Stalin's works were icons of Christ the Saviour, the Mother of God and Saint Nicholas the Miracle Worker. (These icons she had gradually collected from her periodic pilgrimages to Zagorsk outside Moscow.) There were bottles of holy water, as well as a man's wristwatch (presumably that of her husband). Thus, Elena Andreevna in her declining years, while raging at Yeltsin's 'democratic-fascists' who had overturned what was left of her world, had managed improbably to contain adequately the superfluous and contradictory 'scraps' of her life in her buffet cabinet, and realise a momentary accommodation that saw her into the next world.

Conclusion

I would like to conclude by examining how chapters 2–8 have elaborated upon issues raised in chapter 1. Writing the history of people's individual actions at the Narkomfin, within the context of shifting state responses to the domestic realm, has provided me with an opportunity to examine how the material and social world can be differentially constructed across a broad spectrum of scales. In so doing, I have examined the play of micropowers and the highly contentious and 'scrappy' engagements that constitute social life from the minutiae of daily life to shifts in state policy. Thus this book has been an attempt to identify how individuals and groups interact and to examine the conceptual strategies they invoked in order to facilitate their immediate, and at times conflicting, social strategies.

One of the key dynamics I have tried to delineate is the interiorisation and exteriorisation of social life facilitated by changing terms of the material world. Though a binary opposition in a traditional structuralist sense, it was a useful intervention to help understand the material at hand. It had the additional advantage of resonating with other intellectual traditions, both Anglo-American and Soviet as well as local, which similarly deploy structuralist oppositions as tropes with which to order experience and realise contingent social goals. Such an opposition has the advantage of enabling a certain degree of mutual intelligibility while at the same time offering an alternative evaluation as in this study, which has shown how certain conceptual tools (e.g. structuring tropes) can be used differentially to achieve different ends; how these, in turn legitimate the social strategies of individuals and groups and how such strategies could be then be obviated, resisted or partially deployed.

In the endeavour to understand how the material world is configured and what it says about a given a society there is a tendency to forget that this desire to understand is itself a strategy for coping with certain aspects of being; a strategy that is an attempt to empower, utilising ever more effective tools. Thus we create conceptual tools (or *Denkmittel* such as theories of material culture) with which to cope better with our concerns and contingencies. Unfortunately despite the best of intentions there is a tendency to envision these conceptual tools as actually representing what is going on rather than simply a provisional means of coming to terms with what has been experienced. Thus, we fall into the muddles of hypostatisation described by Bauman wherein we believe and operationalise statements like 'structure structures', and as Bourdieu warns us, confuse 'regularity for a rule'. In whatever constituted form, the individual agent – the ultimate and undeniable locus of culture change and innovation – ultimately becomes one of Giddens' 'cultural dupes'. We are left somewhat at a loss in coming to terms with cultural change.

The problem of the 'cultural dupe' has similarly troubled students of Russian and Soviet history, particularly in terms of understanding the legitimacy of society and state and how Stalinist totalitarianism was possible. The Stalin period, despite the devastating toll on human life and its suffering did not arise as the result of an overwhelming external force in the demonic personality of Stalin (as in Conquest 1968, Medvedev 1971). Rather it was made possible because individuals experienced a delimited but nonetheless expanded degree of empowerment and legitimation of their independent actions in daily life. They could at once be allowed to participate more directly in the Stalinist socialist state, and realise relatively freely their individual local goals. If anything, Stalinism offered a guarded reprieve, particularly in the domestic realm, against the rigours of a totalising and rationalising modernism that preceded it.

The history of the Soviet Union with its cataclysmic crises of state and social legitimacy is a process of culture change that many individuals – from the householders of the community of the Narkomfin to politicians and Sovietologists – are still coming to grips with. I have focused here on the domestic realm – a major and contentious arena for the negotiation of state and social legitimacy – using one of the state's most innovative tools to realise that legitimacy: the Narkomfin Communal House and the social project it embodied. In focusing on the domestic realm, I have looked specifically at material culture and its use. My intention was to come to terms with these broader social processes through this conceptual ocular while trying better to understand this tool upon which we students of material culture are so heavily reliant.

In so doing it is apparent that the material world is hardly fixed, inscribed or explicitly signifying; nor is it inherently ambiguous, polyvalent and open. Rather it is both and neither. The material world is, *pace* James, whatever an individual agent or group requires it to be, or more accurately, enables it to become in order to cope with contingencies and realise individual or group interests. Clearly, there is little to be sentimental about, or committed to, as far as these understandings of material culture are concerned. To paraphrase Rorty, these ideas about the material world must 'earn their keep' until the time they lose their effectiveness and are discarded in order to deal with changed contingencies. This is precisely what the inhabitants of the Narkomfin and various state interests did. What is palpable from the discussion at hand is how fluid and unruly such understandings could be and how various denotative and contextual understandings of material culture could be differentially and partially deployed. In these examples, different degrees of social and material exteriorisation and interiorisation, resulted in a variety of often seemingly incommensurable goals over a broad spectrum of contexts: from ensuring state legitimacy and Party control, to the interpersonal relations and conflicts between individuals of the same household. People make do with the conceptual tools at hand and exploit their relative social effectiveness; differentially deploying and destroying entire cosmic understandings of the social and material world in order to cope with the complexities of social life with varying degrees of success. Something like a directing habitus or structuring structure can only seem to exist, therefore, if instantiated by an individual or group of individuals as part of a conscious strategy or tacit complicity to realise a particular social goal. By focusing too much on structure or habitus we lose sight of the 'constitutive outside', the 'remainders' and 'gaps' discussed in chapter 1 that constitute the dynamics of social action and cultural change – we privilege statics over dynamics.

In addition, the material articulation of these dynamics is often quite ephemeral. By applying a little bit of paint, inserting a strategically placed thin wood partition, or simply rearranging the furniture of a room, one can assert and subvert entirely different and contradictory cosmologies of social being, as we have seen in earlier chapters. However, it must be recalled here that material goods were the socially acknowledged terms by which such actions could be taken. Material culture, therefore, must be locally understood to signify in some way in order for that to happen. In the case of European and Soviet societies this materialist preoccupation is well documented. However, this is not always the case. Material objects are neither merely signifying or, for that matter, meaningfully ambiguous. There is no reason to imagine that sometimes a thing just might not signify some thing; may have ambiguous meaning; or might not do anything at all – that is, it may not 'matter', to use Judith Butler's pun.

As was illustrated via a deployment of differing contextual and denotative understandings of material culture, these conceptual understandings were critical in orchestrating social action; asserting and subverting orders of legitimacy which included and excluded certain individuals and groups. Following Bourdieu and Bowen, native denotative understandings narrowly legitimated pre-Revolutionary modernising elites; whereas, in an attempt to counter this social and cultural hegemony, ascendant Stalinist elites asserted a more 'fuzzy' contextual understanding, which dissipated and empowered social action across a broader social spectrum, ensuring the social legitimacy of the Stalinist state. This process was reversed in the wake of Stalin's death and is currently undergoing an additional reversal as well. Both understandings envision material culture correctly, but have nothing to say about the inherent qualities of material culture and the social conditions of its use. There is nothing inherently 'liberating' or moral about such conceptual tools, as many Post-Processual archaeologists and others would have us believe in their assertions of meaningful ambiguity in the constitution of material culture (Shanks and Tilley 1987; 1992). Such conceptualisations are merely amoral enabling devices, functioning locally, temporarily and nothing more. An 'adequate social theory' cannot contain the movements of such devices and thereby keep Smith's so-called 'jackals' at bay.

On a more individual level these understandings could be deployed to legitimate one form of action over another with the result that differing understandings would be applied without consistency except as many and differing local contingencies required. For instance, a K-unit householder invoked prevailing denotative standards of taste and hygiene to legitimate her celebration of the domestic 'hearth'. She achieved this with her frequent wallpaperings, the segmentation of her living space from her in-laws' by thin wood partitions, and a zoned arrangement of furniture within. These interventions at once legitimated her desires to elaborate the domestic 'hearth' and emphasised an interiorising understanding of social action. This contradicted the highly normative, modernist *byt* reformist and exteriorising strategies of her mother-in-law. Her actions were, however, somewhat contradictory. They simultaneously asserted a new, modernist *byt* reformist sensibility, by way of a withdrawal inwards from the original K-unit, while within exploding outwards into segmented arrangements that asserted a revived concern with exteriority. This contradiction was managed by the application of the prevailing rules of taste which legitimated her actions as 'tasteful' and 'modern' whilst enabling her to dismiss her mother-in-law's as 'petit-bourgeois'. In so doing, she creatively employed radically different understandings of material culture with which to realise her goals under very limited circumstances. Her actions simultaneously affirmed prevailing norms of *byt* reform and a return to socialist roots, while asserting her independence in an extended family. The legitimation of her personal independence and autonomous self was inextricable from her affirmation of the revived Leninist project of *byt* reform and state socialism. Though contradictory and unrelated, these local goals affirmed and participated across a broad spectrum of discontinuous social strategies, and simultaneously realised and improbably constituted one another by both 'building socialism' and 'keeping house'.

Her neighbour, in asserting her own independent, married and adult status, similarly proceeded to rid her K-unit as best she could of the decidedly interiorised bourgeois furniture and interior arrangements of her mother. She favoured, instead, exteriorised, dispersed config-urations and objects approved of by *byt* reformers. Not simply an assertion of her self at the expense of her mother, her actions simult-aneously invoked denotative understandings of material culture and the revived project of *byt* reform against the excesses of Stalinism. Thus, her mother would have been criticised for being petit-bourgeois just as other individuals had criticised their 'less enlightened' seniors. At the same time, this restructuring of the domestic realm, with its attendant understanding of social action and state legitimacy, funct-ioned at an even more intimate and emotional level. As this K-unit householder said herself, restructuring was a means of coming to terms with the great losses of Stalinism and the Second World War. These actions were not simply interpersonal, or political. They effected a clean slate, a new life and a new world – to help heal and forget the horrors of the old, while holding out hope for the future.

In yet another way an F-unit householder was able to resist modernist *byt* reformist understandings in the post-Stalin era. She could defend her derided love of embroidery and the deployment of the artefacts of her craft throughout her household, by reasserting a contextualist understanding of material culture. For her nothing could be petit-bourgeois if it was done 'sincerely'. She thereby asserted her individual agency over any normative modernist understandings.

These single sets of actions had ramifications across a broad spectrum of unrelatable and contradictory conflicts and interests. The interventions, restructurings and containments on the part of these and other inhabitants at the Narkomfin could in one movement accommodate the meaningful superfluity of otherwise entirely unreconcilable elements.

It was mentioned earlier how Elena Andreevna quite improbably and 'scrappily' managed just such a temporary containment of superfluity through the device of her buffet cabinet. Smith mentions how such attempts to contain and structure are impulses to control unruly contradictory elements, much in the spirit of Foucault's understanding of discipline. Smith might have understood Elena Andreevna's buffet cabinet in the following light:

> It is out of these scrappy (heterogeneous) elements and the local resolutions and provisional stabilities yielded by their continuous scrappy (more or less conflictual) interactions that we (and, from various perspectives, others) construct our various versions of our 'selves' and, as necessary, explain or justify our actions, goals, and beliefs. It is also out of the scrappy interactions of these scrappy elements – though on a more general scale – that theorists in the different disciplinary traditions cited above construct, from their accordingly different perspectives, their accordingly different general accounts of human behaviour. (Smith 1988:148)

Elena Andreevna's buffet cabinet might appear to some observers as painfully contradictory. Some liberal highly educated Russians I questioned described her as 'deformed' and 'sick', a form of *meshchanstvo*, a grotesque result of seventy-four years of totalitarian socialism. Such responses suggest a certain intellectual 'nausea'; what Smith would call 'a reactionary response to the increasing contemporary destratification of cultural arenas and practices, and a misdiagnosis of the cognitive dislocation, dissonance, and nausea – literally, disgust – experienced as a result by high-culture critics' (Smith 1988:76). Smith argues these responses are the result of a process, *pace* Bourdieu's own notions of distinction (Bourdieu 1984), whereby 'it seems that wherever systems of more or less strictly segregated hierarchical strata begin to break down and differentiations become more numerous, rapid, complex, less predictable, and less controllable, the resulting emergences, mixtures, and minglings will look, from the perspective of those in the historically upper strata, like flattenings, falls, and collapses – in short, like losses of distinction' (Smith 1988:77). Regulatory, rationalising, in short 'disciplining' and fixed conceptual strategies prevent us from coming to terms with such superfluities and partialities, with the result that we feel Smith's 'nausea'. The entire history of *byt* reform – like the entire history of European Enlightenment rationality – has been an attempt to keep such nauseous feelings at bay.

This leaves us to consider the contingencies surrounding fixed axiological strategies of containment. In the Soviet example, the circumstances of these attempts seem clear as well as the conceptual devices used to achieve them. Strategies of exteriorisation and interiorisation had very obvious, contingent and socially programmematic components. An almost structuralist vacillation between a set of binary oppositions seems to have emerged – structuring tropes such as: socialist: petit-bourgeois, male:female, public:private or exteriorisation: interiorisation. This coincidence is not entirely accidental as there is a very strong and important tradition of structuralist thought in the Russian intellectual tradition. The legacy of Lévi-Strauss goes back to Roman Jakobson of the Prague School of Linguistics, and Lévi-Strauss's use of the works of Prince Trubetzkoy (Hymes 1970:291). Both individuals were very prominent in the early development of semiotics in the early twentieth century in Russia and the establishment of the Moscow Linguistic Circle, later disbanded by Stalinist authorities in the late 1920s (Lucid 1977:2). The works of these individuals (so central to Lévi-Strauss) were to provide the foundation for the revived study of semiotics under Khrushchev in the late 1950s and early 1960s, particularly Iurii Lotman's Tartu School of Semiotics. The containing, rationalising and denotative implications of structuralist research were probably intuitively clear to the Stalin-era authorities which earlier rejected them.

It might be interesting, then, to situate analogous shifts in the understanding of material culture in recent archaeological debates. Over the past ten to fifteen years, there has been a noticeable rejection of structuralist approaches with their totalising effects on the interpretation of the material record. Structuration theory (Giddens) and the notion of a habitus (Bourdieu) are more recent attempts to overcome the procrustean effects of such conceptual tools (see Johnson 1989; Parker-Pearson and Richards 1994).

However, in some of the most stridently political and contingently nuanced works, such as Michael Shanks and Christopher Tilley's *Reconstructing Archaeology*, there are revealing contradictory sentiments, such as 'social practice *engraves* [my italics] meaning in material culture and *structures* [my italics] it and that material culture is active (it affects practice) and may operate three-dimensionally' (Shanks and Tilley 1992:132). However, they also assert that

> the rules of the material culture game are not fixed like those of chess but mutable and continuously subject to the possibility of change even though for the most part they may tend to be reproduced. Meaning is not a matter of an immutable relationship between signifier and signified but the spatio-temporal fixation of a chain of signifiers to produce an interpretable meaning. (Shanks and Tilley 1992:132–3)

What such conflicting tensions in their statements reveal is an obvious desire to contain adequately superfluity, but with a certain guilt-ridden anxiety. This is a legacy of the Frankfurt School's problematic of desiring to facilitate free, contingent interpretation, but without the threat of abject relativism. Superfluity was contained in terms of a Marxian inspired but unarticulated social theory, 'a differentiated higher form of freedom', which 'has a decisive voice in the real overcoming, but in no way coincides with it, and predicts the future only abstractly and inexactly' (Horkheimer 1978:438). Smith might argue that these uneasy contradictions might be due 'to the traditional idea that the only thing that prevents people from behaving like beasts or automatons is their being leashed by/to some transcendental or otherwise absolute authority' (Smith 1988:161).

Thus Shanks and Tilley's project for 'a challenge to a socialist political imagination, a challenge which while necessarily rooted in our experience in Britain, applies to a Western world of renewed capitalism' (Shanks and Tilley 1992:265) would be ensured by a '*critical* [my italics] appreciation of different pasts. And the critical element is to deny a disabling relativism – not just anything goes' (Shanks and Tilley 1992:264). They exhibit the fear of what Smith calls the 'objectivist-generated phantom heresy of "relativism"' (Smith 1988:167), which is fuelled by an insistent need to be adequate to a critical social theory and the fixed containing effects such an adequacy would ensure, and the eventual obviation of such 'phantom relativist heresies'.

To counter the abject relativism implied by Derridean deconstruction, the archaeological theorist Timothy Yates (following Ryan, Mark Leone (Leone 1995) and Shanks and Tilley) desires, in the spirit of the Frankfurt School, to force an 'incision' of a Marxist epistemology in the description of Derridean traces and signifying chains, to deconstruct and determine the social and ideological motivations of a particular way in which *différance* is modulated and understood. Yates, argues that a social theory is required in order meaningfullly to establish and describe those traces, those signifying chains which are displaced and articulated by the property of *différance*:

> Deconstruction must possess theories of its own about what a text 'is', how it functions, how and where it is produced and reproduced and to what ends. For Derrida this has been the operation of a metaphysics of presence or logocentrisim, but in order to force the incision, shown as the opening into all systems of presence, we need some theory more closely concerned with what historical irregularities as well as regularities articulate 'texts'. (Yates 1990:276)

However, to attempt such a supplement or appropriation of Marxian socialism (as Shanks and Tilley propose in 'determining'/'describing'/'articulating' what a text 'is') amounts to nothing more than a displacement (differ/deferring), thereby creating one trace in place of another, a vain objectification of some presence of a totalising logic – Marxian, socialist or something else. Not that Derrida would necessarily object to such an appropriation; it is the very essence of *différance*. However, to presuppose that deconstruction can illuminate some final 'original', 'Marxian socialist' trace goes against Derrida's entire project by once again asserting a metaphysic of a 'Marxian' presence over any other. Michel Foucault argued in *The Order of Things* that Marxian epistemology itself is part-and-parcel of a modernist episteme: 'to make the empirical, in man, stand for the transcendental. Despite appearances to the contrary, it is evident how closely knit is the network that links thoughts of the positivist or eschatological type (Marxism being the first rank of these)' (Foucault 1970:321). The entire thrust of Derrida's work was precisely to dismantle all such metaphysics of presence or epistemes (Marxian or otherwise), and not to assert one over the other as more genuine, as Yates, Shanks, Tilley and Ryan propose.

Earlier this century, the great Russian theorist Mikhail Bakhtin expressed a similar concern regarding his structuralist predecessor Ferdinand de Saussure and other colleagues that prefigured concerns for absolute, local contingency later expressed by Smith, Strathern and Rorty:

> My attitude toward structuralism: I am against enclosure in a text. Mechanical categories: 'opposition', 'change of codes' (the many styles

of Eugene Onegin in Lotman's interpretation and in my interpretation).
Sequential formalisation and depersonalisation: all relations are logical
(in the broad sense of the word). But I hear voices in everything and
dialogic relations among them. I also perceive the principle of augment-
ation dialogically. High evaluations of structuralism. The problem of
'precision' and 'depth'. Depth of penetration into the object (thing like)
and depth of penetration into the subject (personal).

Structuralism has only one subject – the subject of the research himself.
Things are transformed into concepts (a different degree of abstraction);
the subject can never become a concept (he himself speaks and responds).
Conceptual meaning is personalistic; it always includes a question, an
address, and the anticipation of a response, it always includes two (as a
dialogic minimum). This personalism is not psychological, but semantic.
(Bakhtin 1986:169–70)

In light of this it is necessary to consider why structuralism is still
problematic. Part of the reason lies in the recurrent fear of the Frankfurt
School, as expressed in Richard Bernstein's criticism of Richard Rorty,
that the abandonment of any criteria or 'adequate social theory' by
which one can justify a political institution leaves us powerless in a
very practical and pragmatic sense to address differing claims to what
constitutes 'liberalism': 'what for one "liberal" is basic for liberty or
freedom is to another "iberal" a mark of coercion' (Bernstein 1987:547).
In short, a certain authority is threatened by the 'phantom heresy of
relativism'; a fear, Smith would argue, of 'someone's acknowledging
the fact and partiality of her perspective would make her authority –
that is, precisely the privilege of her perspective – vulnerable' (Smith
1988:160). However, Smith has argued previously (and it is worth
repeating here) that 'it might be thought that there was some
communal value to ensuring that all authority was always subject to
interrogation and always at risk. All authority: which must mean that
of a parent, teacher, and missionary as well as that of tyrant, pope,
and state flunky' (Smith 1988: 161). Similarly, both Mouffe and Butler
argue that it is precisely 'undecidability' which ensures a continuously
shifting 'constitutive outside' wherein alternative voices can be heard;
that authoritarianism can be countered and social justice ensured by
never allowing anyone the axiological high ground.

Recently some archaeologists commenting on the origins of Europe
such as Ian Hodder (Hodder 1990:301) have exhibited an axiological
urge towards 'containment' as part of a project seeking to establish the
origins of European society, by constituting a line of structural 'traces'

up to the twentieth century at a time when the question of what it means to be European has never been more contentious. More to the point, Hodder appears to attempt a genealogy for the creation of a meta-unity and origin myth – a 'Europeanness', as practised by many different peoples at various times including that of our own. This is the process of separating the 'wild' from the 'domestic' – a structuring trope associated with the emergent adaptive strategies of the European Neolithic. This might also be seen – as the trope suggests – as the ongoing tension between exteriorisation and interiorisation characterising Soviet discourses in the twentieth century. Indeed Soviet theoreticians themselves – in the tradition of Marx, Engels and Morgan – very clearly saw the socialist project as the obviation of such oppositions and contradictions set in motion since the Neolithic.

The dynamics of such a structuring trope can be seen to be banal. To quote Bourdieu, such tropes are 'reducible in the last analysis to a fundamental dichotomy, only because its whole economy, which is based on the principle of the economy of logic, presupposes a loss of rigour for the sake of greater simplicity and generality and because it finds in "polythesis" the conditions required for the correct use of polysemy' (Bourdieu 1977:110). The reduction of a culture's (or desired cultural unity's) 'generative principle' or 'habitus', such as the structuring trope *domus/agrios* proposed by Hodder or the oscillation between binary oppositions, becomes too unwieldy, too vague, too polysemous and ultimately too banal (on the banality of dualisms see Miller 1994:296–7). Or perhaps more directly, because such structural tropes are so polysemous and so 'fuzzy', it is amenable to anyone to exploit to fulfil any particular strategy – including that of the social theorist.

At this juncture it is worthwhile to emphasise that Soviet theoreticians consciously generated and manipulated such tropes to describe the trajectory of the Neolithic to the present and in so doing constitute legitimating state ideologies. After all, the two intellectual traditions of these structuring tropes are intimately linked through the work of Lévi-Strauss. Both function in an aggregative manner, pulling together a recurring myth of European unity (Hodder) and the structural Marxist inevitability of Soviet socialism. This was the final resolution of the structural opposition between the 'wild':'domestic' and 'exteriorisation':'interiorisation' – in an attempt to resolve the structural contradictions of the Neolithic and to overcome them with the realisation of communism, merging future and past utopias. European prehistory and the origins of the structural contradictions of the

Neolithic became central to the myth of socialism. In *Gorod i Byt* (Gradov 1968), the primer for revived *byt* reformist city planning in the 1960s, this continuing mythic contradiction is expressed thus: 'The idea of collective housing and daily life as well as the communal rearing of children arose already in ancient times. And here already two millennia later this idea develops in ceaseless competition with the opposing conception of isolated dwellings and petty housework' (Gradov 1968:30). This point is illustrated by Gradov with two plans of an upper Palaeolithic settlement and one dating from 3000 BC demonstrating communal living, as well as a rendering and plan of a more recent seventeenth-century 'Iroquois' longhouse presented as a 'prototype of corridor planning' as it was first introduced at the Narkomfin Communal House (Gradov 1968:31) (see figure 25). These illustrations served to prefigure the Narkomfin and advance such planning to recreate a pre-capitalist Arcadia at the 'high' historical level of communism. For the Bolshevik (as well as Hodder) the eventual, almost 'modernist', resolution of the *agrios* to the *domus* is a trope comparable to the Bolshevik resolution of 'nature' to 'socialism'. By using these tropes, both Hodder and Soviet theoreticians sought in varying degrees of sincerity and irony 'a guarantee of renewal: not only as a token from the past but as a guide to the future' (Rykwert 1989:191, see Rykwert's work for an excellent analysis of the cultivation of primitivism in the realisation of modernisms and architectural origins in general).

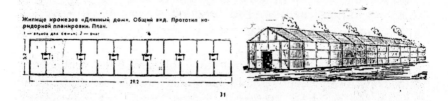

Figure 25 Iroquois dwelling redrawn from Lewis Henry Morgan in Gradov 1968:30

Thus two rather different 'incisions' (to borrow Yates's phrasing) are made possible within these rather 'fuzzy' structuring tropes in order to create two rather different but structurally similar stories. However, an 'adequate social theory', 'habitus' or 'structuration theory' would not be able to make sense of these 'incisions', to separate and distinguish them and to understand their resultant stories as was earlier argued by

Strathern (1991:108). Instead, I would argue that in light of these two undeniably different 'incisions' and the 'prosthetic' conceptual devices they articulated within these structuring tropes, emphasis ought to be shifted away from Strathern's 'prosthetics' deployed within these 'incisions', to the 'incisions' themselves: the spaces, gaps and 'constitutive outsides' in which they play. One should move away from our preoccupation with 'presence' and its attendant metaphysics, and return to a 'semantic personalism' privileging the individual agent as articulated earlier by Bakhtin (Bakhtin 1986:169–70). Because, it is there – in these spaces, gaps and 'incisions' – that individual agency resides and culture change is effected. It is also where the determining contingencies surrounding such manipulations are evident and intelligible, so that we might better come to terms with and understand what was at stake for Soviet theoreticians as well as for others.

The process of aggregation and disaggregation, achieved through different understandings of material culture, emphasising respectively its denotative and contextual qualities, was used variably by Soviet authorities to realise a very specific political objective - namely the exteriorisation and interiorisation of social life founded upon the unifying European myth of Neolithic alienation from 'nature'/'the wild'/'the *agrios*'. So too, for some archaeologists, the conceptually disaggregating dynamic unleashed by their emphasis on deconstruction, facilitated the critical dismantling of 'totalising' conceptual frameworks and asserted instead a 'fuzzy', local, contingent and contextual understanding of material culture kept in check, however, by an 'adequate social theory' (Leone 1995, Shanks and Tilley 1987; 1992). This is not to say that the archaeological Post-Processualist is in some way a Stalinist (as this comparison might suggest). However, both the Post-Processualist and the Stalinist sought similar conceptual tools with which to break up a totalising structure. Both were reactions to different but related modernisms that would prove to be more inclusive; empowering those previously disenfranchised by the creation and assertion of 'fuzzier' conceptual structural dynamics. Rather, it is crucial to point out that these two unrelated political agendas use very similar and related conceptual tools. For this reason, it is essential not to be too entranced by such enabling 'prosthetic' devices and 'theories of material culture'. As Strathern has pointed out, these 'prosthetics' (as her apt trope suggests) are 'alien' to the agent and one's motivations; they merely enable *something* – a 'powerful' and amoral conceptual tool in the Foucauldian sense. What one might do is forget about a unifying 'theory of material culture' and instead focus on the dynamics of such 'theories' within the spaces, gaps and 'incisions' in which they play, in short to examine the purposes to which such tools are used and what their attendant 'costs' are. In this way, the uses of power and its enabling devices might be better understood and then more profitably used to identify, as Smith would have us do, the 'dynamics of the Nazi's [or the Stalinist's] emergence and access to power and, accordingly, a specification of political and other actions that might make that emergence and access less likely, both in one's own neighbourhood and elsewhere' (Smith 1988:155). But it will never guarantee (and we should not want it to) and assuage the inherited legacy of Frankfurt School anxiety: 'nothing can guarantee that the jackals will be kept at bay, neither axiology nor any specific alternative that replaces it' (Smith 1988:155).

Thus this book has been written to constitute these delineating structuring tropes and displace them a little further, while elaborating the subject at hand: the Narkomfin Communal House, and enabling it to resonate across a broad spectrum of other concerns; often radically unrelated (such as the innumerable encounters in the lives of individual inhabitants) while at other times appositely sympathetic. These movements have all been contained and constituted, however, by the consolidating 'trace' of the physical building itself and the communities it has housed. This was done with the hope that it could be a step towards a more satisfactory management of the unsettling superfluity of meaning we encounter as students of Soviet and Russian culture.

Today, however, the situation is as volatile and unsettled as ever. At present the building and site are in an alarming state of decay with almost half of the units empty or abandoned (see figure 26). The successor to the Council of Ministers owns the communal block and the Moscow City Council owns the living block and leases out the laundry facility to one of the new post-communist business enterprises. Attempts have been made to convert the units of the living block into corporate housing for foreign businesses (*Arkhitekturnyii Vestnik*, 1995, no. 2:4). At the same time the house museum of Feodor Shaliapin, which occupies the remaining neo-classical buildings of the original site, is said to be contesting the ownership of the entire area in an attempt to reconsolidate the original pre-Revolutionary lots for its own use. The centrality of the site in Moscow, just off the Garden Ring Road and overlooking the American Embassy compound to the back, makes the complex of the Narkomfin Communal House very attractive in the burgeoning real estate market of post-Soviet Moscow, with many interests scrambling for its control. Indeed, the fragmented ownership,

Figure 26 Exterior Narkomfin Dom Kommuna, 1992, photographed by Aleksei Taits, Moscow.

and the uncertain and contested future of the complex, only reiterates its history, where competing understandings of social and material relations have been contentiously engaged in an ongoing effort to realise the terms and promise of the good life, radically configuring and reconfiguring the material world towards divergent and improbably contradictory ends. I hope this book is a more profitable engagement or 'scrap' over these contentious and unresolvable issues and will thereby enable others unnameable and yet to come. More still, however, this elaboration of the house might help to contain meaningfully and tentatively the experiences of the individuals and families who have lived at the Narkomfin at the spearhead of modernism and those who in the aftermath of this demiurgic project are still struggling to live there now.

Appendix

Full set of as-is floor plans of the Narkomfin Communal House showing known conditions in 1992 (author's drawing). Shaded areas indicate units purged under Stalin in the 1930s.

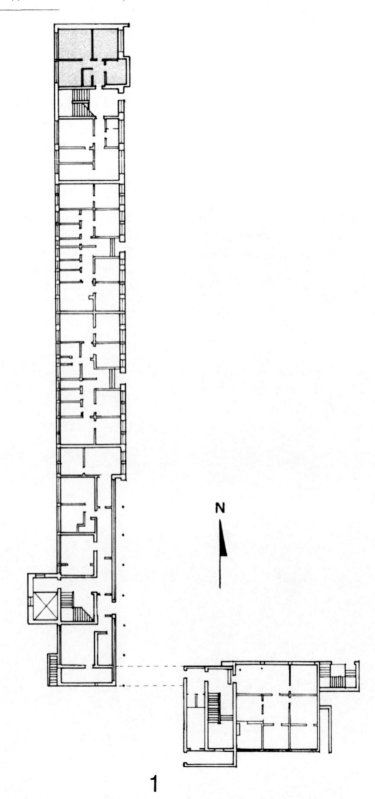

1

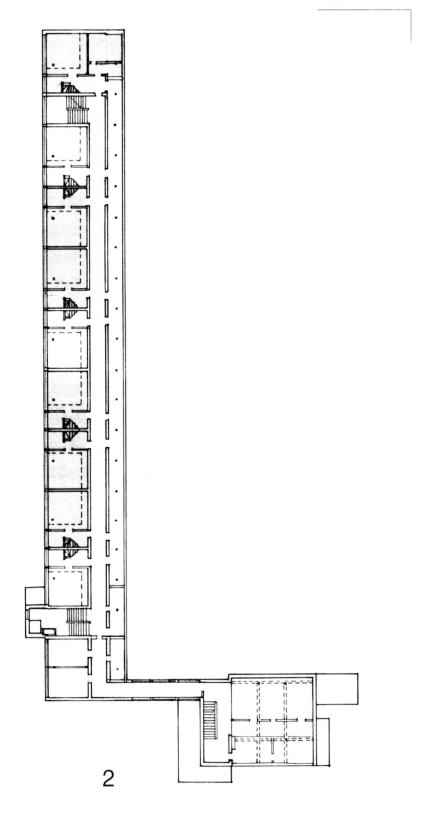

2

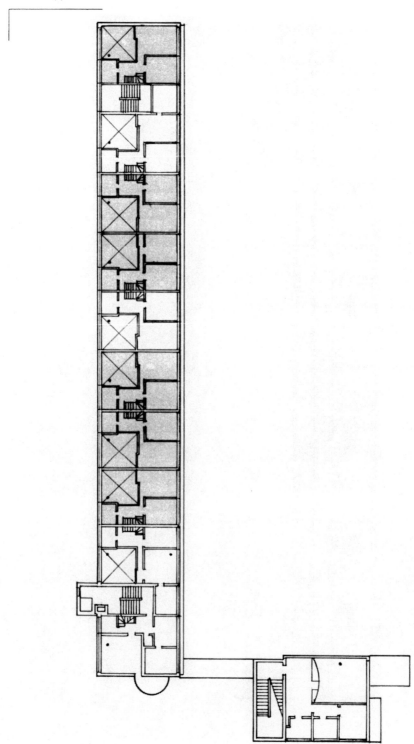

3

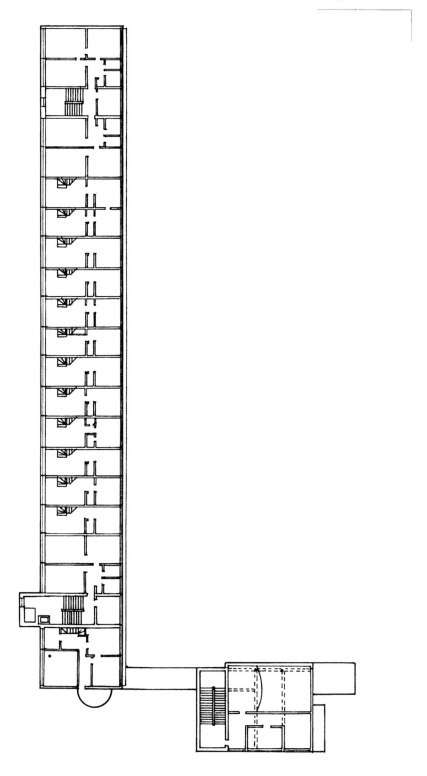

4

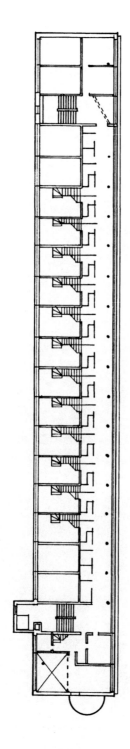
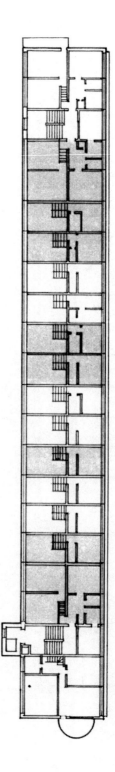

5   6

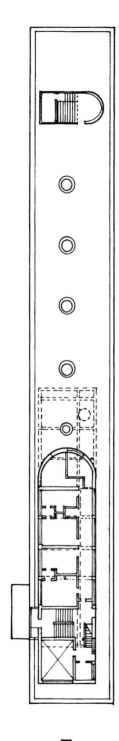
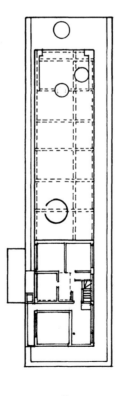

7   8

Sources

Archives Consulted

(1) REU-9, Krasnopresnenskii Raion, Moscow. (2) MGINTA (Moskovskii Gosudarstvennyi Istoricheskii Nauchno-Tekhnicheskii Arkhiv). (3) Arkhiv Instituta 'Mosvodokanal', Moscow. (4) TsGAOR, SSSR (Tsentral'nyi Gosudarstvennyi Arkhiv Oktiabarskoi Revoliutsii), Moscow. (5) TsMADSN (Tsentral'nyi Moskovskii Arkhiv Na Spetsial'nikh Nositeliakh). (6) RGAKFD (Rossiiskii Gosudarstvennyi Arkhiv Kinofotdokumentov). (7) Muzei Istorii i Rekonstruktsii g. Moskvy. (8) Photographic Collection, Ecole d'Architecture, Université de Genève, Switzerland. (9) State Shchusev Architectural Museum, Moscow. (10) TSGAR, RSFSR, Moscow. (11) NDKOH, Narkomfin Dom Kommuna Oral History, (1990-2, Author's Collection)

Bibliography

Agarov, P. (1909), *Ves'ma Poleznyi Sputnik' Kazhdoi Khoziaik v Domashnem' Obikhode*,n.p.

Agienko, A. (1931), *Za Novyi Byt*, Moscow: OGIZ-Moskovskii Rabochii.

Aleksandrov, F.A. (ed.) (1968), *Byt i Kul'tura*, Moscow: Moskovskii Rabochii.

Andreev, P.P. (1893), *Domovedenie*, (n.p.): Pantelevykh'.

Avdeeva, A.A. (1868), *Polnaia Khoziaistvennaia Kniga, chast' 2.*, St Petersburg: Izdatel'stvo Knigoprodavtsa A.F. Feodorova.

Babty, Ian and Yates, Tim, (eds.) (1990), *Archaeology after Structuralism*, London: Routledge.

Baiburin, A.K. (1983), *Zhilishche v Obriadakh i Predstavleniiakh Vostochnykh Slavian*,Leningrad: Nauka.

Bakhterev, M. and Razumovskii, A. (1930), *Kul'turno-Bytovye Tovarishchestva*, Moscow and Leningrad: Molodaia Gvardiia.

Bakhtin, M.M. (1986), *Speech Genres and Other Late Essays*, ed. Caryl Emerson and Michael Holquist, Austin: University of Texas Press.

Barth, Frederik (1987), *Cosmologies in the Making*, Cambridge: Cambridge University Press.

Bauman, Zygmunt (1989), 'Hermeneutics and Modern Social Theory', in *Social Theory of Modern Societies: Anthony Giddens and His Critics*, ed. David Held and John B. Thompson, Cambridge: Cambridge University Press.

Bernstein, Frances (1998), Envisioning Health in Revolutionary Russia: The Politics of Gender and Sexual-Enlightenment Posters of the 1920s. *The Russian Review*, **57**, 191–217.

Bernstein, Richard J. (1987), One Step Forward, Two Steps Backward: Richard Rorty on Liberal Democracy and Philosophy, *Political Theory*, **15(4)**, 538–63.

Blier, Suzanne Preston (1987*)*, *The Anatomy of Architecture*, Chicago: University of Chicago Press.

Bliznakov, Milka (1993), Soviet Housing during the Experimental Years, 1918 to 1933, *Russian Housing in the Modern Age*, ed. William Craft Brumfield and Blair A. Ruble, Cambridge: Cambridge University Press and Woodrow Wilson Centre Press.

Bordiugov, G.A. (1987*)*, Nekotorye Osobennosti Formirovaniia Novoi Kul'tury Byta v Gody Dovoennykh Piatiletok, *Sovetskaia Kultura, 70 Let Razvitiia*.

Boudon, Philippe (1979), *Le Corbusier's Pessac Revisited*, Cambridge, Mass.: MIT Press.

Bourdieu, Pierre (1977), *Outline of a Theory of Practice*, Cambridge: Cambridge University Press.

—— (1984*)* *Distinction*, Cambridge: Cambridge University Press.

—— (1990a), *In Other Words*, Stanford: Stanford University Press.

—— (1990b), *The Logic of Practice*, Stanford: Stanford University Press.

Bown, Mathew Cullerne (1991), *Art under Stalin*, Oxford: Phaidon.

Bowen, John R. (1994), Interpretations plurielles: la pragmatique de l'exegese rituelle dans la Société Gayo, *L'Homme, 132*, **XXXIV (4)**, 77–8.

Boym, Svetlana (1995), *Common Places: Mythologies of Everyday Life in Russia*, Cambridge, Mass.: Harvard University Press.

Broch-Due, Vigdis, Rudie, Ingrid and Bleie, Tone (eds) (1993), *Carved Flesh Cast Selves: Gendered Symbols and Social Practices*, Oxford: Berg.

Brown, Edward J. (1978), Towards a Theory of Soviet Meshchanstvo: Some Reflections Suggested by Vera Dunham's Book, *In Stalin's Time*, *Russian Review*, **37**, 188–96.

Buchli, Victor (1995) Interpreting Material Culture: The Trouble with Text, in Ian Hodder et. al. (eds), *Interpreting Archaeology*, London: Routledge.

—— (1997), Khrushchev, Modernism, and the Fight against Petit-bourgeois Consciousness in the Soviet Home, *Journal of Design History*, **10(2)**, 161–76.

—— (1998), Moisei Ginzburg's Narkomfin Communal House in Moscow: Contesting the Social and Material World, *Journal of the Society of Architectural Historians*, **57(2)**

Budina, O.R. and Shmeleva, M.N. (1989), *Gorod i Narodnye Traditsii Russkikh*, Moscow: Nauka.

Butler, Judith (1993), *Bodies that Matter*, London: Routledge

Carsten, Janet and Hugh-Jones, Stephen (1995), *About the House*, Cambridge: Cambridge University Press.

Central Committee of the Communist Party of the Soviet Union (Bolsheviks) (1939), *History of the Communist Party of the Soviet Union (Bolsheviks)*, Moscow: Foreign Language Publishing House.

Central Committee of the Communist Party (Bolsheviks) of Ukraine, of Workers and Peasants (1929), *Kul'turno-Bytovaia Rabota Sredi Rabotnits i Krest'ianok*, Kharkov: KNIGOSPILKA.

Chizhikova, L.N. (1979), Zhilishche Russkikh, in M.G. Rabinovich (ed.), *Material'naia Kul'tura Kompaktnikh Etnicheskikh Grupp na Ukraine*, Moscow: Nauka.

Chomsky, Noam (1968), *Language and Mind*, New York: Harcourt, Brace and World.

Clements, Barbara Evans (1992), The Utopianism of the Zhenotdel, *Slavic Review*, **51 (3)**, 485–96

Communist Party of the Soviet Union (1961), *Materiali XXII S''ezda KPSS*, Moscow: Gospolitizdat.

Conquest, Robert (1968), *The Great Terror: Stalin's Purge of the Thirties*, New York:

Cooke, Catherine (1974), 'The Town of Socialism', PhD Thesis, University of Cambridge University.

—— (1983), *Russian Avant-Garde: Art and Architecture*, London: Architectural Design and Academy Editions.

—— (1995), *Russian Avant-Garde: Theories of Art and Architecture*, London: Academy Editions.

Constitution of the USSR (1936)

Deetz, James (1977), *In Small Things Forgotten*, New York: Anchor.

Derrida, Jacques (1976), *Of Grammatology*, Baltimore: Johns Hopkins University Press.

—— (1978), *Writing and Difference*, London: Routledge and Kegan Paul.

Deutsche, Rosalyn (1996), *Evictions: Art and Spatial Politics*, Cambridge Mass.: MIT Press.

Donley-Reid, Linda W. (1990), A Structuring Structure: the Swahili House, in Susan Kent (ed.),

Domestic Architecture and the Use of Space, Cambridge: Cambridge University Press.

Dubniak, V. (1931), Za Zdorovoe Zhilishche, *Za Zdorovyi Kul'turnyi Byt: Sbornik Statei*, Moscow: Gosudarstvennoe Uchebno-pedagogicheskoe Izdatel'stvo.

Dunham, Vera (1976), *In Stalin's Time*, Cambridge: Cambridge University Press.

Edelman, Robert (1993), Everybody's Got to Be Someplace: Organizing Space in the Russian Peasant House, 1880 to 1930, in William Craft Brumfield and Blair A. Ruble (eds), in *Russian Housing in the Modern Age*, Cambridge: Cambridge University Press and Woodrow Wilson Centre Press.

Engels, Friedrich (1972), *The Origin of the Family, Private Property, and the State*, New York: Pathfinder Press.

Fitzpatrick, Sheila (1979), Stalin and the Making of a New Elite, 1928–1939, *Slavic Review*, **38 (3)**, 377–402.

—— (1982), *The Russian Revolution: 1917–1932*, Oxford: Oxford University Press.

—— (1985), The Civil War as a Formative Experience, in Abbot Gleason and Peter Kenez (eds.), *Bolshevik Culture* Bloomington: Indiana University Press.

—— (1992) *The Cultural Front*, Ithaca: Cornell University Press.

—— (1994) *Stalin's Peasants: Resistance and Survival in the Russian Village after Collectivization*, Oxford: Oxford University Press.

Foucault, Michel (1970), *The Order of Things*, London: Tavistock.

—— (1977), *Discipline and Punish: The Birth of the Prison*, London: Penguin.

Geertz, Clifford (1980), *Negara: The Theatre State in Nineteenth-Century Bali*, Princeton: Princeton University Press.

Getty, J. Arch and Manning, Roberta T. (1993*)*, *Stalinist Terror: New Perspectives*, Cambridge: Cambridge University Press.

Giddens, Anthony (1979), *Central Problems in Social Theory*, London: Macmillan.

Ginzburg, Moisei (1934), *Zhilishche*, Moscow: Gosstroiizdat USSR.

Glassie, Henry (1975*)*, *Folk Housing in Middle Virginia*, Knoxville, Tenn.: University of Tennessee Press.

Goldman, Wendy Z. (1992), The Utopianism of the Zhenotdel, *Slavic Review*, **51(3)**, 485–96.

—— (1993), *Women, the State and Revolution*, Cambridge: Cambridge University Press.

Gorkii, Maksim (1953), *Zametki o Meshchanstve*, M. Gor'kii Sobranie Sochinenii, tom 23. Moscow: Gosudarstvennoe Izdatel'stvo Khudo-zhestvennoi Literatury.

Gosden, Christopher (1994), *Social Being and Time*, Oxford: Blackwell.

Gradov, G.A. (1968), *Gorod i Byt*, Moscow: Literatury po Stroitel'stvu

Groys, Boris (1992), *The Total Art of Stalinism,* Princeton: Princeton University Press.

Hazard, Jonathan (1939), *Soviet Housing Law*, New Haven: Yale University Press.

Heller, Mikhail and Nekrich, Aleksandr H. (1986), *Utopia in Power*, New York: Summit Books.

Henderson, Susan R. (1996), A Revolution in the Women's Sphere: Grete Lihotzky and the Frankfurt Kitchen, in D. Coleman, Elizabeth Danz and Carol Henderson (eds), *Architecture and Feminism*, Princeton: Princeton University Press.

Hillier, W and Hanson, J. (1984), *The Social Logic of Space*, Cambridge: Cambridge University Press.

History of the Communist Party of the Soviet Union (Bolsheviks) (1939), A Commission of the Central Committee of the Communist Party of the Soviet Union (Bolsheviks) (eds), Moscow: Foreign Languages Publishing House.

Hodder, Ian (1986), *Reading the Past*, Cambridge: Cambridge University Press.

—— (1990), *The Domestication of Europe*, Oxford: Blackwell.

—— (1991), Interpreting Archaeology and its Role, *American Antiquity*, **56**, 7–18.

—— et al. (1995), *Interpreting Archaeology*, London: Routledge.

Holmgren, Beth (1994), *Women's Works in Stalin's Time*, Bloomington: Indiana University Press.

Horkheimer, M. (1978), On the Problem of Truth, in *The Frankfurt School Reader,* Oxford: Blackwell.

Hudson, Hugh D. (1994), *Blueprints and Blood,* Princeton: Princeton University Press.

Hymes, Dell (1970), Linguistic Method in Ethnography: Its Develop-ment in the United States, in P. Garvin (ed), *Method and Theory in Linguistics*, The Hague: Mouton.

Ivanova, A. (1926), *Not Doma*, Moscow: Voprosy Truda.

James, William (1995), *Pragmatism*, New York: Dover Publications.

Johnson, Mathew (1989), Conceptions of Agency in Archaeological Interpretation, *Journal of Anthropological Archaeology*, **8**, 189–211.

—— (1993), *Housing Culture*, London: University College London Press.

Kabakov, Ilya (1989), *Ten Characters*, London: Institute of Contemporary Arts.

—— (1993), *In the Communal Kitchen*, Paris: Galerie Dina Vierny.

Khan-Magomedov, S.O. (1972), *M. Ia. Ginzburg*, Moscow: Literaturi po Stroitel'stvu.

Khlevniuk, O.V. (1983), O Roli Partiino-Gosudarstvennogo Rukovodstva v Pereustroistve Byta na Sotsialisticheskikh Nachalakh v Gody Pervoi Piatiletki. *Iz Raboty Partiino-gosudarstveno*, (no publisher, no place).

Kisel'nikova, N.V. (1985), 'Sushchnost' i Istoricheskie Osobenosti Meshchanskoi Morali', Candidate's Dissertation Moscow: Gosudarstvenyi Universitet im. M.V. Lomonosova, Filosofskii Fakul'tet.

Kostrov, T. (1930), *Kul'tura i Meshchanstvo*, Moscow: Molodaia Gvardiia.

Kotkin, Stephen (1993), Shelter and Subjectivity in the Stalin Period, in William Craft Brumfield and Blair Ruble (eds), *Russian Housing in the Modern Age*, Cambridge: Cambridge University Press and Woodrow Wilson Centre Press.

—— (1995), *Magnetic Mountain*, Berkeley: University of California Press.

Kozhanyi, P. (1924), *Rabochee Zhilishche i Byt*, Moscow: Izdatel'stvo V.Ts.S.P.S.

Kozhanyi, P. and Pyzhova, N. (eds) (1925), *Kak Stroit' Novyi Byt*, Moscow: Voprosy Truda.

Kropotkin, P. (1995), *The Conquest of Bread and Other Writings*. Ed. Marshall Shatz, Cambridge: Cambridge University Press.

Krupskaia, Nadezhda (1930), *O Bytovykh Voprosakh*, Moscow and Leningrad: Gosudarstvennoe Izdatel'stvo.

Kurella, A. (1930), *Krasivaia Zhizn'*, Moscow: Molodaia Gvardiia.

Laqueur, Thomas (1990), *Making Sex: Body and Gender from the Greeks to Freud*, Cambridge, Mass.: Harvard University Press.

Larin, Iu. (1930), Perspektivy Razvitiia Zhilishchnoi Kooperatsii, in Iu. Larin and B. Belousov (eds), *Za Novoe Zhilishche*, Moscow: Izdanie Tsentrozhilsoiuza.

Larin, Iu. and Belousov, B. (1930), *Za Novoe Zhilishche*, Moscow: Izdanie Tsentrozhilsoiuza.

Leone, Mark and Potter Jr., P.B. (1992), Legitimation and the Classification of Archaeological Sites, *American Antiquity*, **57**, 137–45.

—— (1995), A Historic Archaeology of Capitalism, *American Anthro-*

pologist, **97(2)** 251–68.

Levi-Strauss, C. (1966), *The Savage Mind*, London: Weidenfeld and Nicolson.

Lodder, Christina (1983), *Russian Constructivism*, New Haven: Yale University Press.

Lucid, Daniel P. (1977), *Soviet Semiotics*, Baltimore: Johns Hopkins University Press.

McCracken, Grant (1989), *Homeyness*, In *Interpretative Consumer Research*, E. Hirschman, ed. Provo, UT: Association for Consumer Research.

Maiakovskii, V. (1930), *Sobranie Stikhotvorenii v Dvukh Tomakh*, tom 2, Leningrad: Sovetskii Pisatel'.

Marx, Karl (1983), *Capital*, vol. 1., London: Lawrence and Wishart.

—— (1986), *Karl Marx: A Reader*, ed. Jon Elster, Cambridge: Cambridge University Press.

Medvedev, Roy (1971), *Let History Judge: The Origins and Consequences of Stalinism*, New York:

Miliutin, Nikolai (1930), *Problemy Stroitel'stva Sotsialisticheskikh Gorodov*, Moscow: Gosudarstvennoe Izdatel'stvo

—— (1939), Unpublished autobiography

Millar, James (1985) The Little Deal: Brezhnev's Contribution to Acquisitive Socialism, *Slavic Review*, **44 (44)** 694–706.

Miller, Daniel (1994), *Modernity: An Ethnographic Approach*, Oxford: Berg.

Moore, Henrietta (1986), *Space, Text and Gender*, Cambridge: Cambridge University Press.

—— (1990), Paul Ricoeur: Action Meaning and Text, in C. Tilley (ed.), *Reading Material Culture*, Oxford: Blackwell.

—— (1994), *A Passion for Difference*, Cambridge: Polity Press.

Morgan, Lewis Henry (1978), *Ancient Society*, New York: Labor Press.

Mouffe, Chantal (1993), *The Return of the Political*, London: Verso.

—— (ed.) (1996a) *Deconstruction and Pragmatism*, London: Routledge

—— (1996b), Democracy, Power and the 'Political', in Seyla Benhabib (ed.), *Democracy and Difference*, Princeton: Princeton University Press.

Nikiforov, N. (1929), *Protiv Starogo Byta*, Moscow: Moskovskii Rabochii.

Nove, Alec (1982), *An Economic History of the Soviet Union*, London: Penguin.

—— (1988), *The Soviet Economic System*, Winchester, Mass.: Unwin Hyman.

Organovich, M. (1928), *Za Novyi Byt*, Moscow and Leningrad: Molodaia Gvardiia.

Osipovich, M. (1931), *Za Sotsialisticheskuiu Perestroiku Byta*, Moscow: Sovetskoe Zakonodatel'stvo.

Parker, Rozsika (1984), *The Subversive Stich: Embroidery and the Making of the Feminine*, London: Women's Press.

Parker-Pearson, Michael and Richards, Colin (1994), *Architecture and Order: Approaches to Social Space*, London: Routledge.

Radchenko, A. (1928), *Domovodstvo, Vypusk 1, Kak Pravil'no Vesti Svoi Dom*, Moscow: GLAVPOLITPROSVET.

Rappaport, Amos (1982), *House Form and Culture*, Englewood Cliffs NJ: Prentice-Hall.

Riabushin, A.V. (1976), *Zakonomernosti i Tendentsii Razvitia Predmetno-prostranstvennoi Sredi Zhilishche*, Doctoral Dissertation in Theory and History of Architecture, Moscow.

Ricoeur, Paul (1991), *A Ricoeur Reader: Reflection and Imagination*, ed. Mario J. Valdes, New York: Harvester Wheatsheaf.

Rorty, Richard (1980), *Philosophy and the Mirror of Nature*, Oxford: Blackwell.

—— (1991), *Essays on Heidegger and Others*, Cambridge: Cambridge University Press.

Rosenthal, Bernice Glatzer (1994), *Nietzsche and Soviet Culture*, Cambridge: Cambridge University Press.

Rykwert, Joseph (1989), *On Adam's House in Paradise*, Cambridge, Mass.: MIT Press.

Samson, Ross (1990), Introduction, in Ross Samson (ed.), *The Social Archaeology of Houses*, Edinburgh: Edinburgh University Press.

Schapiro, L. (1971), *The Communist Party of the Soviet Union*, New York: Vintage Books.

Semashko, N.A. (1928), *O Svetlom i Temnom v Rabochem Bytu*, Moscow.

—— (1929), *Kul'turnaia Revoliutsiia i Ozdorovlenie Byta*, Moscow: Gosudarstvennoe Meditsinskoe Izdatel'stvo.

—— (n.d.), *Za Uiut, Poriadok, Chistotu v Zhilishche*, Moscow: Tsentral'nyi Institut

Sanitarnogo Prosvesheniia Narkomzdrava SSSR.

Shanks, Michael and Tilley, Christopher (1987*), Social Theory and Archaeology*, Oxford: PolityPress.

—— (1992), *Re-constructing Archaeology*, London: Routledge.

Sheftel', S. (1931*), V Bytovoi Pokhod*, Moscow: Izdatel'stvo 'Vlast' Sovetov' Pri Prezidiume VTsIK.

Sheridan, Alan (1980), *Michel Foucault: The Will to Truth*, London: Tavistock Publications.

Shtein, Viktor (1929), *Za Novyi Byt!*, Leningrad: Izdatel'stvo Krasnaia Gazeta.

Siegelbaum, Lewis H. (1988), *Stakhanovism and the Politics of Productivity in the USSR, 1935–1941,* Cambridge: Cambridge University Press.

Smidovich, S. (1927), *Rabotnitsa i Novyi Byt,* Moscow and Leningrad: Gosudarstvennoe Izdatel'stvo.

Smith, Barbara Herrnstein (1988), *Contingencies of Value,* Cambridge, Mass.: Harvard University Press.

Sorokin, A. and Markovich, I. (1931), *Sotsialisticheskaia Perestroika Byta i Zadachi Rabochei Bytovoi Kommuny,* Moscow and Leningrad: Molodaia Gvardiia.

Sosnovy, Timothy (1952), The Soviet Urban Housing Problem, *The American Slavic and East European Review,* **11**, 288–303.

Sovety Proletarkoi Khoziaike (1924), Ekaterinburg: Izdatel'stvo Uralkniga.

Starostenko, A. M. (1990), *Meshchanstvo Kak Sotsial'noe Iavlenie: Genezis, Sushnost', Osobenosti Proiavlenie Preodolenia,* Moscow: Akademia Obshchestvennikh Nauk Pri TsK KPSS, Kafedry Sotsial'noi Psikhologii i Sotsiologii Politiki.

Stites, Richard (1989), *Revolutionary Dreams,* Oxford: Oxford University Press.

Strathern, Marilyn (1991), *Partial Connections,* Savage, Md.: Rowman and Littlefield Publishers.

STROIKOM, RSFSR (1930), *Typovye Proekty i Konstruktsii Zhilishchnogo Stroitel'stva,* Moscow.

Thomas, Julian (1998), The Socio-semiotics of Material Culture, *Journal of Material Culture,* **3(1)**, 97–108.

Thurston, Robert W. (1986), Fear and Belief in the USSR's 'Great Terror': Response to Arrest, 1935–1939, *Slavic Review,* **45 (2),** 214–37.

Tilley, Christopher (1989), Excavation as Theatre, *Antiquity,* **63**, 275–80.

—— (1994), *A Phenomenology of Landscape,* Oxford: Berg.

Toporokov, A.K. (1929), *Kak Stat' Kul'turnym,* Moscow: Rabotnik Prosveshchenie.

Travin, I. (1979), *Material'no-veshchnaia Sreda i Sotsialisticheskii Obraz Zhizni,* Leningrad: Nauka.

Trotsky, Leon (1972), *The Revolution Betrayed,* New York: Pathfinder Press.

Viola, Lynne (1993), The Second Coming: Class Enemies in the Soviet Countryside, 1927–1935, In J. Arch Getty and Roberta T. Manning, (eds), *Stalinist Terror: New Perspectives,* Cambridge: Cambridge University Press.

Vladimirskii, A. and Sheftel', C. (1931), *Kul'turno-Bytovaia Rabota v Domakh,* ed. N. Semashko, Moscow: Mosoblispolkom.

Willen, Paul Larner (1953), 'Soviet Architecture in Transformation',

Master of Arts Thesis, Faculty of Political Science, Columbia University.

Yates, Timothy (1990), Derrida: There is Nothing Outside of the Text, in C. Tilley (ed.), *Reading Material Culture* Oxford: Blackwell.

Zalesky, Eugene (1980), *Stalinist Planning for Economic Growth, 1933–1952*, Chapel Hill: University of North Carolina Press.

Zarina, M.M. (1928), *Domovodstro,* Moscow and Leningrad: Gosudarstvennoe Izdatel'stvo.

Zarinskaia, I.Z. (1987), *Sotsial'nye i Esteticheskie Aspekty Formirovaniia Zhiloi Predmetnoi Sredy,* Candidate's Dissertation, Moscow: Vsesoyuznyi Nauchno Issledovaditel'skii Institut Tekhnicheskoi Estetiki.

Zaslavsky, Victor (1982), *The Neo-Stalinist State: Class, Ethnicity and Consensus in Soviet Society,* New York: M. E. Sharpe.

Žižek, Slavoj (1992), Eastern Europe's Republics of Gilead, in Chantal Mouffe (ed.), *Dimensions of Radical Democracy,* London: Verso.

Zuikova, E.M. (1974), *Sovershenstvovanie Byta v Usloviiakh Sotsializma,* Moscow: Znanie.

Index

CPSIA information can be obtained at www.ICGtesting.com
Printed in the USA
266919BV00001B/18/P